Both Sides of the River
Merseyside in Poetry and Prose

Also by GLADYS MARY COLES

POETRY

The Sounding Circle
Sinerva And Other Poems
The Snow Bird Sequence
Stoat, in Winter
Liverpool Folio
Studies in Stone
Leafburners: New and Selected Poems
The Glass Island

BIOGRAPHY AND CRITICISM

The Flower of Light: A Biography of Mary Webb
Introductions to Mary Webb's novels *Gone to Earth*
        and *Precious Bane*
Introduction to Mary Webb's essays *The Spring of Joy*
Mary Webb: a new biography
Walks with Writers (with Gordon Dickins)
Mary Webb and Her Shropshire World (forthcoming)

AS EDITOR

Selected Poems of Mary Webb
Mary Webb: Collected Prose and Poems
Poet's Wirral: An Anthology (in preparation)
Poet's England: Lancashire (in preparation)

BOTH SIDES OF THE RIVER

Merseyside in Poetry and Prose

compiled & edited
and with an Introduction

by

GLADYS MARY COLES

HEADLAND

First published in 1993
by
HEADLAND PUBLICATIONS
38 York Avenue
West Kirby, Wirral
Merseyside L48 3JF

A CIP record for this book is
available from the British Library

ISBN
0   903074   65   6

Design: Richard Lloyd-Jones of Nichols Print
Typesetting: Nichols Print, Heswall, Merseyside
Printed in Great Britain by: Pentagon Printing Co, Liverpool

To Merseysiders everywhere,
especially my mother and father

There, stately buildings preside,
the Mersey skyline a child's New York:
the Liver tall, uniquely towered
and topped by twin birds,
giant cormorants in copper,
wings lifted, poised for flight;
one bird looking seawards
pensive, down the estuary,
the other gazing citywards
into another sea....

GLADYS MARY COLES
from *Liverpool Folio*

CONTENTS

INTRODUCTION

Anthologists are, by nature, 'library cormorants', to use Coleridge's image — a particularly apt one, in my case, as the wings of the symbolic Liver Bird seemed to hover over me, urging me on during the five years of research for this book.

My aim was to compile an anthology which would reflect Merseyside's contribution to literature and, at the same time, evoke the area's unique character in its many facets. I was aware of the strong literary tradition of Merseyside, particularly the wealth and diversity of the literature stimulated by Liverpool, the great seaport city at its heart; and I saw how these writings could be brought together to give a sense of development across the centuries, an unfolding narrative of Merseyside and its people from earliest times up to the present day.

While primarily drawing on imaginative writing — poetry, novels, short stories, plays and scripts, songs, ballads and legends — I was also looking for extracts from biographies and autobiographies, letters, diaries, journalism, travel-writing, as well as illuminating documentary and archival material.

My research revealed a surprising number of writers of national and international stature who have either used Merseyside in their work, or who have visited the area and resided for a time, recording their impressions. Added to these are the many established writers who are Merseysiders, by birth or by virtue of having spent there a significant portion of their lives. However, in making selections for this anthology, my criterion was the quality and relevance of the writing, rather than the name of the author. Consequently, work by little-known writers is included alongside that by distinguished names.

The project involved an enormous amount of reading, and even though discarding a great deal, I filled two rooms with my gatherings. Liverpool alone has generated such a quantity of literature and comment (few places can have had so much written about them), that I collected enough material for three anthologies on the city itself.

Merseyside today is, of course, more than Liverpool — an enormous conurbation which includes Wirral. Nonetheless, Liverpool is the *raison d'etre* of Merseyside and its capital, an exciting city, rich in culture and contrasts, whose fortunes directly affect those of the rest of the region. The anthology concentrates attention on Liverpool and the Wirral bank of the Mersey, as the title indicates, focussing on the two sides of the river, the life, places and people on its banks and hinterland, and on the river itself in its journey through time.

In other words, this book is descriptive of the literal and historical Mersey-side, and does not attempt to represent the totality of the huge present-day region. For instance, places on the Wirral Peninsula portrayed here are mainly those along the Mersey coast (such as Birkenhead, Wallasey, New Brighton), rather than those along the Dee. And I decided to include some important places on the upper reaches of the Mersey which are not officially Merseyside — notably Warrington, where the river ceases to be navigable, an ancient crossing point (forded by the Romans, bridged by the Normans, and later fought over during the Civil War); and, on the Wirral coast, Stanlow and Ellesmere Port.

The anthologist cannot hope to please every reader. One of the major difficulties is in completing the selection, as there will always be another 'find' or discovery of a piece of writing which ought to be included, and inevitably such pieces will also come to light when the book has gone to the printers. Equally, there will always be an aspect which has not been touched on.

I was involved as much with exclusions as inclusions, and some of these omissions caused me considerable difficulty. I would have liked, for instance, to quote much more of Herman Melville and Nathaniel Hawthorne, but had to be rigorously selective. Similarly, I found it difficult to omit some very interesting writing by obscure nineteenth century novelists - William Wilson, for example, who wrote vividly of life in Everton and other Merseyside settings, including a Liverpool foundry; or William Edwardes Tirebuck. Ultimately my choice was influenced by the availability of the text today. On the theme of poverty in nineteenth century Liverpool, Silas K. Hocking's *Her Benny* (1879) a story of street waifs, can be obtained by today's readers, whereas James Lockhart Haigh's *Sir Galahad of the Slums* (1907) cannot.

Considerations of space and balance dictated the omission of writers I would otherwise have included: Hall Caine, a Liverpool novelist who regarded the Picton Library as his university; Ralph Waldo Emerson, whose perceptive comment in 1847, 'There is a fierce strength in the streets', has lasting relevance; Oscar Wilde who, returning from America in December 1883, lectured in Birkenhead and spoke of being delighted by the Liverpool fog; and Washington Irving, Mark Twain, Lytton Strachey, John Cowper Powys, James Hanley.

Not all my research took place in libraries. It was exhilarating to become a tourist in my own locality, to walk about as if a visitor, with heightened receptivity. I viewed with renewed admiration Liverpool's fine architecture, statues and monuments, its two inspiring cathedrals - and at this point decided that the anthology would contain visual images. Of, for instance, St George's Hall (1854) - in Sir John Betjeman's opinion 'The finest neo-classical building in

Europe', 490 ft in length, its plateau the scene of many historic gatherings, from suffragette and strike demonstrations to the candlelit wake for John Lennon. Here are the cenotaph and the lion sculptures (I remember as a child being held up to touch their huge paws). Designed by Harvey Lonsdale Elmes in his early twenties, St George's Hall, as Dr Quentin Hughes has said, 'should remain forever the symbol of Liverpool's belief in the ability of youth.' In my picture research I explored the collections of the Walker Art Gallery and the Merseyside Maritime Museum, and photographed some familiar landmarks. The Liver Birds are even more impressive close up, as I discovered from the roof of the *art nouveau* Royal Liver Building where they perch above on their twin cupolas, each bird 18ft high with a wing span of 12ft. From here, at more than 300ft, the view of Birkenhead and Liverpool joined by the Mersey brings to mind John Masefield's description of 'that double city'. The Renaissance style Port of Liverpool Building is strikingly beautiful with its burnished dome, the interior of which bears Psalm 107, 'They that go down to the sea in ships' - another reminder that Liverpool, like Venice, is wedded to the sea.

The anthology is arranged chronologically, in four parts. Part One begins with Geoffrey Tresise's imaginative study of the local dinosaur, Chirotherium, one of the first inhabitants of this area which many centuries later became Merseyside. Poems, novels and other pieces by twentieth century writers evoke these early periods when successive invaders settled in the region. There are legends and a medieval ghost story (translated from Latin by Paul Booth); and part of the middle-English poem on Sir Gawain, who hunts the Green Knight 'in the wilderness of Wirral'.

While Geoffrey Chaucer was the earliest of the many great writers to visit (in 1358, a young member of Prince Lionel's household), he did not mention Liverpool in his work. His contemporary, the author of *Piers Plowman*, possibly also travelled in the vicinity of the Mersey, referring to Halton Castle in his poem: 'Thoro the pass of Haltoun / Poverte might passe whith owte peril of robbyrye.'

The rise of Liverpool commenced with King John's letters patent of August 1207, creating into a borough and port the 'Liverpul' which had previously been merely a small fishing village on a creek (not named in the Domesday survey). King John saw the potential of his new 'free borough on the sea', advantageously positioned on the west coast, with its powerful, tidal river surging out to the Irish Sea, its 'Pool' an inlet, where ships could shelter. After four centuries of slow growth, the maritime and commercial expansion of Liverpool accelerated in the late seventeenth century, when trade with America increased rapidly. This led to the creation of the world's first wet commercial dock in 1715 (Thomas Steers cleverly utilised the mouth of the Pool, the remainder being covered by new streets). The town developed, with fine buildings, attracting travellers such as Daniel Defoe, who came to see 'one of the wonders of Britain'. Like Celia Fiennes before him, he described being ferried across the 'Mersee' from Wirral - they were using one of the oldest ferry services in Europe, begun by the Benedictine monks of Birkenhead Priory (founded 1150). The ferry service continues to this day (world-famous in the words of the moving song by Gerry Marsden).

Social life and the theatre were thriving in mid-eighteenth century Liverpool, described by Samuel Derrick of Bath. The arts were flourishing in this period of enormous mercantile development, an ever-growing prosperity gained largely through the iniquitous Slave Trade, known as the "Africa Trade". Extracts of poetry and prose describe the triangular system, the slave ships and the emotions which slavery and its profits aroused. Here, a poem by a present-day young Liverpool poet, Paul Cosgrove, accompanies the work of William Roscoe, one of the finest poets of the eighteenth century, a Liverpool philanthropist and M.P., a founder of the Society for the Abolition of the Slave Trade. Part One ends with the Abolition in 1807, and Thomas de Quincey's description of 'a prodigious fire' which destroyed the Goree warehouse.

In Part Two, the vastly expanded port and town, with its extremes of wealth and poverty, splendid buildings and appalling slums, and the river thronged with sailing ships and steamships, are seen through the eyes of various visiting writers, novelists and poets, ranging from Thomas Carlyle to Francis Kilvert; from Charles Dickens to Sir Arthur Conan Doyle (Sherlock Holmes solving a Mersey murder); from Felicia Hemans (with a surprisingly sharp and almost feminist poem about girls at prayer in a Wavertree school) to John Masefield. Herman Melville, arriving in 1839, was amazed by the Mersey, 'an arm of the sea', and described the impact Liverpool made on him and other sailors, in his autobiographical novel *Redburn* (1849). Nathaniel Hawthorne, the U.S. Consul in Liverpool, commuted daily across the Mersey from Rock Ferry to his office on the waterfront - his *English Notebooks* are rich in impressions of people and places on both sides of the river. His attitude was ambivalent, as he was fascinated but repelled by what he saw, deliberately choosing to walk through the most poverty-stricken areas, observing street life. It is interesting that Emily Brontë derived Heathcliff from these Liverpool streets.

By this date Birkenhead had begun its growth, based on the development of Laird's Shipyard, pioneering iron ships; and the new resort of New Brighton thrived at the estuary mouth, where the Mersey spills into Liverpool Bay. Cunard and many other shipping lines were based in Liverpool, the 'Port of a Thousand Ships', one of the largest in the world. White cargoes of cotton had replaced the tragic black cargoes, the Industrial Revolution promoting commercial success, with a new slavery in Lancashire mills. Mass emigration and immigration brought in thousands of people of different nations and races, to create the cosmopolitan character of Liverpool. In the second half of the nineteenth century it became predominantly Celtic, with a huge proportion of Irish settlers (in the wake of the 1840 potato famine), a continuing influx of Welsh, especially from nearby North Wales, and increasing numbers of Scottish seeking employment. Here too was the first Black community in Europe. This mix of peoples, particularly the Celtic, was to result in the distinctive Liverpudlian character, quick-witted, imaginative, story-telling, warm-hearted, with a sustaining humour and resilience in the face of adversity, and a strong sense of community. This character was not given a literary voice until the next century.

There was less need for twentieth century writers in Part Two, the few exceptions being Frank Milner's insights into the growth of Liverpool as a centre of Art (a tradition strongly maintained ever since); an extract from Jimmy McGovern's penetrating radio play on Gerard Manley Hopkins' *Felix Randal*; Kit Wright's poem on an extraordinary Liverpool 'Mole'; and poems by Elizabeth Bartlett, Gwyn Parry and myself, illustrative of the immigrant population (my own mixed ancestry is Scandinavian, Welsh, Italian, Irish).

The twentieth century falls naturally into two sections, 1960 being the watershed. Part Three covers the decades when Liverpool was at its zenith, known as 'the second city of the British Empire' (city status was given in 1880), gateway to America, ocean liners and cargo vessels queuing to enter the Mersey, the new waterfront buildings a magnificent skyline. Yet there was also a dire legacy of slums and poverty, unemployment and strikes, given graphic description in the work of George Garrett, a Liverpool-Irish writer and docker. Extracts from the diaries and letters of writers such as Wilfred Owen, Olaf Stapledon and George Orwell, autobiographical writings of Siegfried Sassoon, Graham Greene, J. B. Priestley, Helen Forrester, novels by Nicholas Monsarrat, Malcolm Lowry, John Brophy and Beryl Bainbridge, capture essential aspects of Merseyside in the years which include two World Wars. This section closes with an extract from Alun Owen's *No Trams to Lime Street*, a television play, significant in the author's use of the Liverpool accent and idiom, which he had to defend at the time and which can now be seen as a milestone in the growth of Merseyside's sense of identity (and a foundation for Phil Redmond's long-standing television success, *Brookside*).

Increasingly, as the century progresses, writers from Merseyside emerge to prominence in every form of writing - poets, novelists, short story writers and scriptwriters for stage, radio and television. Part Four consists almost entirely of Merseyside authors and, significantly, there are many more poets. Other contributors also have strong Merseyside associations, such as Edward Lucie

Smith who compiled *The Liverpool Scene*, Ian Nairn who writes, with an architect's love, of the city's 'superb buildings', the poet Simon Rae (whose mother is from Liverpool) contributing a compassionate poem on the Hillsborough tragedy; and I have included poems about the Albert Dock by two writers from America and Holland who attended my Creative Writing School in the Summer Academy at Liverpool University.

Undoubtedly, in the 1960s and 70s a new confidence in the Merseyside identity developed as a result of the phenomenal success of the Beatles; in the wake of Merseybeat came the Mersey Sound poets (Adrian Henri, Roger McGough, Brian Patten), the words and music of The Scaffold (Roger McGough, Mike McCartney, John Gorman), the television writer Carla Lane (first successful with *The Liver Birds*), Willy Russell, Alan Bleasdale, Jim Hitchmough, Ramsey Campbell, Keith Birch (whose *The Merseysiders* was the first local radio soap opera) and many more who are represented in the anthology. Social comment, sharp humour and a strong local flavour characterise much of this work, approximating to a regional literature which has national, sometimes international, impact.

In spite of economic decline and unemployment, literary expression and the arts as a whole flourished in the 1980s - and continue to burgeon. Merseyside has, in the late twentieth century, a potent literary presence and the most intense concentration of arts activity outside London. A vibrant and creative city, Liverpool continues to change and redevelop, and is today a major centre of education, the media and tourism, with one of Europe's busiest Freeports. The literary tradition of Merseyside, part of its rich cultural heritage, will certainly continue into the twenty-first century.

It is my hope that this anthology will help to widen public perception of Merseyside - and Liverpool in particular - promoting an understanding beyond the clichéd images. An anthology is a book to be dipped into, but which should also be a unified whole when read in sequence. Here, in holding a mirror to Merseyside through the ages, the evolution of life in Britain is reflected, literature illuminating history.

Gladys Mary Coles, 1993

I am grateful to many people for their help, and I wish particularly to thank: Michael Stammers, Keeper of the Merseyside Maritime Museum; Frank Milner, Head of Education at the Walker Art Gallery and Lady Lever Gallery; Marij Van Helmond, Curator of Regional History, Merseyside Maritime Museum;

Dr. Geoffrey Tresise, Curator of Earth and Physical Sciences, Liverpool Museum; Paul Booth, Senior Lecturer, Dept. of History, Liverpool University; Philip Key, Arts Editor of the *Daily Post*; Joe Riley, Arts Editor of the *Liverpool Echo*; - each of whom contributed specialist pieces to the anthology.

My thanks are extended also to: Joseph Sharples, Assistant Curator of Fine Art, the Walker Art Gallery; Tony Tibbles, Curator of Maritime History, Merseyside Maritime Museum; Gail Cameron, Assistant Curator of Maritime History, M.M.M.; David Hillhouse, Principal Museums Officer, Wirral Museums; Staff of the Maritime Record Centre; Staff of the University of Liverpool Sidney Jones Library also Special Collections and the Continuing Education Library; Staff of the Liverpool Central Libraries Record Office and Local History Library; Staff of the Birkenhead Central Library, Local Studies; Staff of Clwyd Library Services.

Kind interest and encouragement from Willy Russell, Simon Rae, Jim Hitchmough, Keith Birch, Adrian Henri, Diane Massey, William Leece, Roger McGough, Nick Batey, Dewi Roberts, Paul Catcheside, Phil Taylor, Ron Travis and Angela Heslop, were greatly appreciated. And, for suggesting the title, a special thank you to Theresa Griffin.

I wish to thank all the authors, photographers and owners of copyright material who have generously allowed me to use their work. I am grateful to the E. Chambré Hardman Trust, Keith G. Medley, Steve Barnes of Living Memories Ltd., Margaret Roberts of Peter Kaye Photography, and Patrick Maloney of Maritime Prints for permissions and for trusting me with uniquely valuable material; also the Trustees of the National Museums and Galleries on Merseyside, and the Liverpool Daily Post and Echo Ltd.

For their part in the production of the book in its various stages, I express my thanks to Richard Lloyd-Jones, Lawrence Nichols, Dave Jones, Ken Almond, Steve Fitzsimmons, John Traynor, Bill McNab, Emlyn Evans and Alun Williams.

Finally, I gratefully acknowledge on behalf of Headland Publications, financial assistance from Merseyside Arts, which helped this project to get underway. And I express my gratitude to the Foundation for Sport and the Arts for a grant which provided assistance towards printing the large number of illustrations which enhance the text.

G. M. C.

PART ONE

"Free borough upon the sea"

<small>LETTERS PATENT OF KING JOHN, 1207</small>

'What it may grow to in time,
I know not ...'

<small>DANIEL DEFOE, 1708</small>

"The Liverpoolians,
Free and Open as the Ocean
on which They Get their Riches"

<small>CATHERINE HUTTON, 1788</small>

Dinosaurs

The Hand-Animal Chirotherium, and others (Triassic)

In June 1838, workmen quarrying building stone in the Storeton Quarries near Birkenhead discovered the raised outlines of what appeared to be human hands on the underside of some of the sandstone slabs. So began one of the most baffling geological detective stories - the Case of the Invisible Dinosaur....

GEOFFREY TRESISE
The Invisible Dinosaur (1990)

The 'foot-prints' are impressed in marl, which also shows sun-cracking, ripple-marking and occasional rain-pitting. They have been covered by sand, now sandstone, which has taken natural casts. The animal which crawled over the muds was a great reptile called Chirotherium, and other smaller prints were made by a lizard, Rhynchosaurus. The muddy shore on which the prints were made was dried by the sun, and sands blowing over it filled up the foot-prints and preserved them when otherwise they soon would have been washed out. ...

There are two sets of prints to each animal, one much smaller than the other and obviously left by his front legs which were rarely placed on the ground. Probably he would drag himself out of the lake on all fours and then go off on his two hind legs. The size and distance apart of the prints gives an idea of the size of the animal. Curved lines made by the dragging of his tail are occasionally seen, proving that he had a large tail which was usually carried off the ground but sometimes dragged after him ... an animal about six feet high and twelve feet from snout to tail, poised somewhat like a Kangaroo, walking instead of hopping. Some of the foot-prints have been found so perfectly preserved that traces of scales are visible showing that his skin was scaly.

On the same marl bed as the foot-prints are a number of impressions of plants like the modern Horsetail (Equisitum) only larger. These probably grew round the lake and formed the chief food of the Chirotherium ...

Unfortunately he never left his skeleton for us to complete the picture, but bones are rarely preserved in sandstone as percolating waters soon dissolve them completely.

DAVID E. OWEN
The Story of Mersey and Deeside Rocks (1939)

Tribes and the Calder Stones
(Neolithic and Bronze Age)

The Calder Stones (among) the oldest works of human hands to be found in Liverpool ... formed the stone burial-chamber of a barrow ...

A great chieftain was dead; he had passed into the land of his fathers. Amidst the wailings and lamentations of his people, the hallowed corpse would be carried to some spot close to the grave it was to occupy. Perhaps a tall wooden funeral pyre would be erected, and the body placed reverently upon its summit. The high priest or holy man of the tribe would then set the great pile alight, and its flickering flames would soon flare up, consuming the corpse and silhouetting the weird, skin-clad figures of the mourners against the horizon. As the last flames died down, the charred bones would be gathered from the smouldering heap, scooped into a special urn and, to the accompaniment of mystic chanting and incantations, be placed in the dark rock-cavern which had been prepared for them.

One of the Calder Stones

RICHARD WHITTINGTON-EGAN
Liverpool, This is My City (1972)

Celts and Romans

I am called Marcus Geladius, and I am writing this account because the Britain I live in today is so different from the civilized, prosperous land of my childhood, that I want my grandchildren and great-grandchildren to know what life was like then and why it has changed to what it is now ...

On the last day of their lives my father and mother had been hunting on the peninsula that separates the Dee from the Seteia Aest on the north-east side, an unnavigable river with a marshy estuary. That peninsula is thickly wooded, with two ranges of low hills and patches of open heath; the place is sparsely inhabited, and abounds with game; very different from the narrow valleys and knotted hills that lay south and west of our estate. My parents had just returned across the Dee in two barges with their hunt servants and horses, when one of those chilly fogs with a thick fishy smell crept up from the estuary, and out of it, unseen by the signal stations on the banks or the catapult crew on the sacred island at the river mouth, came a narrow black craft, rowed swiftly upstream with fifteen oars a side. I know those fogs well, and have been caught by them often when sailing in the estuary with my cousins, Dron and Coryn. The black ship made for the small stone quay where our boats and barges were usually moored, and ran aground on a sandbank. Thirty or more Irish warriors leapt out and waded ashore, killed my father and mother and all their servants save Gorra, the chief huntsman, a tough old Ordovician who put an arrow through the throat of the nearest raider, escaped into the woods, climbed the steep track to our house on the crest, and gave the alarm. My grandmother dispatched a mounted messenger to the commandant of the XXth at Deva, then calmly arranged a screen of archers behind the tall shrubs that bordered our ornamental gardens. The raiders, panting uphill on a slippery path, walked into that ambush and were slain. Not one reached the house. A few years later she told me about it, though neither of us then realized that it was an early warning of disasters that were destined to change our lives and fortunes ....

JOHN GLOAG
The Eagles Depart (1973)

Dove Point, Meols

Sometimes, winter gales
storming the coast
find,
beneath shifting sands,
stumps of oak and ash
where once a Roman Legion camped.
Sometimes a coin,
Nerva or Constantine.

Sometimes, north winds
striding the waves
sing,
through flying spume,
wild airs the Roman Legion sang
before the altar stone
of Mithros or Jupiter.

Sometimes, through sea mist,
sandalled feet
that knew the seven hills
seem near,
near -

DORA KENNEDY

The Story of Ingimund, Norse Invader of Wirral, c.902-907

....the expulsion of the Norse hosts from Ireland...Hingamund their leader...to the island of Britain (Anglesey). The men of Britain assembled against them, and they were driven by force from the territories of the men of Britain. Afterwards Hingamund with his forces came to Edelfrida queen of the Saxons, for her husband, that is Edelfrid, was at the time in a disease...Now Hingamund was asking lands of the queen in which he would settle, and on which he would build huts and dwellings, for he was at this time weary of war. Then Edelfrida gave him lands near Chester (Wirral), and he stayed there for a time...the result of this was, when he saw the city full of wealth and the choice land around it, he desired to

4

possess them. Afterwards Hingamund came to the leaders of the Norsemen and Danes; he made a great complaint in their presence, and he said that they were not well off without good lands, and that it was right for them all to come to seize Chester and to possess it with its wealth and its lands. Many great battles and wars arose on account of that. This is what he said: "Let us beseech and implore them first, and if we do not get them willingly in this way let us contest them by force." All the leaders of the Norsemen and Danes agreed to this....

ANNALS OF IRELAND. THREE FRAGMENTS
in *Scandinavian England* by F.T. Wainwright (1975)

The Battle of Brunanburh, 937

> King Athelstan, the lord of warriors,
> Patron of Heroes, and his brother too,
> Prince Edmund, won themselves eternal glory
> In battle with the edges of their swords
> Round Brunanburh; they broke the wall of shields...
>   ...There the Norseman's chief
> Was put to flight, and driven by dire need
> With a small retinue to seek his ship.
> The ship pressed out to sea, the King departed
> Onto the yellow flood and saved his life ...

Extract from the Old English poem *The Battle of Brunanburh*
selected by RICHARD HAMER in *A Choice of Anglo-Saxon Verse* (1970)

Was Brunanburh Bromborough?

Anglo-Saxon Chronicle: "AD 937, This year, Athelstane, and Edmund his brother, led a force to Brunanburh, and there fought against Anlaff, and Christ helping, had the victory, and slew five kings and seven earls."

Anlaff, son of Sithric, was a Danish nobleman, on whom Athelstan had conferred the title of King of Northumberland. On the death of Sithric, Anlaff and his brother Godfrid assumed the sovereignty without waiting for the consent of Athelstan, who soon expelled them. Anlaff then entered into a conspiracy with Constantine, King of Scotland, and having collected a great body of Danish pirates, whom he found in the Irish Sea, and some Welsh princes, who were in fear of the growing power of Athelstan, he made, in conjunction with the forces of the Scottish King, an irruption into England, where they were signally defeated at Brunanburh. What place seems more likely as a meeting-place of the Welsh princes and pirates roving in the Irish Sea than Cheshire, or that the famous battle was fought alongside the Mersey here? Athelstan showed his goodwill by conferring on Chester the privilege of coining money, a privilege it retained until William and Mary ruled in England.

WILLIAM T. PALMER
The River Mersey (1944)

1207 and SO ON

They tell us King John was a bad King,
But was he misunderstood?
For when he came up to Lancashire
He did us a power of good.

Then good brother Richard was fighting
Away on the Holy Crusade,
He made fun of the Barons, ground down the serfs,
And grabbed all the taxes they paid.

They took him to Runneymede Island,
A place in the south, I believe,
They said, "Gracious Monarch, Illustrious Sir,
Sign here or we'll see you don't leave."

"I will not be bullied," the King cried,
"In the north I'll find warmer hearts,
I'll call in at Liverpool on the way up
And look into this matter of charts."

The Mayor met him down by the river,
Quoth the King, "I've not come to barter,
Just hand me a purse of gold each year,
A quill, and I'll sign that old Charter."

When the news was read out from the parchment,
Which was then the Plantagenet Times,
There were high jinks all over the hamlet,
Four hawks and six falcons in fines.

They brought out this bird called the Liver,
And put that twig in its beak,
Then they cried out, "To all generations
Will this symbol of gratitude speak;

For it isn't a fluke or a herring,
Which we know that bird should feed on,
But his emblem, a sprig of Plantagenet Broom,
In honour of Bad King John."

Ancient Corporate Seal of Liverpool
(Destroyed 1743)

DORA KENNEDY

6

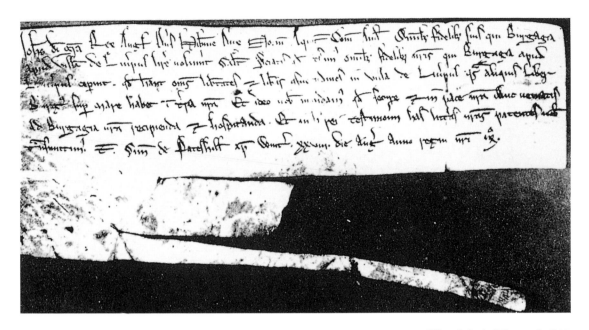

King John's 'Charter', 1207

TRANSLATION: *John by the grace of God King of England, Lord of Ireland, Duke of Normandy and Aquitane, Count of Anjou, to all his loyal subjects who may wish to have burgages in the township of Liverpul greeting. Know ye that we have granted to all our loyal subjects who shall take burgages in Liverpul that they shall have all the liberties and free customs in the township of Liverpul which any free borough on the sea has in our land. And therefore we command you that in safety and in our peace ye come thither to receive and occupy our burgages. And in testimony hereof we transmit to you these our letters patent. Witness Simon de Pateshill. At Winchester the 28th day of August in the 9th year of our reign [1207].*

The Cistercian Abbey of Stanlow (Stanlaw), 1178-1296
Poem by an unknown Stanlaw Monk

Stanlaw! where I hope to lie
When my hour shall come to die,
Hard thy lot and brief thy fame
Still thou teachest by thy name —
Stan and Law together blending
Name all neighbour names transcending.
Law is Hill—I lift my eyes
To the hills beyond the skies.
Stan is Stone - O! Corner Stone!
What art thou but Christ alone ?
Altar stone, on thee there lies
That blest Bread of Sacrifice.
Stanlaw! 'tis the Lord above
Gave thy name to tell his love.

Trans. from Latin by the Rev. F. G. Slater, Vicar of Ince

7

The First Ferry

It is a frosty November morning sometime in the 12th century. A small group of monks in loose black gowns with baggy sleeves and cowls coming to a point over their heads, are wading through the shallows of the Mersey as they manoeuvre a small boat towards a primitive jetty on what is now known as the Birkenhead side of the river. She is a craft with both sail and oars. Perched unhappily upon the jetty is a heavy-jowelled merchant. He blows into his palms but he cannot drum his numb feet for warmth lest the frail structure gives beneath him. The expression on his twitching features alternates between impatience and anxiety as he grimly observes the performance before him. But anxiety is the dominant partner. For that pot-bellied citizen of commerce, those many years ago, was doing something that very few people had done before him but that millions would do after him . . . taking a ferry across the Mersey.

DAVID CHARTERS
*Ferries Forever: A Closer Look
at the Mersey Ferries of Past and Present* (1984)

Birkenhead Priory

Birkenhead Priory in 1790, from an old drawing.

1st Royal Charter, Edward II, 1318
...granted that the prior and monks 'may erect sufficient Houses on their own proper ground at Birkened, in the place of the passage aforsaid, or as near as can conveniently be done for entertainment of such men and hold the same to them and their successors forever. And that the men about to dwell in these Houses may buy and sell victuals for the sustenance of the men about to pass over the said Arm of the Sea...'

2nd Royal Charter, Edward III, 1330
...granted that the prior and monks 'and their successors forever may have there the Passage over the said Arm of the Sea as well for men as for horses and other things whatsoever, and may receive for that Passage what is reasonable without let or hindrance...'

The Forests of Wirral

... the Hundred was afforested by Randel de Meschines, fourth Earl of Chester, who, as a reprisal for some predatory expeditions of the men of Wirral, ordered their farms to be destroyed, and afforested the whole district, appointing Alan Sylvestre to the office of bailiff or chief ranger. The bailiwick of the forest was afterwards held by the Stanleys of Storeton and Hooton.

"For nearly two centuries and a half, the inhabitants of the forest and the small villages on its borders, continued the mere serfs of the barons, ever ready to embark in any expedition against their more civilised, or more opulent, neighbours. At length the citizens of Chester suffered so much from the proximity of the forest, and the shelter it afforded to the freebooters, that they complained to Edward the Black Prince, then Earl of Chester, at whose request his father ordered it to be disforested." (Mortimer)

HAROLD EDGAR YOUNG
A Perambulation of the Hundred of Wirral (1909)

From Blacon Point to Hilbree,
A squirrel may leap from tree to tree.

Old Rhyme

The Wirral Horn

from *Sir Gawain and the Green Knight* (late 14th century)

He had no friend but his horse in the forest and hills,
no man on his march to commune with but God,
till anon he drew near unto Northern Wales.
All the isles of Anglesey he held on his left,
and over the fords he fared by the flats near the sea,
and then over by the Holy Head to high land again
in the wilderness of Wirral: there wandered but few
who with good will regarded either God or mortal.
And ever he asked as he went on of all he met
if they had heard any news of a knight that was green
in any ground thereabouts, or of the Green Chapel.
And all denied it, saying nay, and that never in their lives
a single man had they seen that of such a colour could be.

trans. J. R. TOLKIEN
from *Sir Gawain and the Green Knight* (1975)

9

A Medieval Ghost Story, 1373

A story relating to the celebration of Mass, told by Master Richard de Puttes in 1373.

There was once a man who lived in Haydock in Lancashire, who had kept a mistress who had borne him sons. She had died, however, and he had subsequently married another woman. Some time later, he was going to a smithy to have his plough-irons (that is, the coulter-knife and ploughshare) fettled and sharpened. The blacksmith in question lived at Hulme, a village which is about two miles away from Haydock. On his return from there, at night time, the man passed a cross at the side of the road in Newton-le-Willows, when he suddenly felt an extreme attack of fear and horror coming over him. While he stood there, stricken with terror, he looked round and saw an apparition like a dark shadow. He called upon the thing not to do him any harm, and asked it what it might be. A voice came out of the shadow and said to him,

"Be not afraid. I am the woman who was your lover. I have been permitted to come back to you to seek your help."

The man then asked how things were with her.

"Bad", she replied. "But if you wish, you can help me."

He answered, "I will gladly do anything I can. Just tell me what to do."

She said, "I can only be delivered from the bitter punishment which is being inflicted on me by means of Masses celebrated by worthy priests."

To which he said, "I will have Masses said for you, even if I have to spend all my goods."

She replied, "Don't be afraid. Just put your hand on my head, and take what you find there."

He did what she asked, and took a handful of deep black hair. Now the woman, when she was alive, had had a head of fine golden locks. She spoke again, and said to him, "When you have had as many Masses said for me as there are hairs in this handful, then I will be released from punishment."

He agreed to this, thereupon she said to him, finally, "Come to this place at such and such a time and you will learn what has happened to me."

Then she vanished.

The man then took the handful of hair and put it for safe-keeping in a hole in a door-post. Then he immediately sold half his property, and with the money he raised from it he journeyed far and wide, looking for priests and having large numbers of Masses said. At times he would come back, and have a look at the handful of hair, and so it went on until every strand had turned to gold. Finally, at the appointed time, he came to Newton Cross, and waited there for some time. Suddenly, he saw a light in the distance, moving quickly towards him. When it had reached him, a voice spoke from out of the light, which thanked him many times and said, "Blessed be you amongst all men. You have delivered me from the extremity of pain, and now I am going to bliss."

After a few more words had passed between them, she left him and sped away.

trans. PAUL BOOTH,
Preacher's Common-Place Book

Liverpool Castle in 1442. *The sandstone castle was built by William de Ferrers, Sheriff of Lancaster, c. 1207-35. An earlier castle existed at West Derby.*

Lyrpole and Wyrale:
John Leland, the King's Antiquary, visits c.1536-39

Lyrpole, alias Lyverpoole, a pavid towne, hath but a chapel. Walton a iiii miles of, not far from the sea is a paroche chirch. The king hath a castelet there, and the Earl of Darbe hath a stone howse there. Irisch merchants cum much thither, as to a good haven. After that Mersey water cumming towards Runcorne in Cheshire, is (called) Runcorne Water. At Lyrpole is smaul custome payed, that causith marchantes to resorte thither. Good marchandis at Lyrpole, and much Irish yarrn that Manchester men do buy there.

Wyrale begynnith lesse than a quarter of a mile of the very cite self of Chester... Weste Kirkeby a village hard on the shore. And half a mile lower is Hillebyri, as the very point of Wyrale.

This Hillebyri at the flood is al environid with water as an isle, and than the *trajectus* is a quarter of a mile over and 4 fadome depe of water, and at ebbe a man may go over the sand. It is about a mile in cumpace, and the grounde is sandy and hath conies. There was a celle of monkes of Chestre, and a pilgrimage of our Lady of Hilbyri .... It is by estimation a XVI mile from the point of Hilbery to crosse strait over to the next shore in Lancastershire.

For Lyrpole lyith a X miles into the lande from the mouthe of Mersey Water, and lytle lak of XX from the very barre of Mersey that lyith in the mayne se ....

From Hilbyri to cumpace about the shore of Wyral on Mersey side to Walesey village on the very shore, wher men use much to salten hering taken at the se by the mouth of Mersey, is a seven or eight miles.

Thens a 2 myles to the fery house on Wyrale shore, and there is a *trajectus proximus* to Lyrpole a 3 miles over.

Aboute half a quarter of mile upward hard on Wyral shore is Byrk(et) a late a priory of a XVI monkes as a celle to Chester without any village by it.

Al the shore grounde of Wyral apon De side ys highe bankid, but not veri hilly grounde. And so ys the bank of Wyrale onto Birket on Mersey side.

JOHN LELAND Itinerary, c.1536-39

Speke Hall (centre), built by the Norris family, completed 1598, with additions 1605 and 1612. The Brasses of Henry Norris (left) and his wife Clemence (right) (1524) in Childwall Church.

Curtailing of Liverpool street entertainers, 1571

We agree that no players of interludes, jugglers, jesters or wandering people bryngyng into this towne any monstrouse or straunge beasts, or other visions royde or rayre, to theyre lucre and distress of the queens subjects without licence of Mr Maior tyme beyng.

Liverpool Town Books

Racing at Liverpool, 1577

This year on the holy day of the Ascension, there was a running of horses at Liverpool for a silver bell given by Mr Ed Torbock, to be run for every year under the patronage of the Mayor.

Liverpool Town Books

An early play in which Liverpool is mentioned, ̀performed by Lord Strange's players in 1590

Since fortune hath thus spitefully crost our hope, let us leave this quest and harken after our King, who is at this daie landed at Lirpole.

from Fair Em, the Miller's Daughter of Manchester, with the Love of William the Conqueror, a Pleasant Comedie. (c. 1590)

A Plague, Liverpool, 1558

1558. It is ordered that all persons who may happen to be visited with the pestilence in the said town, that every of them shall depart out of their houses and make their cabbins on the heath, and there to tarry from the feast of the Annunciation of our Lady until the feast of St. Michael the Archangel; and from the said feast of St. Michael until the said feast of the Annunciation of our Lady, to keep them on the back side of their houses, and keep their doors and windows shut on the street side until such time as they have license from the Mayor to open them, and that they keep no fire in their houses, but between 12 and 3 of the clock at afternoon and that no other person or persons be of family conversation or dwell with them upon pain of imprisonment, and to keep their own houses, and that they walk in no street except for a reasonable cause, and their houses to be cleaned or dyght with such as shall be appointed by Mr Mayor for the safeguard of the Town.

TOWN CLERK OF LIVERPOOL, *Town Books*

A Great Storm, December 1565

.... abowte x or xi of the clocke that Sondaye at nyght sodenlie spronge and rose the marveliust and terribliest storm of wynd and wether that continued abowt six howres or lytyll lesse, as well upon land as water, to the great hurte of the cominalte, and theyr howsies and barnes, wyth many wynd mylne cleyne overthrowen and all to broken, wyth great hurt upon churchies and chapells...and other hurtes of glasse wyndowys ... a part of our chapell wall of this towne next the full sea marke brostyn and wasshyn out...

TOWN CLERK OF LIVERPOOL, *Town Books*

Liverpool, 1650 (by Herdman)

A Great Frost, Wallasey, 1683

A great frost soe that people went over the pooll anywhere at any time of the tide and it was thought by severall that a man at low water at some time might have gone over to Liverpoole, all passage out of these parts to Liverpoole was by Warrington or fidler's ferry, where they went over on Ise.

Parish Records, St Hilary, Wallasey

The Legend of The Boot (The Boot Inn, Liscard)

A Wallasey Highwayman

Our Good Queen Bess did rule this realm when honest Jack was hoste unto this Inne, well helped by lusty wife and bucksome daughter Joan. One wilde dark night when all were snoring snug abed, a fierce wilde horseman bedaubed with muck and blood did gallope to the door and make a thunderous thump thereon; when our hoste did open unto him he rushed intoe the house, a big jack boot in one hand and a great horse pistol in t'other, calling wild foul wordes for instant meat and drink. He had a beastly savage look and our hoste did eye him well whilst meat and drink went bolting down his wolfish maw. Thinks Jack there's booty in that boot; for when he thumped it on the board there was a chink of gold, the pistol too was bye.

Our honest Jack was cute and bold, and when he brought more wine he wilful spilt it on the man, and when he turned in wrath, Jack whipped the pistol to his sconce and called for lusty wife and bucksome daughter Joan and they did bind the robber safe and sure and made the gold-lined boot secure. This scarce well done when in there bounced three gentlemen, one with bloody sconce and bootless leg, who, when he saw the robber bound was glad, but soon began to wail his boot. Now did our hoste begin to crow and bid his women bring the gold-lined boot. The gentleman was then in hearty mood and gave ten guineas to our hoste and ten more to lusty wife and bucksome Joan. He gave the robber to the gibbet and the Boot to be a sign to this Inne while it doth stand.

from The Boot Inn

Litherpole, commonly called Lirpole...
William Camden's Description, 1586

The Mersey spreading and presently contracting its stream from Warrington falls into the ocean with a wide channel very convenient for trade, where opens to view Litherpole, commonly called Lirpole, from a water extending like a pool, according to the common opinion, where is most convenient and most frequented passage to Ireland; a town more famous for its beauty and populousness than for its antiquity; its name occurs in no ancient writer except that Roger of Poictou who was lord, as then stated, of Lancaster, built a castle here, the custody of which has now for a long time belonged to the noble and knightly family of Molineux, whose chief seat is in the neighbourhood of Sefton ... This Roger held, as appears by Domesday Book, all the lands between the rivers Ribble and Mersey.

WILLIAM CAMDEN
Britannia (1586)

from *Hey for Lancashire !*

Scarce could the labouring Muse salute this lively Shire,
But strait such shouts arose from every Mosse and Mere,
And Rivers rushing downe, with such unusuall noyse,
Upon their peably sholes, seem'd to expresse their joyes,
That Mersey (in her course which happily confines
Brave Cheshire from this Tract, two County Palatines)
As ravish'd with the newes, along to Lerpoole ran,
That all the Shores which lye to the Vergivian*,
Resounded with the shouts ...

Thus chiefe of Merseys traine, away with her I runne,
When in her prosperous course she watreth Warrington,
And her faire silver load in Lerpoole downe doth lay,
A Road none more renownd in the Vergivian Sea.

*The Irish Sea.

MICHAEL DRAYTON
from *Poly-Olbion* (1613, 1622)

15

John Middleton, the Childe of Hale (1578-1623)

The local gentry gaudied me
to bring before the freakish king.
Tobacco, witches he was hot against.
Wrestling though
he liked; and I was prodigy enough.
I earned a purse of twenty pound
for putting out
his champion's thumb.

At Brasenose then
they went about my measurements;
full-length in all my lendings
painted me in oils,
while jackdaw scholars pecked about
my cowpat hands. I told them lies:
that dozing in a sandy place
I woke this size, burst all my clothes
like gorsepods in the summer's heat,
and stepping forth at nine-foot-three
met and hurled a fuming bull
head-first into Mersey silt.

And I was landmark after this
among the clods and fields of Hale.
But still my head undutifully turned
towards the river's runs of gold
each time I saw a sunset pour
its crucible. And sometimes too
the river glistened like a brand-
new knife, gulls threw their wings
like money thrown up carelessly.

It was then I longed
for marvels to be home among,
over the horizon's rim
where tall men walk ungawped-at.

At night I crawled into my mother's house
on hands and knees like some great dog.

John Middleton,
the Childe of Hale.

MATT SIMPSON

Sexual Overtones, 17th Century Alehouse Songs

Occasionally there are references to alehouse songs with very definite sexual overtones. A good illustration comes from the Old Swan in Petticoat Lane, West Derby, concerning the landlady, Hanna Horrocks, and her daughter.

> There stands a House in Darby
> Not far from the Old Swan
> The wife will play at Tarly
> With Jos the serving man
> Old Mother Rump and her daughter plump
> They never will refuse it.
>
> But Robin the Baker, a man of round wit,
> He often goes thither to get a fresh bit,
> Old Mother Rump and her daughter plump
> They never will refuse it.

So the song continues through a number of verses.

Standards in alehouses where songs of this nature were sung and gossip exchanged could lead to strained relations between husband and wife, for most men spent the bulk of their time in drinking with others of the same sex. Husbands who staggered home after a night's drinking often attacked their wives in a brutal fashion. When in 1630 Thomas Hough of Runcorn returned home after a day's drinking he attacked his wife Anna, 'beating her severely that her arms, legs and thighs were black and blew'.

JOHN ADDY
Sin and Society in the Seventeenth Century (1989)

The Civil War: Some Reports

Prince Rupert (encamped on Beacon Hill, Everton), 1643 - of Liverpool and its castle, occupied by Roundhead soldiers: 'a mere crow's nest which a parcel of boys might take'.

Adam Martindale (chief clerk to the Parliamentary foot regiment): The Royalists 'did slay almost all they met with to the number of three hundred and sixty, and, amongst others, diverse of their owne friends, and some artificiers, that never bore arms in their lives, yea, one poore blind man.'

Town Clerk: 'We finde that a great company of Inhabitants were Murthered and slaine by Prince Rupert's forces...the names of the Murtherers we cannot as yet be certified of any of them'.

Oliver Cromwell, on the Battle of Winwick, 10 August, 1648: 'We lay that night in the field close by the enemy, lying very wet and dirty, where we had some skirmishing...The next morning the enemy marched towards Warrington, made a stand at a pass near Winwick; we held them in some dispute till our army was come up, they maintaining the pass with great resolution for many hours; but our men, by the blessing of God, charged home upon them, beat them from their standing, where we killed about a thousand of them, and took (as we believe) about two thousand prisoners, and prosecuted them home to Warrington Town, where they possessed the bridge. As soon as we came thither, I received a message from Lieutenant-General Bailey, desiring some capitulation, to which I yielded, and gave him these terms: That he should surrender himself and all his officers and soldiers prisoners of war, with all his arms, ammunition, and horses, upon quarter for life, which accordingly is done...And thus you have their infantry ruined.'

Edward Moore of Bank Hall laments the death of his three sons from smallpox, 1672

Two days before my wife's coming to London it pleased God to visit my daughter with the small pox and when she mended my eldest son William fell sick who after five days died: a child so generously bemoaned as I think the like never was in our parts - whilst he was sick 50 or 60 people a day of my tenants coming or sending to see him. But when he was gone, and having another child lying a dying in the house I resolved to bury him very private between 12 and 1 of the clock at night.

And when night came, I resolved to carry him in my coach privately only with 40 or 50. But truly before he went out of the house there were not so little as 800 people.

And about a mile from Liverpool, on foot, the Mayor with the mace and wand, the aldermen and the common council and at least 700 or 800 people met the corpse so that when we came to the church there was not so little as 1,600 people...I believe the like lamentation was not seen about us at any funeral in man's memory....

Truly I bore the affliction pretty well till I saw and heard such a great and general lamentation amongst my neighbours. And such a sad and mournful tone through the whole church I thought then that my heart would have broke ... To lose him though but 14 years old had found so true and general a resentment at his grave by all his neighbours... .when I came home I fell sick and kept my bed near three weeks...

Then in 4 days my youngest son Thomas died, who was buried at one of the clock, as the former, with many hundreds that met him. Then my wife sent her two sons that yet were to the parsonage house an mile and a half from us where it pleased God after some 5 or 6 days to visit my son Fenwick with the small pox and after 4 days he died and I buried him at another church in a buriel place belonging to Bank Hall.

EDWARD MOORE
Letter to his cousin

Edward Moore names one of his Liverpool streets

The reason why I named it Bridges Alley was because it lay betwixt two bridges, the one at the west end, where never water runs under, made for to spin under; the other at the east end is my tenant, Thomas Bridge, a drunken fellow; upon which these verses were made as follows: -

> In old, bridges for water were,
> But these are made for other fare;
> The one for spinning, and, it's said,
> The other's for the drunken trade.
> Let this be set to England's wonder;
> Two bridges, and no water under!

EDWARD MOORE
Moore Rental

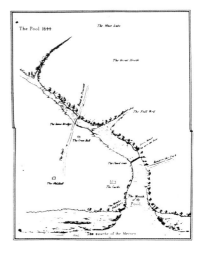

The Pool, 1644

William III and His Army Sail from Hoylake to Ireland, 1690
extracts from the diary of Dr Rowland Davies

Saturday 26th April 1690
We dined at our lodgings in Chester and, after dinner, they all grew very busy in sending their things away to Hoylake where lay our recruits of horse, being four hundred, and the Nassau and Brandenburgh regiments . . .

Sunday 27th April
In the morning, all our sparks were in a great hurry, the wind presenting fair . . .

Saturday 3rd May
In the afternoon I put my trunks, bed, saddle, and hat-case on board Mr Thompson's boat, and sent them to Hoylake, where they were shipped off with the Major's things.

Tuesday 6th May
In the morning we took horse for Hoylake, and passing by Neston, we came there about one o'clock. At our coming we found the commissary at the parson's at dinner with Count Scravenmore, where we waited on him, and got an order for a ship to carry eighteen horses and twenty-three men. Then we dined at one Barker's where it cost us each two shillings, and in the evening we went to a farmer's house, where Frank Burton and I lay together. The surgeon, being of our quarters, we supped at the Major's quarters, about a quarter of a mile from us, and parted in the evening, with a resolution to be on board at nine in the morning; but the Major's tumbril having a wheel broken within two miles of Chester, it gave us some trouble.

Wednesday 7th May
In the morning we breakfasted at our quarters, and paid for ourselves and horses

three shillings each. Then about nine o'clock came on board, and at eleven shipped our horses, all but the major's carriage, which was not yet come up. The major and I walked a mile on the strand, and went into two islands in the bay, and then came on board, all the rest of the company being on board another ship drinking; they all came to us in the evening, and we lay on board all night.

Thursday 8th May
Sir William Russell, Frank Burton and I went on shore to a French suttler's, and at our return, the major's tumbril came up. In the afternoon we shipped it, and came down to the road's mouth, where we lay at anchor all night.

Friday 9th May
In the morning we set sail, the wind being ENE, and steered NW by N; we had but little wind, and got not out of sight of Wales all day.

William III left Kensington on 4th June, arrived at Chester on the 10th, stayed the night at Gayton and on leaving knighted Sir William Glegg, his host.

Wednesday 11th May
His majesty, accompanied by his royal highness the prince of Denmark and several other persons of quality, embarked at Highlake and the same afternoon went out to sea: but the wind wavering, made not much way that day. . .

DR ROWLAND DAVIES

'London in Miniature', 1698

From Burton ... I went to the ferry 9 miles to the River Meresy, another great river indeed much broader and a perfect sea for 20 mile or more; it comes out of Lancashire from Warrington and both this and the Dee empts themselves into the sea almost together a few leagues from Leverpoole, which poole is form'd by a poynt of land that runs almost round the entrance from the sea, being narrow and hazardous to strangers to saile in in the winter, the mouth of the river by reason of the sands and rocks is a gate to the river; this I ferry'd over and was an hour and halfe in the passage, its of great bredth and at low water is so deep and salt as the sea almost, tho' it does not cast so green a hew on the water as the sea, but else the waves toss and the rocks great all round it and is as dangerous as the sea; its in a sort of Hoy that I ferried over and my horses, the boate would have held 100 people.

Leverpool ... is built just on the river Mersy, mostly new built houses of brick and stone after the London fashion; the first original was a few fishermens houses and now is grown to a large fine town and but a parish and one Church, tho' there be 24 streetes in it; there is indeed a little Chappell and there are a great many Dessenters in the town; its a very rich trading town the houses of brick and stone built high and even, that a streete quite through lookes very handsome, the streetes well pitched; there are abundance of persons you see very well dress'd

20

and of good fashion; the streetes are faire and long, its London in miniature as much as ever I saw anything; there is a very pretty Exchange stands on 8 pillars besides the corners which are each treble pillars all of stone and its railed in over which is a very handsome Town Hall; over all is a tower and cupillow thats so high that from thence one has the whole view of the town and the country round; in a clear day you may see the Isle of Man.

CELIA FIENNES
The Journeys of Celia Fiennes,
Ed. Christopher Morris (1947)

The 'pretty Exchange'

from the **Diary of Nicholas Blundell of Little Crosby**

August, 1709.
18th My Wife and I began our Journey toward Whitchourch, we came too late for the Boats at Leverpoole so we went over at Runkhorne, after which we lost our way...
20th We dined at Chester & thence went to the Rock hous, but the Boat was gon, so we got a Smoke made, but no Boat coming to us, we went to the Wood Side, where Mr Darcy Chantrell came to us & got a Boat for us so we came home.

August, 1710.
31st I went to Netherton and spoke to Edward Hawkseye to come work for me, thence I went to Leverpoole & drunk at the Mariners Armes with Thomas Brownbill &c: I bought a fanciful Ring of Mugg Mettle to drink out of, & brock it ere I got it home. Till the 17th bad heasy weather or Rain almost every day, from 17th till the end of this Month veary good weather except now & then some Little Raine.

September, 1710.
9th Dr Cawood went hence to Leverpoole with Intention to have gon for Ireland but the Wind being cross he came back, I went with him, we dined at Mrs Lawsons, there was in the same Roome with us at Different times Robert Bootle & his Son, Richard Rose, Mr Molineux of the Grange, &c :, we drunk at the Woolpack with Mr Plumb, Patrick Kelly, &c:. My Ditchers found a Basket Hilted Sword & a Lock of a Gun or Pistoll as they were ditching between the Long Garden & the Bleaching Yord, tis probable they had laine there since the time of the sivell Wars.

10th Mr Aldred dined & suped here. My Wife read to me in a Spirituall book.

11th Dr Cawood went in the Morning to the Sea Side in hopes to have met the Ship which he designes to goe in for Ireland but he mist of her and towards Evening he went againe, my Wife & I went then with him but we all came back againe.

12th Dr Cawood took Shiping at Leverpoole for Ireland. I went to Leverpoole for some Lat Nailes, I drunk at the Woolpack with Dr Tarlton & with Mr Morphew at his own house.

13th One from Leverpoole. I Suppose the Huntsman was here to enquire for some of Leverpoole Hounds as were strayed here away as he was told. I planted some Hollins in the Stock-roots as were taken up in the Hollin Hedge where the way is designed to be into the New Orcherd.

December 1711

10th I met Sir Francis Anderton, Mr Steven Anderton &c: a Coursing in Formby, we had very fine spourt; Sir Francis Anderton, I, &c; Rid down to the Sea Side & saw them take Flooks; Mr Steven Anderton and Mr Flemming Rid a Rase upon the Sands. I dined about four of the Clock at Cattys in Formby with Mrs Blundell of Ince, Sir Francis Anderton, Mr Flemmin, &c:. I layed the wager there with Mr Steven Anderton about the Number of Holes in a Flagelet.

NICHOLAS BLUNDELL
The Great Diurnal of Nicholas Blundell Vol. One, 1702 - 1711

'One of the wonders of Britain'
Daniel Defoe visits 'Liverpoole', c. 1708

I entred Lancashire at the remotest western point of that county, having been at West-Chester upon a particular occasion, and from thence ferry'd over from the Cestrian Chersonesus, as I have already call'd it, to Liverpoole. This narrow slip of land, rich, fertile and full of inhabitants, tho' formerly, as authors say, a meer waste and desolate forest, is called Wirall, or by, some Wirehall. Here is a ferry over the Mersee, which, at full sea, is more than two miles over. We land on the flat shore on the other side, and are contented to ride through the water for some length, not on horseback but on the shoulders of some honest Lancashire clown, who comes knee deep to the boat side, to truss you up, and then runs away with you, as nimbly as you desire to ride, unless his trot were easier; for I was shaken by him that I had the luck to be carry'd by more than I car'd for, and much worse than a hard trotting horse would have shaken me.

Liverpoole is one of the wonders of Britain, and that more, in my opinion, than any of the wonders of the Peak; the town was, at my first visiting it, about the year 1680, a large, handsome, well built and encreasing or thriving town; at my second visit, anno I690, it was much bigger than at my first seeing it, and, by the report of the inhabitants, more than twice as big as it was twenty years before that; but, I think, I may safely say at this my third seeing it, for I was surpriz'd at the view, it was more than double what it was at the second; and, I am told, that it still visibly encreases both in wealth, people, business and buildings: What it may grow to in

22

time, I know not ...

The town has now an opulent, flourishing and encreasing trade, not rivalling Bristol, in the trade to Virginia, and the English island colonies in America only, but is in a fair way to exceed and eclipse it, by encreasing every way in wealth and shipping. They trade round the whole island, send ships to Norway, to Hamburgh, and to the Baltick, as also to Holland and Flanders; so that, in a word, they are almost become like the Londoners, universal merchants.

The trade of Liverpoole consists not only in merchandizing and correspondencies beyond seas; but as they import almost all kinds of foreign goods, they have consequently a great inland trade, and a great correspondence with Ireland, and with Scotland, for their consumption, exactly as it is with Bristol; and they really divide the trade with Bristol upon very remarkable equalities.

The new church built on the north side of the town is worth observation. 'Tis a noble, large building, all of stone, well finish'd; has in it a fine font of marble placed in the body of the church, surrounded with a beautiful, iron pallisado; the gift of the late Mr. Heysham, a merchant of London, but considerably concerned in trade on this side, and for many years member of Parliament for Lancaster. There is a beautiful tower to this church, and a new ring of eight very good bells.

The town-house is a fine modern building, standing all upon pillars of free-stone; the place under it is their Tolsey or Exchange, for the meeting of their merchants; but they begin to want room, and talk of enlarging it or removing the Exchange to the other part of the town, where the ships and the merchants business is nearer hand.

In a word, there is no town in England, London excepted, that can equal Liverpoole for the fineness of the streets, and beauty of the buildings; many of the houses are all of free stone, and compleatly finished; and all the rest (of the new part I mean) of brick, as handsomely built as London itself.

DANIEL DEFOE
A Tour through the Whole Island of Great Britain (1721 - 26)

The First Wet Dock, (1715)

... the ships lye aground before the town of Liverpool; 'tis bad riding afloat before the town, by reason of the strong tides that run here; therefore ships that ride afloat ride up at the Sloyne, where there is less tide.

CAPTAIN GRENVILLE COLLINS
Coasting Pilot (1693)

Liverpoole's situation being on the north bank of the river, and with the particular disadvantage of a flat shore. This exposed the merchants to great difficulties in their business; for though the harbour was good, and the ships rode well in the offing, yet they were obliged to ride there as in a road rather than a harbour. Here was no mole or haven to bring in their ships and lay them up, (as the seamen call it) for the winter; nor any key for the delivering their goods, as at Bristol,

Biddiford, Newcastle, Hull, and other sea ports: Upon this, the inhabitants and merchants have, of late years, and since the visible encrease of their trade, made a large basin or wet dock, at the east end of the town, where, at an immense charge, the place considered, they have brought the tide from the Mersee to flow up by an opening that looks to the south, and the ships go in north; so that the town entirely shelters it from the westerly and northerly winds, the hills from the easterly, and the ships lye, as in a mill-pond, with the utmost safety and convenience. As this is so great a benefit to the town, and that the like is not to be seen in any place in England but here, I mean London excepted, it is well worth the observation and imitation of many other trading places in Britain who want such a convenience, and, for want of it, lose their trade.

DANIEL DEFOE
A Tour through the Whole Island of Great Britain (1721 - 26)

Liverpool Pottery Rhyme, 18th Century
Inscription on a Liverpool ware jug:

Bucks View of Liverpool, 1728

At last it pleased His Majesty
To give peace to the Nation,
And honest hearts
From foreign parts
Came home for consolation,
Like lightning - for I felt new life
Now safe from all alarms
I rushed and found my Friend and Wife
Locked in each others Arms,
Yet fancy not
I bore my lot
Tame like a lubber - No
For seeing I was finely tricked
Plump to the devil I boldly kick'd
My Poll and my Partner Joe.

William Roscoe's boyhood

Roscoe was born in the quiet modest house of the Old Bowling Green, Mount Pleasant, near what is now the corner of Hope Street. Shortly after his birth, his family moved from the Old Bowling Green to another house with a bowling-green lower down, where his father kept a tavern and looked after a large market-garden. Roscoe senior is reputed to have been formerly a butler at Allerton Hall. Roscoe was happy in his family circle and, when he lost his mother at an early age, he addressed some of his poetic lines to her memory...

At the age of six he was sent to a day school kept by a Mr Martin in Paradise Street, one of the new streets erected on the drained site of the upper reaches of the Pool of Liverpool which were cut off from the river when the Old Dock was constructed in the mouth of the Pool 1710-15. The Dock was an immediate success and contributed to the rapid expansion of Liverpool during Roscoe's boyhood. Roscoe enjoyed his early schooldays and wrote a glowing account of Mr Martin: "To his care, and the instruction of a kind and affectionate mother, I believe I may safely attribute any good principle which may have appeared in my conduct during my future life."

GEORGE CHANDLER
William Roscoe of Liverpool 1753-1831 (1953)

Leverpoole, 'this very opulent town', 1760
To the Earl of Corke

Leverpoole, **Aug. 2, 1760**

MY LORD,

As I have, no where, met with any accurate account of this very opulent town, perhaps my endeavour to give your lordship something of that sort, may not prove disagreeable.

Leverpoole stands upon the decline of a hill, about six miles from the sea. It is washed by a broad rapid stream called the Mersee, where ships lying at anchor are quite exposed to the sudden squalls of wind, that often sweep the surface from the flat Cheshire shore on the west, or the high lands of Lancashire that overlook the town on the east; and the banks are so shallow and deceitful, that when once a ship drives there is no possibility of preserving her, if the weather prove rough, from being wrecked, even close to the town.

About three years since, a ship outward bound for America, richly laden, being badly piloted, struck and went immediately down. Her mast is still plainly to be seen; but she being effectually sucked in by the heavy sandy bottom, all attempts to weigh her up have been ineffectual.

This is the reason that so few ships anchor in the road; for the merchants endeavour to get them immediately into dock, where they lie very secure. The docks, which are three in number, have been built with vast labour and expense: they are, flanked with broad commodious quays surrounded by handsome brick houses, inhabited for the most part by sea-faring people, and communicating with the town by drawbridges and flood-gates, which a man must be wary in crossing over, as they are pretty narrow.

When the tide is full in, the bridges are drawn up, and the gates thrown open, for the passage of vessels inward and out. The corporation is now about widening the entrance to the docks, which is so narrow, that ships have sometimes run foul of each other, going out and in.

Leverpoole seems to be nearly as broad as it is long. The streets are narrow, but tolerably well built: the place is populous, though inferior in this respect to Bristol. Some of the houses are faced with stone, and elegantly finished.

The Exchange is a handsome square structure of gray stone, supported by arches. Being blocked up on two sides with old houses, it is so very dark, that little or no business can be transacted in it; but the merchants assemble in the street opposite to it, as they used to do before it was erected, and even an heavy shower can scarcely drive them into harbour. It was built at a great expense under the inspection of Messrs. Wood, the father and son. I need not tell your lordship that these are the celebrated architects, to whose correct taste and great genius Bath owes some of her finest ornaments and most useful improvements. In the upper part of the Exchange are noble apartments, wherein the corporation transact public business. The court-room is remarkably handsome, large and commodious; here the mayor tries petty causes, and has power to sentence for transportation. The assembly-room, which is also upstairs, is grand, spacious, and finely illuminated: here is a meeting once a fortnight to dance and play cards; where you will find some women elegantly accomplished, and perfectly well dressed. The proceedings are regulated by a lady stiled the Queen, and she rules with very absolute power.

The play-house, which is very neat, will hold about eighty pounds. Here a company of London performers exhibit during the summer-season, and acquire a great deal of money. I saw several pieces really well done. Holland, Shuter, and Mrs. Ward, who are at the head of the business, being very industrious, and careful to please, meet with great success; not more however than they deserve. The dances are admirably executed by Grimaldi, Maranesi, and Signora Provensalla. The scenes are prettily painted, the clothes very rich, and everything carried on with amazing propriety. They play three times a week; and behind the boxes there is a table spread, in the manner of a coffee-house, with tea, coffee, wines, cakes, fruit and punch; where a woman attends to accommodate the company, on very moderate terms, with such refreshment as they may prefer.

The infirmary is neat and handsome, and here the poor are taken particular care of. Dr. Green, who is a man of learning, perfectly skilled in his profession, shewed me, in a small garden behind this house, in which he attends, a curious exotic, not unlike the common heath-fir: he called it the Frost-plant; it being covered with a shining coat, that glitters in the sun: it is cold to the touch, and dissolves under the hand.

SAMUEL DERRICK

Letters of Samuel Derrick Esq,
Master of Ceremonies at Bath (1767)

Prologue for the opening of the Theatre Royal, Williamson Square, June 1772 (extract)

Long too has Mersey rolled her golden tide,
And seen proud vessels in her harbour ride;
Oft on her banks the Muse's sons would roam,
And wished to settle there a certain home;
Condemned, alas! to hawk unlicensed bays,
Contraband mummeries, and unlicensed plays!
Your fostering care at length relieved their woes,
Under your auspices this Staple rose.
Hence made free merchants of the lettered world,
Boldly adventuring forth, with sails unfurled,
To Greece, and Rome, Spain, Italy, and France,
We trade for play and opera, song and dance....

Theatre Royal

GEORGE COLMAN

Extract from another Prologue written for the same occasion

Where Mersey's stream long winding o'er the plain,
Pours his full tribute to the circling main,
A band of fishers chose their humble seat;
Contented labour blessed the far retreat:
Inured to hardship, patient, bold, and rude,
They braved the billows for precarious food:
Their straggling huts were ranged along the shore,
Their nets and little boats their only store.
    At length fair Commerce found the chosen place,
    And smiled approving on the industrious race.
    Lo! as she waves her hand, what wonders rise,
    Stupendous buildings strike the astonished eyes:
    The hollowed rock receives the briny tide,
    And the huge ships secure from Neptune ride;
    With busy toil the crowded streets resound,
    And wealth, and arts, and plenty, spread around.
The Muses next a willing visit paid;
They came to Pleasure's and to Virtue's aid;
A graceful ease and polish to impart,
Refine the taste and humanize the heart....
    This night the Muses' messenger I come,
    To bid you welcome to their new-raised dome:
    Well pleased the stately building they survey,
    And here their annual summer visit pay...
    O kindly cherish still their generous arts,
    And shew their noblest praises—in your hearts.

GEORGE PERRY

The Legend of the Mermaid of Black Rock (Perch Rock)

Master Robinson saw a beautiful mermaid reclining upon Black Rock one stormy night. Unconcerned about the inclement weather she combed her long golden hair and then with a smile came on board his stricken ship. He begged her to be a comfort and assistance to him in his low condition and so caught hold of her Comb and Green Girdle that was about her waist. She replied "Sir you ought not to rob a young woman of her riches and then expect a favour at her hands; but if you will give me my comb and girdle again, what lies in my power I will do for you." Gratefully he returned her possessions and she led him safe to land. Some days later she came to his father's house where he lay, placed a ring upon his finger and began to sing as she departed. Soon afterwards Master Robinson fell unconscious and died 'to the Wonderful Admiration of all the people who saw the young man.'

from Chap-books of Eighteenth Century Liverpool
retold by MAURICE HOPE *in Castles in the Sand (1982)*

Wreckers and Smugglers

Wallasey for wreckers,
    Poulton for trees,
Liscard for honest men,
    And Seacombe for thieves.

Traditional Rhyme

'God bless Father, God bless Mother
and God send us a wreck before morning.'

Old Wallasey Prayer

'Very Fiends'

On stormy days and nights, crowds might have been seen hurrying to the shore with carts, barrows, horses, asses, or oxen even, which were made to draw timber, bales, boxes or anything that the raging waters might have cast up. Many a half-drowned sailor has had a knock on the sconce (head) whilst trying to obtain a footing that has sent him reeling back into the seething water, and many a house had been suddenly replenished with eatables and drinkables and furniture and garniture, where previously bare walls and wretched accommodation only were visible.

Then for smuggling. Fine times the runners used to have in my young days. Scarcely a house in North Wirral that could not provide a guest with a good stiff glass of brandy or Holland's. The fishermen used to pretend to cast their nets to take the fish that abounded on our coasts, but their fishing was of a very different kind.

JAMES STONEHOUSE
Recollections of a Nonagenarian (1863)

Mother Redcap's

In the eighteenth and early nineteenth centuries there was a considerable amount of smuggling along the Wirral coast ... Until the heavy tax on salt was removed in 1825, very large quantities were smuggled and immense fortunes made ...

On a much smaller scale, rum, sugar and tobacco were landed from incoming vessels and found a ready market amongst those who asked no questions. The headquarters of the smugglers was a little public house on the shore, known as Mother Redcap's because of the red cap always worn by the woman who kept it.

In the latter half of the eighteenth century there were only a few farms between the village of Seacombe and the Magazines, so that Mother Redcap's (originally built in 1559) stood very much alone. No road led to it; the only approach by the shore. Behind it lay Liscard Moor and further inland still stretched Bidston Moss, little frequented wastes ideal for smuggling purposes ... Outside stood a pole surmounted by an unusual weather-vane; it did not indicate the wind's direction but the state of things inside Mother Redcap's. Pointing towards the house, it signified, "All's well; come in"; if pointing away from the pub, it told those in the know, "Danger; keep out."

From another post hung a painted sign depicting "Old Mother Redcap" holding a frying-pan over a fire, and underneath these doggerel lines:

> "All ye that are weary come in and take rest,
> Our eggs and our ham they are of the best,
> Our ale and our porter are likewise the same
> Step in if you please and give 'em a name."

Mother Redcap.

The front door was of five-inch oak, studded with square-headed nails and backed by several iron bars dropping into sockets, a formidable obstacle to quick entry. If an unwanted visitor forced the door he stepped on to a trapdoor which gave way and deposited him in the cellar some eight feet below. There were many cellars and tunnels underneath the site in which could be hidden not only contraband goods but sailors and others keeping out of the clutches of the notorious press-gang. Merchant sailors used to cross the river to hide in the cellars of the inn until their ships were ready to sail. Coming into port they would often take to their boats well out in the estuary, land in Cheshire and go into hiding. Many a ship had to be brought into port by a scratch crew of riggers and carpenters sent out by the owners for that purpose.

Opposite the inn was a good anchorage known as "Red Bet's" often used by privateers. Their officers and crews frequented Mother Redcap's; they had complete confidence in the old lady and on returning from a voyage would leave their pay and prize-money with her until they wanted it. It was believed, and still is, that a large sum of money lies hidden in the house and grounds, as only a few days before Mother Redcap died a rich prize was brought into port which yielded every sailor on board at least £1,000. Very little was found in her possession on her death and the treasure, if it exists at all, has never been discovered.

NORMAN ELLISON
The Wirral Peninsula (1955)

Birkenhead Priory in 1777

Far on the view—at soften'd distance seen,
Whilst rolls the stream its copious waves between,
There—long deserted by the sable band,
A lonely abbey glooms upon the strand:
When once the towering arch, in Gothic state
Rose high; and frown'd recluse the iron grate:
But shook by time, the lofty columns fall,
The wide roof drops, and sinks the mouldering wall;
The hollow gale thro' every cavern flies,
And the dull owl repeats her midnight cries.

WILLIAM ROSCOE
from *Mount Pleasant* (1777)

John Wesley's Visits to Liverpool

Tuesday, 15 April, 1755

I rode to Warrington. At six in the morning... I preached to a large and serious congregation, and then went on to Liverpool, one of the neatest, best-built towns I have seen in England. I think it full twice as large as Chester... Two thirds of the town ... have been added within these forty years. If it continue to increase in the same proportion, in forty years more it will nearly equal Bristol. The People in general are the most mild and courteous I ever saw in a seaport town; as indeed appears by their friendly behaviour, not only to the Jews and Papists who live among them, but even to the Methodists (so called).

Wednesday, 4 August, 1762

I rode to Liverpool, where also was such a work of God as had never been known there before. We had a surprising congregation in the evening, and, as it seemed, all athirst for God.

Monday, 16 July, 1764

[Liverpool] I preached on the 'one thing needful', and the rich behaved as seriously as the poor. Only one young gentlewoman laughed much. Poor thing! Doubtless she thought, 'I laugh prettily.'

Monday, 14 April, 1777

[Liverpool] Many large ships are now laid up in the docks, which had been employed for many years in buying or stealing poor Africans, and selling them in America for slaves. The men-butchers have now nothing to do at this laughable occupation. Since the American war broke out, there is no demand for human cattle. So the men of Africa, as well as Europe, may enjoy their native liberty.

JOHN WESLEY (1703-91)
Journal, Ed. N. Curnock (8 vols 1909-16)

Liverpool, 1777
from 'Mount Pleasant'

How numerous now her thronging buildings rise!
What varied objects strike the wandering eyes !
Where rise yon masts her crowded navies ride,
And the broad rampire checks the beating tide;
Along the beach her spacious streets extend,
Her areas open, and her spires ascend;
In loud confusion mingled sounds arise,
The docks re-echoing with the seamen's cries,
The massy hammer sounding from afar,
The bell slow-tolling, and the rattling car;
And thundering oft the cannon's horrid roar,
In lessening echos dies along the shore.

There with the genuine glow of COMMERCE fir'd,
Her anxious votaries plod the streets untir'd, ...

Ah ! why, ye Sons of Wealth, with ceaseless toil,
Add gold to gold, and swell the shining pile ?
Your general course to happiness ye bend,
Why then to gain the means neglect the end?
To purchase peace requires a scanty store,—
—O spurn the groveling wish that pants for more !—
And thirst not with the same unconquer'd rage,
Till nature whitens in the frost of age;
But rather, on the present hour rely,
And catch the happier moments ere they fly; ...

Far as the eye can trace the prospect round,
The splendid tracks of opulence are found:
Yet scarce an hundred annual rounds have run,
Since first the fabric of this power begun;
His noble waves inglorious, MERSEY roll'd,
Nor felt those waves by labouring art controul'd;
Along his side a few small cots were spread,
His finny brood their humble tenants fed;
At opening dawn with fraudful nets supply'd,
The paddling skiff would brave his spacious tide,
Ply round the shores, nor tempt the dangerous main,
But seek ere night the friendly port again.

Now o'er the wondering world her name resounds,
From Northern climes, to INDIA'S distant bounds...

Far to the right, where Mersey duteous pours
To the broad main his tributary stores;
Ting'd with the radiance of the golden beam,
Sparkle the quivering waves: and 'midst the gleam
In different hues, as sweeps the changeful ray,
Pacific fleets their guiltless pomp display:
Fair to the sight, they spread the floating sail,
Catch the light breeze, and skim before the gale;
Till lessening gradual on the stretching view,
Obscure they mingle in the distant blue;
Where in soft tints the sky with ocean blends,
And on the weaken'd sight, the long prospect ends.

Yet lovelier scenes the varied prospect cheer,
Where CESTRIA'S plains in long extent appear,
There shine the yellow fields with corn o'erspread;
There lifts BRITANNIA'S oak its towering head:
Swells the brown hill, the sloping vales retire,
And o'er the woodland peeps the rural spire;
Above the rest the CAMBRIAN mountains rise,
Close the long view, and mingle with the skies.

WILLIAM ROSCOE
from *Mount Pleasant* (1777)

The Custom House from Traffords Wyent (Rooker engraving).

To be sold at auction at George's Coffee House, betwixt the hours of six and eight o' clock, a very fine negro girl about eight years of age, very healthy, and hath been sometime from the coast. Any person willing to purchase the same may apply to Captain Robert Syers, at Mr Bartley Hodgett's Mercer and Draper near the Exchange, where she may be seen till the time of sale.

Williamson's Liverpool Advertiser, 1765

A fine negro boy, to be sold by auction. He is 11 years of age; the auction will take place at the Merchants' Coffee House, Old Church Yard. Sale to commence at 7 o'clock, by candle light. By order of Mr. Thomas Yates, who hath imported him from Bonny.
Auctioneer, James Parker.

Liverpool Chronicle.

Launch of a Slaver in 1775

My father was owner and commander of the *Mary Ellen.* She was launched on the 4th of June, my birthday, and also the anniversary of our revered sovereign, George III. We used to keep his majesty's birthday in great style. The bells were ringing, cannon fired, colours waved in the wind, and all the schools had holiday ... The *Mary Ellen* was named after and by my mother. The launch of this ship is about the first thing I can remember. The day's proceedings are indelibly fixed upon my memory. We went down to the place where the ship was built, accompanied by our friends. We made quite a little procession, headed by a drum and fife. My father and mother walked first, leading me by the hand. I had new clothes on, and I firmly believed that the joy bells were ringing solely because our ship was to be launched.... It was a pretty sight to see the *Mary Ellen* launched. There were crowds of people present, for my father was well known and very popular. When the ship moved off there was a great cheer raised. I was so excited at the great " splash " which was made, that I cried, and was for a time inconsolable, because they would not launch the ship again, so that I might witness another great " splash." I can, in my mind's eye, see " the splash " of the *Mary Ellen* even now. I really believe the displacement of the water on that occasion opened the doors of observation in my mind. After the launch there was great festivity and hilarity. I believe I made myself very ill with the quantity of fruit and good things I became possessed of. While the *Mary Ellen* was fitting-up for sea, I was often taken on board. In her hold were long shelves with ring-bolts in rows in several places. I used to run along these shelves, little thinking what dreadful scenes would be enacted upon them. The fact is that the *Mary Ellen* was destined for the African trade, in which she made many very successful voyages. In 1779, however, she was converted into a privateer.

JAMES STONEHOUSE [b. 1770]
Recollections of Old Liverpool by a Nonagenarian, (1863)

Iron

Cold iron fashioned into instruments of torture
Grotesque arrangements of man's engineering
Coarse, uneven black and brutal
What hell inspired us to have used these
Shackles, chains, spikes for bodily pain
Encumbered African limbs clad in iron, suppressed
Black skin chaffed by black iron
Red tears pour from wounds
Hungry, not satisfied, the iron incisors sink deeper
Far from home black bodies become drums to be beaten
Mother Africa cannot caress her weeping children
The fleshy umbilical cord replaced by links of iron
And drowned by the clatter of Birmingham forges
The world doesn't hear the screams
Echoes of greed resound in a triangular shape
Liverpool's heritage! 'our once proud city'
Our past is drenched in blood
The knife still drips

PAUL COSGROVE

Get Slaves honestly if you can,
And if you cannot get them honestly,
Get them.

Old Saying

from *Liverpool and Slavery*
by a Genuine 'Dicky Sam'

Memorable are the cutting words of George Frederick Cooke, tragedian, born 17th April, 1756, died 26th September, 1812. At the Liverpool Theatre one night, as was usual on many occasions with him, he staggered on the stage drunk; when the audience perceived this, they loudly hissed and hooted him. Cooke steadying himself, shouted most vociferously, "I have not come here to be insulted by a set of wretches, of which every brick in your infernal town is cemented with an African's blood."...

The system of trade carried on by the Liverpool African traders ran as follows:—Ships were built and fitted to carry slaves; the cargoes consisted of Manchester and Yorkshire woollen goods, hatchets, cutlasses, knives, gunpowder and trinkets, pistols, muskets, &c., from Birmingham and Sheffield; these they bartered for slaves—men, women, and children—on the west coast of Africa; they then carried their cargoes of slaves to the West Indies, who were sold for specie, sugar, and rum, and the latter commodities were sold in Liverpool, thus making three profits to the merchants in one voyage...

* * *

In the office of Thomas Clarke, three gentlemen were busily engaged in conversation. One says, "Shall it be equal shares ?" "Certainly!" say the other two; "and we will deal fairly this time," to which the former replied—" Let there be no cheating of any kind; here is my hand on it, here is mine, and here is mine."

"Now, gentlemen, sign the agreement." Signed—Thomas Ratcliffe, William James, John Simmons, Owners of the good ship "Thomas," of Liverpool; Captain Peter Roberts (better known as " Bully" Roberts).

"Now, captain, when can you be ready to start fully equipped for a good voyage ?" demanded Mr. James, who had been an old slave captain; to which Captain Roberts answered—" Nineteenth of next month."

On the date named everything was ready; the owners and captain were in good humour; the good ship "Thomas" lay in the Salt House Dock; some friends of the owners came down to inspect the ship, and were much surprised to see the hold of the ship so curiously fitted with partitions. One of the ladies ventured to ask Mr. James if it was not cruel to pack so many poor people in so little room. "No!" replied the old slaver, "they rather like it. You see, Mrs. Simmons, they are badly treated in their own country—I mean, the people, as you call them; we don't call them that: to us they are only slaves." Only slaves !

Mr. James did not wish to be bothered with questions like these. He sometimes felt it was wrong to buy and sell the slaves; but then it was profitable, and that satisfied his conscience. He was like a great many more of his day, and a conscience was a thing he could not afford to keep. There were several other vessels being fitted out for the African trade, as it was called, but, nearer the truth, would have been—slave dealers, buyers and sellers of human beings, with instincts and passions like ourselves.

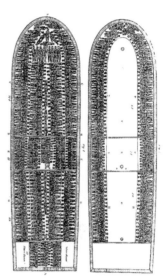

The Slave Ship 'Brookes'

At flood-tide, on the 19th of June, 1767, the captain stood on the quarter-deck to receive his last instructions from Mr. James, who undertook the management of the ship's cargo, and all arrangements until she cleared the dock...

The Chief Accra was one of the principal men catchers and slave dealers in Old Calabar. The chief led his party up the river in canoes; Roberts' crew was assisted and considerably enlarged by natives ... It was not long before the two villages were in flames, out rushed the frightened negroes for safety, when they were immediately pounced upon by Accra's men, and bound hand and foot with ropes and chains ... to the ship "Thomas" of Liverpool, Captain Roberts; Accra would receive in exchange for the slaves ... the pistols and gunpowder which had been brought for his special favour ...

from *Liverpool and Slavery by a Genuine 'DICKY SAM'* (1884, reprint 1984)

The Wrongs of Africa

Deep freighted now with human merchandize,
The vessel quits the shore; prepar'd to meet
The storms, and dangers, of th' Atlantick main:
Her motion scarce observ'd save when the flood
In frequent murmurs beats against her prow.

Whilst groans and loud laments, and scalding tears,
Mark'd the keen pangs of others. - Female shrieks,
At intervals, in dreadful concert heard,
To wild distraction manly sorrow turn'd;
And ineffectual, o'er their heedless limbs,
Was wav'd the wiry whip that dropp'd with blood.

WILLIAM ROSCOE
from *The Wrongs of Africa* (1787-8)

The former Captain of a Slave Ship describes conditions on his vessel

The cargo of a vessel of a hundred tons, or little more, is calculated to purchase from two hundred and twenty to two hundred and fifty Slaves . . . the Slaves lie in two rows, one above the other, on each side of the ship, close to each other, like books on a shelf. I have known them so close, that the shelf would not easily contain one more . . . the poor creatures, thus cramped for want of room, are likewise in irons, for the most part both hands and feet, and two together, which makes it difficult for them to turn or move, to attempt either to rise or to lie down, without hurting themselves or each other . . . The heat and smell of these rooms, when the weather will not admit of the slaves being brought upon deck, and of having their rooms cleaned every day, would be almost unsupportable to a person not accustomed to them . . . They are kept down by the weather to breathe a hot and corrupted air, sometimes for a week: this, added to the galling of their irons, and the despondency which seizes their spirits when thus continued, soon becomes fatal. And every morning perhaps, more instances than one are found, of the living and the dead, like the Captives of Mezentius, fastened together.

JOHN NEWTON
Thoughts upon the African Slave Trade (1788)

Roscoe's condemnation of this infamy

Shame to Mankind! But shame to BRITONS most,
Who all the sweets of Liberty can boast;
Yet, deaf to every human claim, deny
That bliss to others, which themselves enjoy:
Life's bitter draught with harsher bitter fill;
Blast every joy, and add to every ill;
The trembling limbs with galling iron bind,
Nor loose the heavier bondage of the mind.

Yet whence these horrors ? this inhuman rage,
That brands with blackest infamy the age ?
Is it, our varied interests disagree,
And BRITAIN sinks if AFRIC'S sons be free?
—No—Hence a few superfluous stores we claim,
That tempt our avarice, but increase our shame;
The sickly palate touch with more delight,
Or swell the senseless riot of the night.—
—Blest were the days ere Foreign Climes were known,
Our wants contracted, and our wealth our own;
When Health could crown, and Innocence endear,
The temperate meal, that cost no eye a tear:
Our drink, the beverage of the chrystal flood,
—Not madly purchas'd by a brother's blood—
Ere the wide spreading ills of Trade began,
Or Luxury trampled on the rights of Man.

WILLIAM ROSCOE
from *Mount Pleasant* (1777)

Anti-Abolition Song

If our slave trade be gone, there's an end to our lives:
  Beggars all we must be, our children and wives:
No ships from our port their proud sails e'er would spread,
  And our streets grown with grass, where cows might be fed.

Captain Crow took the last slave ship out from Liverpool, 1807.

Captain Hugh Crow

18th Century Art and Artists in Liverpool

Fleetwood Hesketh of Meols by Joseph Wright (1769)

The growing prosperity of Liverpool in the 18th Century and its strong visual appeal attracted artists to depict the port and its people.

Joseph Wright of Derby (1734-97) played an important part in Liverpool's artistic history. Between late 1768 and summer 1771 he was based in Liverpool where he depicted several of the port's leading slave-owning merchants as well as wealthy landowners from the Lancashire hinterland. Joseph Gildart, *a former Lord Mayor of Liverpool,* Fleetwood Hesketh of Meols *and his wife* Frances Bold, *the coal heiress, are among the finest of this group. Wright was a friend of Joseph Tate, an early member of the sugar-plantation dynasty. Wright's presence in Liverpool helped galvanise local artists and contributed to attempts to set up a local Academy.*

- Frank Milner

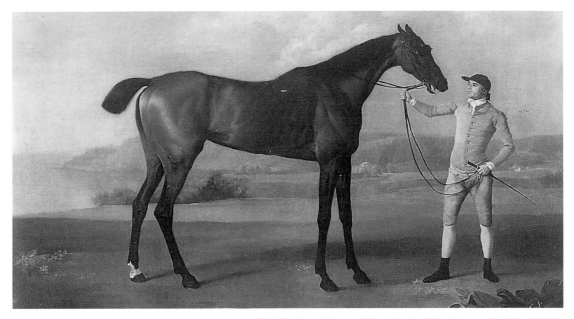

'Molly Longlegs and her Jockey' by George Stubbs (1762)

Of all the artists born in Liverpool, none has been more important than George Stubbs, the greatest animal painter of the 18th Century (1724-1806). He succeeded in raising the quality and status of sporting art by his anatomical precision and subtle use of expression and gesture. He gained a European reputation with the publication in 1776 of The Anatomy of the Horse. Molly Longlegs and her Jockey, *is representative of the best of his single horse portraits and has a diagrammatic clarity that exaggerates the horse's distinctive bloodpoints.*

- FRANK MILNER

Liverpool from Seacombe (1768/9)
by Michael Angelo Rooker

Rooker specialised in topographical watercolours. He and his father were associated with the Liverpool publisher and historian George Perry, whose poem The Prophecy of Commerce *contains a proud description of Liverpool, comparable to Rooker's expansive view.*

> *"... O Mersey! fairest of my numerous train*
> *Pleased, I behold through time's perspective glass*
> *Thy banks adorned with Lerpool's rising towers!*
> *A naval forest crowds her spacious docks..."*

from *"Hoyle Lake,"* 1794

Dear scene ! that stretch'd between the silver arms
Of Deva and of Mersey, meets the main.
And, when the sun-gilt day illumes its charms,
Boasts of peculiar grace, nor boasts in vain.

Though near the beach, dark Helbrie's lonely isle
Reposes sullen in the wat'ry way
Hears round her rocks the tides, returning, boil.
And o'er her dusky sandals dash their spray.

Mark to the left, romantic Cambria's coast,
Her curtain'd mountains rising o'er the floods.
While seas on Orm's beak'd promontory burst,
Blue Deva swells her mirror to the woods.

If to thy quiet harbour, gentle Hoyle,
The shattered navy through the tempest flies.
Each joyous mariner forgets his toil,
And carols to the vainly angry skies.

How gay the scene, when Spring's fair mornings break,
Or Summer-noons illume the grassy mound,
When anchor'd navies crowd the peopled lake,
Or deck the distant ocean's skiey bound.

Like leafless forests, on its verge extreme,
Rise the tall masts, or spreading wide their sails,
Silvering and shining in the solar beam,
Stand on that last blue line, and court the gales.

The peopled lake, of song and lively cheer,
And boatswain's whistle bears the joyful sound,
While rosy pennants, floating on the air,
Tinge the soft seas of glass that sleep around ...

ANNA SEWARD

The 1797 Coat of Arms and the Liver Bird

King John left a lasting reminder of his fleeting interest in Liverpool. The Liver Bird, no less. This most famous, tufted, long-necked, long-legged, web-footed emblem of Liverpool may lack a proven pedigree but it is nothing if not regal to look at; the generally accepted theory is that whilst it never came out of any egg it can boast regal origins.

The ancient corporate seal of the town bore the representation of a bird with a twig in its beak. This is thought to be the eagle of St John the Divine carrying a broom-sprig (this intended as a compliment to King John who used the eagle on his coinage). The original seal was destroyed, however, and a crudely-made copy found later raised ornithological doubts. For a sea-board town it obviously had to be a sea-bird, and more than anything else it looked like a cormorant. Its beak, therefore, was probably holding laver (a type of seaweed). So, when the grant of a new Coat of Arms was made in 1797, the heraldic description was:-

'Argent a Cormorant in the beak a branch of seaweed called Laver all proper, and for the Crest, on a wreath of the colours a Cormorant, the wings elevated, in the beak a branch of Laver proper.'

ALAN BRACK
Liverpool - The Official Book (1978)

Thomas de Quincey at Everton

... the multiform scene ... in all its elements was not unfrequently realised for me on the gentle eminence of Everton. Obliquely to the left lay the many-languaged town of Liverpool; obliquely to the right, the multitudinous sea ... The town of Liverpool represented the earth, with its sorrow and its graves left behind, yet not out of sight, nor wholly forgotten. The ocean, in everlasting but gentle agitation, yet brooded over by dove-like calm, might not unfitly typify the mind, and the mood which then swayed it.

A Fire at Liverpool, 1802

... a prodigious fire occurred at Liverpool: the Goree, a vast pile of warehouses close to one of the docks, was burned to the ground. The huge edifice, eight or nine stories high, and laden with most combustible goods, —many thousand bales of cotton, wheat and oats in thousands of quarters, tar, turpentine, rum, gunpowder, &c., — continued through many hours of darkness to feed this tremendous fire. To aggravate the calamity, it blew a regular gale of wind; luckily for the shipping, it blew inland, —that is to the east; and all the way down to Warrington, eighteen miles distant to the eastward, the whole air was illuminated by flakes of cotton, often saturated with rum, and by what seemed absolute worlds of blazing sparks, that lighted up all the upper chambers of the air. All the cattle lying abroad in the fields through a breadth of eighteen miles were thrown into terror and agitation. Men, of course, read in this hurrying overhead of scintillating and blazing vortices the annunciation of some gigantic calamity going on in Liverpool; and the lamentation on that account was universal. But that mood of public sympathy did not at all interfere to suppress or even to check the momentary bursts of rapturous admiration, as this arrowy sleet of many-coloured fire rode on the wings of hurricane, alternately through open depths of air or through dark clouds overhead.

THOMAS DE QUINCEY
from *The Confessions of an English Opium Eater*, (1821)

PART TWO

"Liverpool, the young giant"

JAMES STONEHOUSE, 1863

"that immense place, which stands like another Venice, upon the waters... intersected by those numerous docks"

LORD ERSKINE

"the deepest poverty and misery in my district"

GERARD MANLEY HOPKINS, 1881

The Lass of Liverpool

Where cocoas lift their tufted heads,
And orange blossoms scent the breeze,
Her charms the mild Mulatto spreads,
And moves with soft and wanton ease,
And I have seen her witching wiles,
And I have kept my bosom cool,
For how could I forget thy smiles,
O! lovely lass of Liverpool.
The softest tints the conch displays,
The cheek of her I love outvies,
And the sea breeze 'midst burning rays,
Is not more cheering than her eyes;
Dark as the petrel is her hair,
And Sam, who calls me love-sick fool,
Ne'er saw a tropic bird more fair
Than my sweet lass of Liverpool.

Tho' doom'd from early life to brave
The feverish swamp, and furious blast,
Tho' doom'd to face the foam-capt wave,
And mount the yard and quivering mast;
Tho' doom'd to brave each noxious soil,
And train'd in stern misfortune's school,
Yet still, O ! 'twould be bliss to toil
For thee, sweet lass of Liverpool.
And when we reach the crowded pier,
And the broad yards are quickly mann'd,
O! should my lovely girl be near,
And sweetly smile, and wave her hand,
With ardent soul, I'd spring to shore,
And scorning dull decorum's rule,
To my fond bosom o'er and o'er
Would press the lass of Liverpool.

EDWARD RUSHTON
Poems (1806)

William Ewart Gladstone's Childhood

A speech at Rodney Street: October, 1812.

Much entertaining went on in my father's house, where Mr Canning himself was a guest; and on a day of a great dinner I was taken down to the dining room. I was set upon one of the chairs, standing, and directed to say to the company 'Ladies and Gentlemen'.

Schooldays:

I was not a devotional child. I have no recollection of early love for the House of God and for Divine Service: though after my father built the church at Seaforth in 1815, I remember cherishing a hope that he might bequeath it to me, and that I might live in it. I have a very early recollection of hearing preaching in St. George's Liverpool, but it is this: that I turned quickly to my mother and said, 'When will he have done?'....

(The Rev. Rawson's school) afterwards rose to considerable repute...But I think this was not so much due to its intellectual stamina as to the extreme salubrity of the situation on the pure dry sands of the Mersey's mouth, with all the advantages of the strong tidal action and fresh and frequent north-west winds. At five miles from Liverpool Exchange, the sands, delicious for riding, were one absolute solitude, and only one house looked down on them between us and the town...

Among our greatest enjoyments were undoubtedly the annual Guy Fawkes bonfires, for which we always had liberal allowances of wreck timber and a tar-barrel. I remember seeing, when about eight or nine, my first case of a dead body. It was the child of the head gardener Derbyshire, and was laid in the cottage bed by tender hands, with nice and clean accompaniments. It seemed to me pleasing, and in no way repelled me; but it made a deep impression....

I have seen wild roses growing upon the very ground that is now the centre of Bootle. All that land is now partly covered with residences and partly with places of business and industry; but in my time but one single house stood upon the space between Primrose Brook and the town of Liverpool.

WILLIAM GLADSTONE
Autobiography (1880)

Have you anything to declare?....

William Cobbett arrived at Liverpool on the 20th of November 1819, after an absence from England of two years and five months. He was met, on landing, by some readers of his Register, who regarded him as a political authority. Among them was Egerton Smith, the editor of the *Liverpool Mercury*, whom he afterwards turned against, and abused under the name of "Bott Smith", on account of something that he had said about the bott disease in horses. A crowd attended him to the custom-house to which his luggage had been conveyed for inspection. When the officers proceeded to open the last package, they found something wrapped in woollen. Cobbett stepped forward, and said, "These are the mortal remains of the immortal Thomas Paine". The crowd pressed round to look into the receptacle. "Great indeed must that man have been," said Cobbett, in his account of the affair, "whose very bones attracted such attention." The officers very readily passed the package back into Cobbett's possession.

Remaining in Liverpool for a few days, he consented, at the request of several persons calling themselves reformers, to address a meeting there, at which he spoke chiefly on two subjects - the bones of Tom Paine, and the condition of the House of Commons. He was heard with a mixture of applause and hissing, and there was much strife of parties.

THE REV. JOHN SELBY WATSON
Biographies of *John Wilkes and William Cobbett* (1870)

Thomas Creevey at Knowsley Hall, 1822

Croxteth, Dec 15th.

... We all dined at Knowsley last night. The new dining-room is opened: it is 53 feet by 37, and such a height that it destroys the effect of all the other apartments. You enter it from a passage by two great Gothic churchlike doors the whole height of the room. This entrance is in itself fatal to the effect. Lady Derby (like herself) when I objected to the immensity of the doors, said: "You've heard Gen. Grosvenor's remark upon them have you not? He asked in his grave pompous manner - 'Pray are those great doors to be opened for every pat of butter that comes into the room?'"

At the opposite end of the room is an immense gothic window, and the rest of the light is given by a skylight, mountains high. There are two fireplaces; and the day we dined there, there were 26 wax candles over the table, 14 on it and ten great lamps on tall pedestals about the room; and yet those at the bottom of the table said it was quite petrifying in that neighbourhood, and the report here is that they have been obliged to abandon it entirely from the cold ... My lord and lady were all kindness to me, but only think of their neither knowing nor caring about Spain or France nor whether war or peace between these two nations was at all in agitation!

THOMAS CREEVEY
The Creevey Papers ed. John Gore, (1903, 1948)

EDWARD LEAR AT KNOWSLEY HALL 1832
Four successive Earls of Derby commissioned Lear to work at Knowsley Hall, painting the menagerie. Lear amused the Earl's grandchildren by composing humorous rhymes, which became his **A Book of Nonsense**.

There was an Old Man with a beard,
who said, 'It is just as I feared! -
Two Owls and a Hen, four larks and a Wren,
Have all built their nests in my beard!'

"The Mole of Edge Hill"
from 'The Losing of Liverpool'

Remember the useful endeavour of Joseph Williamson,
The mole of Mason Street,
Who constructed surprises beyond the aspiring of man
Beneath his feet,
Whose element was the Underworld, whose Plutonic
Shade is the sand—
Stone forest of deep-down disremembered darkness
Felled by his hand,
Or umber and ochre meadow reaped for the aid
Of supervised labour,
His underfed Irish: tread softly on Joseph's ghost,
Your downstairs neighbour,

Whose thought was sound
When inside-out and upside-down he fashioned
His burial mound.

Who wandered from Warrington in at the age of eleven
In 1781,
Was lord of his own strange, dripping and literal suburb
Before he was done,
Who, youngest apprentice of Thomas Moss Tate,
Esquire,
Tobacco Importer,
Twenty years later had eaten the family business
And married its daughter
To come in exceptional wealth to an odd retirement,
His cellar floor,
Whereunder he started to dig up that darkness whereby
He spread some more,
For who can explain
The excavation of nothing whatever for neither
Light nor gain?

In wombs and catacombs below
The air: in brownish-purple tombs

Of sombre echo where no moon
Illumined him among the bare

Wet-whispered caverns, dreamed-out rooms:
The waif of Warrington, I do

Believe, looked for his mother there.

KIT WRIGHT

Felicia Hemans returns from North Wales
to live in her birthplace, Liverpool

From a letter written at Wavertree, 1828:
... waveless horizon! how it wearies the eyes...it is a dull uninventive nature all around here, tho' there must be somewhere little fairy nooks, which I hope by degrees to discover.

Felicia Hemans visits a Girls' School in Wavertree -
lines from her poem 'Evening Prayer at a Girls' School in Wavertree'

Hush! 'tis a holy hour. The quiet room
   Seems like a temple, while yon soft lamp sheds
A faint and starry radiance, through the gloom
   And the sweet stillness, down on fair young heads,
With all their clustering locks, untouched by care,
   And bowed, as flowers are bowed in night, in prayer....

Though fresh within your breasts the untroubled springs
   Of hope make melody where'er ye tread,
And o'er your sleep bright shadows, from the wings
   Of spirits visiting but youth, be spread;
Yet in those flute-like voices, mingling low,
   Is woman's tenderness - how soon her woe!

Her lot is on you - silent tears to weep,
   And patient smiles to wear through suffering's hour,
And sumless riches, from affection's deep,
   To pour on broken reeds - a wasted shower!
And to make idols, and to find them clay,
   And to bewail that worship. Therefore pray!

FELICIA HEMANS

Felix Mendelssohn in Liverpool, 1829

At the end of July, their tour completed, the 20 year old composer and his friend Klingemann returned to England by way of the Lakes, and spent a few days in Liverpool en route to North Wales. At such a time there was presumably no music for them to hear in the city, but the travellers found plenty of diversion in visits to the water-front and the Crown Street depot of the as yet unfinished Liverpool and Manchester Railway.

At the docks they were invited aboard a smart American ship, in whose main saloon stood an excellent Broadwood pianoforte; and upon this instrument Mendelssohn tried out the manuscript of the 'Easter Sonata' he had written in Scotland as a gift for his sister Fanny - later renamed the Fantasia in F sharp minor, Op.28.

Felix's youthful interest in the newly invented steam machinery of the age, already much stimulated by the little paddle steamers then plying between Glasgow and the Isles, was further gratified by a trip on a goods train through the recently excavated tunnels leading from Crown Street to the docks - though at this time the wagons descended by gravity to river level and were hauled back by cables attached to a stationary engine at Edge Hill. All of this Mendelssohn describes in considerable detail in his letters to his family.

So though the composer's untimely death prevented his closer association with our city planned at the time of the opening of the Philharmonic Hall in 1849, when he was to have directed a specially composed cantata based on Milton's 'Comus', he did at least enjoy a fleeting visit twenty years earlier, and can even be said to have made music here, if in a purely private manner.

STAINTON DE B. TAYLOR
Two Centuries of Music in Liverpool (1976)

Lime Street in 1818 (James Taylor Eglinton). The junction of St. John's Lane and Lime Street (formerly Lime Kiln Lane).

The Rocket

No speed ...

No speed with this can fleetest horse compare,
No weight like this canal or vessel bear:
As this will Commerce every way promote,
To this let sons of Commerce grant their vote.

THOMAS GRAY

The opening of the Liverpool and Manchester Railway, 1830
'The Rocket'

... We were introduced to the little engine which was to drag us along the rails. She consisted of a boiler, a stove, a small platform, a bench and behind the bench a barrel containing enough water to prevent her being thirsty for fifteen miles. She goes upon two wheels, which are her feet, and are moved by bright steel legs called pistons ... a snorting little animal which I felt rather inclined to pat.

FRANCES ANNE KEMBLE
Record of a Girlhood (1878)

The first railway accident

At length the line was completed, and ready for the public ceremony of the opening, which took place on the 15th of September, 1830. This important event

Olive Mount Cutting

attracted a vast number of spectators from all parts of the country. Strong palings were erected for miles along the deep cuttings near Liverpool, to keep off the pressure of the multitude, and prevent them falling over in their eagerness to witness the passing trains. Constables and soldiers were there in numbers to assist in keeping the line clear. The completion of the railway was justly regarded as an important national event, and the ceremony of the opening was celebrated accordingly. The Duke of Wellington, then Prime Minister, Sir Robert Peel, Secretary of State, Mr. Huskisson, one of the members for Liverpool, and an earnest supporter of the project from its commencement, were amongst the number of distinguished public personages present.

Eight locomotive engines constructed at the Stephenson works had been delivered and placed upon the line, the whole of which had been tried and tested, weeks before, with perfect success. The various trains of carriages accommodated in all about six hundred persons. The 'Northumbrian' engine, driven by Mr. George Stephenson himself, headed the procession; then followed the 'Phoenix', driven by Robert Stephenson; the 'North Star' by Robert Stephenson Senior (brother of George) ; the 'Rocket', by Joseph Locke; the 'Dart', by Thomas L. Gooch; the 'Comet' by William Allcard; the 'Arrow', by Frederick Swanwick; and the 'Meteor', by Anthony Harding. The procession was cheered in its progress by thousands of spectators - through the deep ravine of Olive Mount; up the Sutton incline; over the great Sankey viaduct, beneath which a multitude of persons had assembled - carriages filling the narrow lanes, and barges crowding the river; the people below gazing with wonder and admiration at the trains which sped along the line, far above their heads, at the rate of some twenty-four miles an hour.

At Parkside, about seventeen miles from Liverpool, the engines stopped to take in water. Here a deplorable accident occurred to one of the most distinguished of the illustrious visitors present, which threw a deep shadow over the subsequent proceedings of the day. The 'Northumbrian' engine, with the carriage containing the Duke of Wellington, was drawn up on one line, in order that the whole of the trains might pass in review before him and his party on the other. Mr. Huskisson had, unhappily, alighted from the carriage, and was standing on the opposite road, along which the 'Rocket' engine was observed rapidly coming up. At this moment the Duke of Wellington, between whom and Mr. Huskisson some coolness had existed, made a sign of recognition, and held out his hand. A hurried but friendly grasp was given; and before it was loosened there was a general cry from the bystanders of "Get in, get in!" Flurried and confused, Mr. Huskisson endeavoured to get round the open door of the carriage, which projected over the opposite rail; but in so doing he was struck down by the 'Rocket', and falling with his leg doubled across the rail, the limb was instantly crushed. His first words, on being raised, were, "I have met my death", which unhappily proved too true, for he

Parkside Station

expired that same evening in the neighbouring parsonage of Eccles. It was cited at the time as a remarkable fact, that the 'Northumbrian' engine conveyed the wounded body of the unfortunate gentleman a distance of about fifteen miles in twenty-five minutes, or at the rate of thirty-six miles an hour. This incredible speed burst upon the world with the effect of a new and unlooked-for phenomenon.

SAMUEL SMILES
The Story of the Life of George Stephenson (1860)

Thomas Carlyle visits his Liverpool relatives, October 1838

... Our voyage to Liverpool was prosperous enough; a calm, chill evening...about midnight we discerned the Rock of Liverpool, and all its multifarious lights rising round us, - one great blaze among the rest which we ascertained afterwards to be a huge Fire, still going on tho' in a subdued state; and finally, amid immense yoho-ing, bullyragging and other tumult, we saw ourselves, about one in the morning, all run safely into moorings in the Dock, and at liberty to land if we liked. To the last moment it was uncertain with me what I would do: however, a porter offering himself "for eighteen pence, Sir," to the Angel Hotel, I set off with him, several others following on the same quest of a bed to sleep in. The Angel, or Wellington, or whatever it was, would not take us in; but some Royal Hotel, close by, did: there, after kicking our heels for a good while, in the empty lobby, in the dead of night, and relying mainly on Patience and the goodwill of "Boots" (for he had our fate in his hands), the wearied individuals did, I suppose, get into some kind of sleeping-cribs; I at least did, and could bolt the door upon myself about two in the morning, and: Here I will be private till the morrow if it please Heaven. I supped on your brandy and one of Mary's crackers; indeed, you may tell her and yourself that nothing of the sort could have been usefuller than your kind gifts proved: thanks to your kind hearts for them! Your pocket-comb was right serviceable too; I found I had forgot the other. Tell my Mother not to fret herself in the smallest about it, as I know she has been doing; I got an excellent one since I came hither. In fine all was right enough. The sooty smell of Liverpool awoke me in the morning about eight; I dressed and walked off to Maryland Street for breakfast: too early still by an hour.

Thomas Carlyle

And on a visit to Liverpool with his wife:
I found time to be impressed by the seeming efficiency of the inhabitants; they appeared to me to be remarkably go-ahead people. Streets, streets, streets! Market places, churches, theatres, shops...I confess amazement at the preponderance of public houses...As I observed comparatively little insobriety, I considered that many of these places relied on foreign seamen for their trade...a gratifying thought because I rather like Liverpool and its people.

Letters of Thomas Carlyle
ed. Edwin Marrs Jnr. (1968)

Thomas Carlyle wrote imaginatively of Liverpool as it was in the Twelfth Century: 'The Creek of the Mersey gurgles, twice in the four-and twenty hours, with eddying brine, clangorous with Sea-fowl; and it is a Lither-Pool, a lazy or sullen Pool, no monstrous pitchy City, and Seahaven of the world!'
In *Past and Present* (1843)

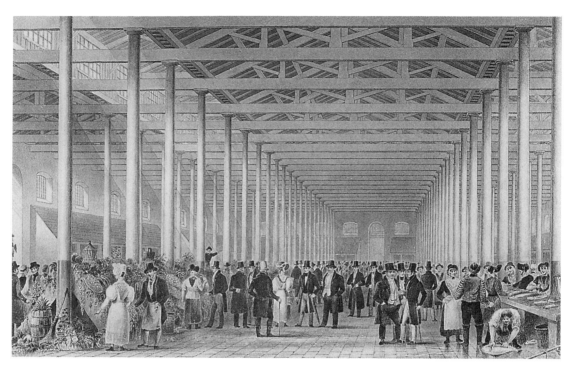

St John's Market, c. 1830 (Robert Barrow)
Designed by John Foster Jnr., opened 1882, lit by gas. A pioneering building: the first large-scale indoor market
in Britain; columns of cast-iron. One of many Liverpool markets, it specialised in food.

St. James' Cemetery, probably 1830s (Robert Barrow)
The domed memorial to Huskisson and small Greek style temple are seen.
The site of the future Anglican Cathedral.

Herman Melville arrives in Liverpool on his first voyage from America, 1839. Extracts from his autobiographical novel, **Redburn.**

The Highlander approaches

After running till about midnight, we *"hove-to"* near the mouth of the Mersey; and next morning before day-break, took the first of the flood; and with a fair wind, stood into the river; which, at its mouth, is quite an arm of the sea. Presently, in misty twilight, we passed immense buoys, and caught sight of distant objects on shore, vague and shadowy shapes, like Ossian's ghosts.

As I stood leaning over the side, and trying to summon up some image of Liverpool, to see how the reality would answer to my conceit; and while the fog and mist, and gray dawn were investing every thing with a mysterious interest, I was startled by the doleful, dismal sound of a great bell, whose slow intermitting tolling seemed in unison with the solemn roll of the billows. I thought I had never heard so boding a sound; a sound that seemed to speak of judgment and the resurrection, like belfry-mouthed Paul of Tarsus.

It was not in the direction of the shore; but seemed to come out of the vaults of the sea, and out of the mist and fog....

I soon learned from my ship-mates that this was the famous *Bell-Buoy*, which is precisely what its name implies; and tolls fast or slow, according to the agitation of the waves. In a calm, it is dumb; in a moderate breeze, it tolls gently; but in a gale, it is an alarum like the tocsin, warning all mariners to flee. But it seemed fuller of dirges for the past, than of monitions for the future; and no one can give ear to it, without thinking of the sailors who sleep far beneath it at the bottom of the deep.

As we sailed ahead the river contracted. The day came, and soon, passing two lofty land-marks on the Lancashire shore, we rapidly drew near the town, and at last, came to anchor in the stream.

Looking shoreward, I beheld lofty ranges of dingy warehouses, which seemed very deficient in elements of the marvelous; and bore a most unexpected resemblance to the warehouses along South-street in New York....There they stood; a row of calm and collected warehouses... these edifices I must confess, were a sad and bitter disappointment to me.

But it was different with Larry the whaleman: who to my surprise, looking about him delighted, exclaimed, "Why, this 'ere is a considerable place - I'm *dummed* if it ain't quite a place - Why, them 'ere houses is considerable houses. It beats the coast of Afriky, all hollow; nothing like this in Madagasky, I tell you - I'm dummed, boys, if Liverpool ain't a city!"

Shipping and the Docks

I know not how many hours I spent in gazing at the shipping in Prince's Dock, and speculating concerning their past voyages and future prospects in life. Some had just arrived from the most distant ports, worn, battered and disabled; others were all a-taunt-o - spruce, gay, and brilliant, in readiness for sea.

Every day the *Highlander* had some new neighbor. A black brig from Glasgow, with its crew of sober Scotch caps, and its staid, thrifty-looking skipper, would be replaced by a jovial French hermaphrodite, its forecastle echoing with songs, and its quarter-deck elastic from much dancing.

On the other side, perhaps, a magnificent New York Liner...would give way to a Sydney emigrant ship, receiving on board its live freight of shepherds from the Grampians, ere long to be tending their flocks on the hills and downs of New Holland.

I was particularly pleased and tickled, with a multitude of little salt-droghers, rigged like sloops, and not much bigger than a pilot-boat, but with broad bows painted black, and carrying red sails, which looked as if they had been pickled and stained in a tan-yard. These little fellows were continually coming in with their cargoes for ships bound for America; and lying, five or six together, alongside of those lofty Yankee hulls, resembled a parcel of red ants about the carcass of a black buffalo.....

Another very curious craft often seen in the Liverpool docks, is the Dutch galliot, an old-fashioned looking gentleman, with hollow waist, high prow and stern, and which, seen lying among crowds of tight Yankee traders, and pert French brigantines, always reminded me of a cocked hat among modish beavers.....

There was the hull of an old sloop-of-war, which had been converted into a mariner's church. A house had been built upon it, and a steeple took the place of a mast...I used to see an old pensioner of a tar, sitting on a camp-stool, reading his Bible. On Sundays he hoisted the Bethel flag, and like the *muezzin* or cryer of prayers on the top of a Turkish mosque, would call the strolling sailors to their devotions....

Surrounded by its broad belt of masonry, each Liverpool dock is a walled town, full of life and commotion; or rather, it is a small archipelago, an epitome of the world, where all the nations of Christendom, and even those of Heathendom, are represented. For, in itself, each ship is an island, a floating colony of the tribe to which it belongs.

Here are brought together the remotest limits of the earth; and in the collective spars and timbers of these ships, all the forests of the globe are represented, as in a grand parliament of masts. Canada and New Zealand send their pines; America her live oak; India her teak; Norway her spruce; and the Right Honorable Mahogany, member for Honduras and Campeachy, is seen at his post by the wheel....

A Liverpool dock is a grand caravansary inn ... Here ships are lodged at a moderate charge and payment is not demanded till the time of departure....they take their ease in their watery inn.

Three Sailors

East Quay, Prince's Dock, 1833 (Samuel Austin)
'For miles you may walk along that river-side, passing dock after dock, like a chain of immense fortresses:-
Prince's, George's, Salt-House, Clarence, Brunswick, Trafalgar, King's, Queen's, and many more.... Nothing
can exceed the bustle and activity displayed along these quays during the day...
HERMAN MELVILLE

Storm in the Mersey, 1836 (Samuel Walters)

The old church of St Nicholas and the Dead-House

The floating chapel recalls to mind the "Old Church", well known to the seamen of many generations, who have visited Liverpool. It stands very near the docks, a venerable mass of brown stone, and by the town's people is called the Church of St. Nicholas. I believe it is the best preserved piece of antiquity in all Liverpool.

Before the town rose to any importance, it was the only place of worship on that side of the Mersey; and under the adjoining Parish of Walton was a chapel-of-ease; though from the straight-backed pews, there could have been but little comfort taken in it.

In old times, there stood in front of the church a statue of St. Nicholas, the patron of mariners; to which all pious sailors made offerings, to induce his saintship to grant them short and prosperous voyages. In the tower is a fine chime of bells....Thirty or forty years ago, these bells were rung upon the arrival of every Liverpool ship from a foreign voyage. How forcibly does this illustrate the increase of the commerce of the town! Were the same custom now observed, the bells would seldom have a chance to cease....

...At noon, when the lumpers employed in loading and unloading the shipping, retire for an hour to snatch a dinner, many of them resort to the grave-yard; and seating themselves upon a tomb-stone use the adjoining one for a table. Often, I saw men stretched out in a drunken sleep upon these slabs; and once, removing a fellow's arm, read the following inscription...HERE LYETH YE BODY OF TOBIAS DRINKER....

In the basement of the church is a Dead House, like the Morgue in Paris, where the bodies of the drowned are exposed until claimed by their friends, or till buried at the public charge.

From the multitudes employed about the shipping, this Dead House has always more or less occupants. Whenever I passed up Chapel-street, I used to see a crowd gazing through the grim iron grating of the door, upon the faces of the drowned within. And once, when the door was opened, I saw a sailor stretched out, stark and stiff, with the sleeve of his frock rolled up, and showing his name and date of birth tattooed upon his arm...

I was told that standing rewards are offered for the recovery of persons falling into the docks; so much, if restored to life, and a less amount if irrecoverably drowned. Lured by this, several horrid old men and women are constantly prying about the docks, searching after bodies. I observed them principally early in the morning, when they issued from their dens, on the same principle that the rag-rakers and rubbish-pickers in the streets, sally out bright and early; for then, the night-harvest has ripened.

...in 1588 the Earl of Derby, coming to his residence, and waiting for a passage to the Isle of Man, the corporation erected and adorned a sumptuous stall in the church for his reception ...in the time of Cromwell's wars, when the place was taken by that mad nephew of King Charles, Prince Rupert, he converted the old church into a military prison and stable; when, no doubt, another 'sumptuous stall' was erected for the benefit of the steed of some noble cavalry officer....

St Nicholas' church.

Dock-Wall Beggars: 'the remarkable army of paupers'

...the singular beggary practiced in the streets frequented by sailors...the remarkable army of paupers that beset the docks at particular hours of the day.

At twelve o' clock the crews of hundreds and hundreds of ships issue in crowds from the dock gates to go to their dinner in the town. This hour is seized upon by multitudes of beggars to plant themselves against the outside of the walls, while others stand upon the curbstone to excite the charity of the seamen. The first time that I passed through this long lane of pauperism, it seemed hard to believe that such an array of misery could be furnished by any town in the world.

Every variety of want and suffering here met the eye, and every vice showed here its victims....Old women, rather mummies, drying up with slow starving and age; young girls, incurably sick, who ought to have been in hospital; sturdy men, with the gallows in their eyes, and a whining lie in their mouths; young boys, hollow-eyed and decrepit; and puny mothers, holding up puny babes in the glare of the sun, formed the main features of the scene.

I remember one cripple, a young man rather decently clad, who sat huddled up against the wall, holding a painted board on his knees. It was a picture intending to represent the man himself caught in the machinery of some factory, and whirled about among spindles and cogs, with his limbs mangled and bloody. This person said nothing, but sat silently exhibiting his board....

... as you passed along...the clamorous petitions of the more urgent ... beset you on every hand ... I cannot say that the seamen did much to relieve the destitution. Very few of them had much money to give ... As an example of their sympathy with suffering among members of their own calling, I must mention the case of an old man, who every day, and all day long, through sunshine and rain, occupied a particular corner, where crowds of tars were always passing. He was an uncommonly large, plethoric man, with a wooden leg, and dressed in the nautical garb; his face was red and round; he was continually merry; and with his wooden stump thrust forth...he sat upon a great pile of monkey jackets ... to receive the coppers thrown him. And plenty of pennies were tost into his poor-box by the sailors ... He was an old man-of-war's man, who had lost his leg at the battle of Trafalgar; and...exhibited his wooden one as a genuine specimen of the oak timbers of Nelson's ship, the *Victory*.

Dockside Streets and the Sailor Ballad-Singers

In the evening, especially when the sailors are gathered in great numbers, these streets present a most singular spectacle, the entire population of the vicinity being seemingly turned into them. Hand-organs, fiddles, and cymbals, plied by strolling musicians, mix with the songs of the seamen, the babble of women and children, and the groaning and whining of the beggars. From the various boarding-houses, each distinguished by gilded emblems outside - an anchor, a crown, a windlass, or a dolphin - proceeds the noise of revelry and dancing; and from the open casements lean young girls and old women, chattering and laughing with the crowds in the middle of the street....

... one of the most curious features of the scene is the number of sailor ballad-singers, who, after singing their verses, hand you a printed copy, and beg you to buy. One of these persons ... I observed every day standing at a corner in the middle of the street. He had a full, noble voice, like a church-organ and his notes rose above the surrounding din .... He was full of marvelous adventures, and all sorts of nautical enormities. He was a monomaniac upon these subjects; he was a Newgate Calendar of the robberies and assassinations of the day, happening in the sailor quarters of the town; and most of his ballads were upon kindred subjects. He composed many of his own verses, and had them printed for sale on his own account. To show how expeditious he was at this business, it may be mentioned that one evening on leaving the dock to go to supper, I perceived a crowd gathered about the *Old Fort Tavern;* and mingling with the rest, I learned that a woman of the town had just been killed at the bar by a drunken Spanish sailor from Cadiz. The murderer was carried off by the police before my eyes, and the very next morning the ballad-singer...was singing the tragedy in front of the boarding-houses, and handing round printed copies of the song, which, of course, was eagerly bought up by the seamen.

Negro Sailors and Visiting Sailors

...one thing that struck me...the absence of negroes...in these streets...the looks of interest with which negro-sailors are regarded when they walk the Liverpool streets. In Liverpool indeed the negro steps with a prouder pace, and lifts his head like a man; for here, no such exaggerated feeling exists in respect to him, as in America. Three or four times, I encountered our black steward, dressed very handsomely, and walking arm in arm with a good-looking English woman. In New York, such a couple would have been mobbed in three minutes; and the steward would have been lucky to escape with whole limbs. Owing to the friendly reception extended to them, and the unwonted immunities they enjoy in Liverpool, the black cooks and stewards of American ships are very much attached to the place and like to make voyages to it...

...of all sea-ports in the world, Liverpool, perhaps, most abounds in all the variety of land-sharks, land-rats, and other vermin, which make the hapless mariner their prey. In the shape of landlords, bar-keepers, clothiers, crimps, and boarding-house loungers, the land-sharks devour him, limb by limb; while the land-rats and mice constantly nibble at his purse....

And yet, sailors love this Liverpool; and upon long voyages to distant parts of the globe, will be continually dilating upon its charms and attractions, and extolling it above all other sea-ports in the world. For in Liverpool they find their Paradise - not the well-known street of that name - and one of them told me he would be content to lie in Prince's Dock till *he hove up anchor* for the world to come.

HERMAN MELVILLE
Redburn (1849)

The Grand Steeplechase (later the Grand National)

The First Grand Steeplechase, 1839

At last the great day arrived, bright and clear with a chill breeze blowing across from the Mersey. Liverpool had for days been agog with talk of the contest and thousands of excited visitors flocked into the area. Parties were held at the country houses, including Croxteth and Knowsley, hotels for miles around were booked up and there were reports of some hostelries accommodating their guests four to a bed. Lynn's prediction that the City's trade would benefit from a 'Grand Steeplechase' was being proven in the best possible way.... Who was going to win?... LOTTERY, a nine-year-old bay gelding who was to become the most brilliant steeplechaser in the early years of the sport.

REG GREEN
A Race Apart: The History of the Grand National (1988)

5th March, 1845

At Aintree to see the Steeple Chase. After a smart run of a mile for £50 given by Lord Sefton, fifteen horses started for the grand Steeple Chase. The day was very cold and frosty, but the ground, though dry and very hard, not very objectionably so. It was an animated race, and a horse named 'Cure-all', nothing thought of, took it very cleverly; the old grey horse 'Peter Simple' coming in second.

Diary of GEORGE HOLT ESQ.

There was an early tradition of horse-racing in the area:- races during the reign of Elizabeth I; at Crosby, along the sands, for the 'Crosby Bell'; at Leasowe (attended by the Duke of Monmouth in 1683); at Maghull; and then at Aintree, where William Lynn leased the land and built a grandstand (1829).

Liverpool's popularity as a sea-bathing resort along the North Shore

The floating bath

Liverpool has become a town of considerable resort as a sea-bathing place; and the inhabitants from the interior of Lancashire resort hither in great numbers during the summer months to enjoy this salubrious and gratifying exercise. The floating bath, which is moored during the season off George's Pier Head, affords excellent accommodation to those who prefer this novel mode of immersion, and on the shore machines are provided as at Scarborough, Brighton and Ramsgate, for conveying the visitors into the briny waves and returning them in safety to the shore. Since the removal of the old baths to make way for the quays at the Prince's Dock, the bath accommodation is somewhat diminished, but a complete suite of new baths is now erecting on the west side of George's Dock, which will, when completed, be an ornament to the town...

T. BAINES *The History of Liverpool* (1852)

Long lines of bathing 'machines' stood in readiness...while stalwart bathing men and women - amphibious creatures - were in attendance... There was a sort of conventional separation between the sexes but the male bathers entered the water and disported there in *puris naturalibus...*

J. A. PICTON *City of Liverpool Municipal Archives, 2 vols.,* (1883 and 1886)

The North Shore (British School, 19th C.)

Franz Liszt makes music in Liverpool, 1840

The Concert Hall, Bold Street.

In 1840 Franz Liszt, then aged 29 and at the apex of his fame as a concert virtuoso, was persuaded to join John Orlando Parry, a Welshman of varied talents (including harp-playing, composing and singing comic songs and promoting concert tours) in a tour of the British Isles which began at Reading...and paused at Liverpool en route for Ireland...

Extracts from the diary of John Orlando Parry:

Dec. 1st. Left Chester at 11 - arrived Birkenhead at 1/4 to 1 - had Oysters Pickled, Bread and Cheese in the open air at the Hotel garden!! We enjoyed it very much - Liszt treated us all - Boat arrived - crossed to Liverpool - Liszt all alive on board - put on his Hungarian great bear skin cloak - Everyone thinking he was a little touched ... dressed and went to the Theatre Royal where the Concert was held - 'twas Subscription Concert - belonging to Mr Ashton. Liszt was tremendously received...the house was so full many left directly Liszt had played his last piece.

Dec. 2nd. Liverpool to Preston...I and Liszt stayed to see Mr Ashton to try and get some money for Lewis - walked about Liverpool - bought some spectacles for Liszt - at 2^{1}/$_{2}$ we went to railway and at 5 were...at Preston...

After giving concerts in Preston, Rochdale and Manchester, Parry brought his company back to Liverpool for embarkation on the Dublin packet, spending a weekend sightseeing in the city. Among the places he visited was the School for the Blind in Commutation Row, where he attended a concert:

When they all rose up to sing the Te Deum of Handel, it was of all things the most overpowering to see near 40 blind people singing with the greatest precision, with a blind person at the organ....We then went through a subterranean passage to their chapel to hear the organ, which is a very fine one, and beautifully played by the maestro - he is also blind!

At the Lyceum Reading Room Parry met Wilson, proprietor of the Bold Street Concert Hall:

He is an uncommon nice man and showed us his concert room. It is very large, and comfortably as well as elegantly fitted up. It will hold 1,200 sitting down and 1,400 when all the corners are filled.

Dec. 16th....on board the *Prince* - Dublin steamer...Oh, my! Oh, Lor! I was dreadfully ill...

STAINTON DE B. TAYLOR
Two Centuries of Music in Liverpool (1976)

from *Liverpool*

Liverpool, the good old town, we miss
  The grand old relics of a reverend past, -
Cathedrals, shrines that pilgrims come to kiss, -
  Walls wrinkled by the blast.

Some crypt or keep, historically dear,
  You find, go where you will, all England through:
But what have we to venerate, - all here
  Ridiculously new.

We have our Castle Street, but castle none;
  Redcross Street, but its legend who can learn;
Oldhall Street, too, we have, the old hall gone;
  Tithebarn Street, but no barn.

Huge warehouses for cotton, rice, and corn,
  Tea and tobacco, log and other woods,
Oils, tallow, hides that smell so foully foreign,
  Yea, all things known as goods, -

These we can show, but nothing to restore
  The spirit of old times, save here and there
An ancient mansion with palatial door,
  In some degenerate square.

Then rise the merchant princes of old days,
  Their silken dames, their skippers from the strand,
Who brought their sea-borne riches, not always
  Quite free from contraband.

And these their mansions, to base uses come, -
  Harbours for fallen fair ones, drifting tars;
Some manufactories of blacking, some
  Tobacco and cigars.

We have a church that one almost reveres, -
  St Nicholas, nodding by the river-side, -
In old times hailed by ancient mariners
  That came up with the tide.

And there's St Peter's, too, not quite so frail,
  Yet old enough for antiquated thoughts:
Ah, many a time I lean against the rail
  To hear its sweet cracked notes....

Yet all is so ridiculously new,
  Except, perhaps, the river and the sky,
The waters and the immemorial blue
  Forever sailing by.

Ay, they are old, but new as well as old,
  For old and new are just the same sky dream, -
One metal in a slightly different mould,
  the same refiltered stream.

ROBERT LEIGHTON

A German visitor, J.G. Kohl, writes in 1842 of Liverpool, the Cheshire Shore, the Rock Lighthouse

I went on that same evening to Liverpool, and at ten o' clock arrived on the 'Cheshire shore', on the south side of the Mersey, opposite to the great town itself. This 'Cheshire shore' has risen and flourished simultaneously with Liverpool, and rural houses of entertainment, and villages rich in country seats have been gradually scattered along the river-side, serving to the townspeople as watering-places, and as places of residence and amusement...To each little place on the opposite side of the Mersey, a steamboat plies from Liverpool as a ferry. At certain hours of the day, about twelve of these ferry steamers assemble at the same wharf to take in their several cargoes, and at a given signal they all start, scattering themselves in different directions over the Mersey, like a pack of cards over a table.

We arrived at the chief of these ferries called Birkenhead, where we and our luggage were packed with railroad speed into a steamer, and within view of the widely spreading and brightly illuminated Liverpool, we glided swiftly over the dark waters of the Mersey. Every moment the echo of the noise made by our paddles as they struck the water, announced that we were passing some stately vessel lying at anchor....

Close to the custom-house lie the docks, and these offer to the stranger a spectacle of commercial bustle, and a multitude of splendid harbour and marine works, unequalled, I believe, in the world, not even excepting those of London.

I cannot tell how many flags were hoisted...at the different piers of Liverpool, to inform the passengers where to look for the Glasgow boat, the Isle of Man boat, the Dublin boat, the Cork boat, the Pembroke boat, and all the rest of them. I, for my part, ranged myself under the flag of Bangor, the most frequented place of transit, to those about to visit North Wales...Newsmen offered us the news of the same morning. Others had telescopes for those who wished to contemplate the Welsh coast at their ease. Oranges and gingerbread, with other delicacies of the same kind, were hawked about...The steamers, meanwhile, were humming, hissing and shrieking around us...

'The mouth of the Mersey' is armed with light-houses, land marks, beacons, telegraph stations, and private signal poles, as a mouth with teeth. The Rock Lighthouse is the most important, the most solid, and the handsomest of all these erections, so I was not surprised to learn that Mr Foster had contributed the design. It is built of hard granite from the island of Anglesey. The stones are all dovetailed into one another, and the whole has been united into one solid mass by a cement of volcanic origin. The coloured light thrown out at night upon the ocean, is said to be one of the most brilliant along the whole English coast. When we passed the place, the windows were carefully closed, that the powerful reflecting mirrors might not, by concentrating the rays of the sun, act as a burning-glass, and so perhaps give occasion to a fire somewhere or other....

We were soon out at sea, but even there on the waste of salt-water I saw more smoking chimneys all at one glance than I had seen altogether on the Steppes of Southern Russia. The chimneys...were those of the various steamers hastening to and from Liverpool. Each observed its line of way, as strictly as if it had been marked out for her by a regular macadamised road....

J.G. KOHL
Ireland, Scotland and England (1844)

64

The growth of the Port, the Population - and Poverty
1801: population 77,000; 1861: population 444,000

...the cellars, sinks and hovels of the wretched lanes and courts near the river....in some parts of the town, inhabited by laborers, and poor people generally. I used to crowd my way through masses of squalid men, women and children, who at this evening hour, in those quarters of Liverpool, seem to empty themselves into the street, and live there for the time... Poverty, poverty poverty...

HERMAN MELVILLE
Redburn (1849)

Liverpool cellars

The cellars are dwellings underground, having no windows and no communication with the outside air excepting by the door, the top of which is sometimes not higher than the level of the street. When the door of such a cellar is closed, light and air are both excluded. Access to the door is by a narrow flight of steps descending from the street. The roof is so low that a person of moderate height cannot stand upright. There is frequently no floor except the bare earth. There is usually one apartment (10 to 12 square feet) but in some cases there is a back cellar used as a sleeping room... All the cellars are dark, damp, ill-ventilated and dirty. There are upwards of 8,000 inhabited cellars in Liverpool and I estimate their occupants at from 35,000 to 40,000.

DR W. H. DUNCAN, 1842
Public Medical Officer for Liverpool (the first in Britain)

Liverpool Poorhouse

'The patients wore the same shirts for seven weeks; bedding was changed and washed once a month; food was at starvation level; spirits entered the Infirmary freely. The number of patients was very large, 1350 rising at times to 1,500.' - of Liverpool Workhouse Infirmary. FLORENCE NIGHTINGALE

Charles Dickens at the Adelphi Hotel: His Voyage to America, 1842

Adelphi Hotel. Liverpool. Monday 3rd January 1842.

My Dear Fred

    We came down here in great comfort and in good spirits ... Fanny came early this morning, stops all night, and sees us sail tomorrow.

    Tomorrow the *Britannia* lies a mile or so off, to be *out* of the way of the shipping, and *in* the stream. We go out to her in a small steamer, at One. She sails directly we get aboard. The passengers friends accompany them in the small steamer aforesaid, and return when the anchor is weighed. They talk of seventy, but I don't believe it. They expect, too, a very fine passage. God send they may be right.

    Our cabin is something immensely smaller than you can possibly picture to yourself. Neither of the portmanteaus could by any mechanical contrivance be got into it. When the door is open, you can't turn round. When it's shut you can't put on a clean shirt, or take off a dirty one. When it's day, it's dark. When it's night, it's cold ... the beds, with pillows, sheet, and blankets complete, might be sent from one place to another through the Post Office, with only a double stamp. I believe it's the best, notwithstanding, both in respect of the motion, and its contiguity to the lady's cabin, where Anne will be. That is really a comfortable room, larger than the breakfast room in Devonshire Terrace; well-lighted, sofa'd, mirrored, and so forth. From *its* door to *our* door, is literally but a step; and not a wide one either.

    Captain Hewitt was not on board; and all hands were very busy, stowing away meat and greens, and an enormous cow, for milk. The stewardess is a Scotch woman, and has crossed the Atlantic seventeen times. She is quite young withal, and buxom enough...

Your truly affectionate brother,
Charles Dickens.

Letters of Charles Dickens (6 vols), ed. House, Storey and Tillotson (1974)

Cunard's paddle steamer The Britannia *passes the Pier Head on her maiden voyage to Boston, America. 4th July, 1840.*
(*C. E. Turner*)

Charles Dickens in the Liverpool Police Force
POOR MERCANTILE JACK - Chapter V in *The Uncommercial Traveller*

Is the sweet little cherub who sits smiling aloft and keeps watch on the life of poor Jack, commissioned to take charge of Mercantile Jack, as well as Jack of the national navy? If not who is? What is the cherub about, and what are we all about, when poor Mercantile Jack is having his brains slowly knocked out by penny weights, aboard the brig *Beelzebub,* or the barque *Bowie-knife* —when he looks his last at that infernal craft, with the first officer's iron boot-heel in his remaining eye, or with his dying body towed overboard in the ship's wake, while the cruel wounds in it do " the multitudinous seas incarnadine"?

Is it unreasonable to entertain a belief that if, aboard the brig *Beelzebub* or the barque *Bowie-knife,* the first officer did half the damage to cotton that he does to men, there would presently arise from both sides of the Atlantic so vociferous an invocation of the sweet little cherub who sits calculating aloft, keeping watch on the markets that pay, that such vigilant cherub would, with a winged sword, have that gallant officer's organ of destructiveness out of his head in the space of a flash of lightning?

If it be unreasonable, then am I the most unreasonable of men, for I believe it with all my soul.

This was my thought as I walked the dock-quays at Liverpool, keeping watch on poor Mercantile Jack. Alas for me! I have long outgrown the state of sweet little cherub; but there I was, and there Mercantile Jack was, and very busy he was, and very cold he was; the snow yet lying in the frozen furrows of the land, and the north-east winds snipping off the tops of the little waves in the Mersey, and rolling them into hail-stones to pelt him with. Mercantile Jack was hard at it, in the hard weather: as he mostly is in all weathers, poor Jack! He was girded to ships' masts and funnels of steamers, like a forester to a great oak, scraping and painting; he was lying out on yards, furling sails that tried to beat him off; he was dimly discernible up in a world of giant cobwebs, reefing and splicing; he was faintly audible down in holds, stowing and unshipping cargo...he was standing by at the shoot of the Cunard steamer off tomorrow, as the stocks-in-trade of several butchers, poulterers, and fishmongers poured down into the ice-house; he was coming aboard of other vessels with his kit in a tarpaulin bag, attended by plunderers to the very last moment of his shore-going existence....all the rigging in the docks was shrill in the wind, and every little steamer coming and going across the Mersey was sharp in its blowing off, and every buoy in the river bobbed spitefully up and down, as if there were a general taunting chorus of "Come along, Mercantile Jack! Ill lodged, ill fed, ill used, hocussed, entrapped, anticipated, cleaned out. Come along, Poor Mercantile Jack, and be tempest-tossed till you are drowned!"

The uncommercial transaction which had brought me and Jack together was this: I had entered the Liverpool police force, that I might have a look at the various unlawful traps which are every night set for Jack. As my term of service in that distinguished corps was short, and as my personal bias in the capacity of one of its members has ceased, no suspicion will attach to my evidence that it is an admirable force. Besides that, it is composed, without favour, of the best men that can be picked, it is directed by an unusual intelligence. Its organisation against Fires I take to be much better than the metropolitan system, and in all respects it tempers its remarkable vigilance with a still more remarkable discretion.

Jack had knocked off work in the docks some hours, and I had taken, for purposes of identification, a photograph likeness of a thief, in the portrait-room at our local head police-office (on the whole, he seemed rather complimented by the proceeding), and I had been on police parade, and the small hand of the clock was moving on to ten, when I took up my lantern to follow Mr. Superintendent to the traps that were set for Jack. In Mr. Superintendent I saw, as anybody might, a tall, well-looking, well-set-up man of a soldierly bearing, with a cavalry air, a good chest, and a resolute, but not by any means ungentle, face. He carried in his hand a plain black walking-stick of hard wood: and whenever and wherever, at any after-time of the night, he struck it on the pavement with a ringing sound, it instantly produced a whistle out of the darkness, and a policeman. To this remarkable stick I refer an air of mystery and magic which pervaded the whole of my perquisition among the traps that were set for Jack.

We began by diving into the obscurest streets and lanes of the port. Suddenly pausing in a flow of cheerful discourse before a dead wall, apparently some ten miles long, Mr. Superintendent struck upon the ground, and the wall opened, and shot out, with military salute of hand to temple, two policemen - not in the least surprised themselves, not in the least surprising Mr. Superintendent.

"All right, Sharpeye?"

"All right, sir."

"All right, Trampfoot?"

"All right, sir."

"Is Quickear there?"

"Here am I, sir."

"Come with us."

"Yes, sir."

So, Sharpeye went before, and Mr. Superintendent and I went next, and Trampfoot and Quickear marched as rear-guard. Sharpeye, I soon had occasion to remark, had a skilful and quite professional way of opening doors - touched latches delicately, as if they were keys of musical instruments - opened every door he touched, as if he were perfectly confident that there was stolen property behind it - instantly insinuated himself, to prevent its being shut.

Sharpeye opened several doors of traps that were set for Jack, but Jack did not happen to be in any of them. They were all such miserable places that really, Jack, if I were you, I would give them a wider berth. In every trap somebody was sitting over a fire, waiting for Jack. Now, it was a crouching old woman, like the picture of the Norwood Gipsy in the old sixpenny dream-books; now, it was a crimp of the male sex, in a checked shirt and without a coat, reading a newspaper; now, it was a man crimp and a woman crimp, who always introduced themselves as united in holy matrimony; now, it was Jack's delight, his (un)lovely Nan; but they were all waiting for Jack, and were all frightfully disappointed to see us.

"Who have you got up-stairs here?" says Sharpeye generally. (In the Move-on tone.)

"Nobody, surr; sure not a blessed sowl." (Irish feminine reply.)

"What do you mean by nobody? Didn't I hear a woman's step go up-stairs when my hand was on the latch?"

"Ah! sure, thin, you're right, surr, I forgot her. 'Tis on'y Betsy White, surr. Ah! you know Betsy, surr. Come down, Betsy darlin', and say the gintlemin."

Generally, Betsy looks over the banisters (the steep staircase is in the room) with a forcible expression in her protesting face of an intention to compensate herself for the present trial by grinding Jack finer than usual when he does come. Generally, Sharpeye turns to Mr. Superintendent, and says, as if the subjects of his remarks were wax-work:

"One of the worst, sir, this house is. This woman has been indicted three times. This man's a regular bad one likewise. His real name is Pegg. Gives himself out as Waterhouse."

CHARLES DICKENS
The Uncommercial Traveller (1860)

The Founding of Blackburne House, an 'Educational Establishment for Women', 1844
That those who are our best teachers,and whose lessons are oftenmost heeded in life, should be well taught themselves, is a proposition that few reasonable men will gainsay.
After taking the chair at the opening meeting of the Mechanics' Institute, 26 February, 1844
....took the chair at a large assembly of The Mechanics' Institute at Liverpool... having been received with tremendous and enthusiastic plaudits... did immediately dash into a vigorous, brilliant, humorous, pathetic, eloquent, fervid, and impassioned speech...received by Thirteen Hundred Persons with frequent, vehement, uproarious, and deafening cheers...
After acting in Bulwer Lytton's play 'Not So Bad As We Seem' at the Philharmonic Hall, 1852
I left Liverpool at four o' clock in the morning, and I am so blinded by excitement, gas, waving hats and handkerchiefs that, believe me, I can hardly see to write, but nevertheless it was a night of triumph.
CHARLES DICKENS

Charles Dickens

Van Diemen's Land

You rambling boys of Liverpool,
    I'd have you to beware:
When you go a-hunting
    With your dog, your gun, your snare,
Watch out for the gamekeeper,
    Keep your dog at your command,
And think of all the hardships
    Going to Van Diemen's Land.

We had two Irish lads on board,
    Jimmy Murphy and Paddy Malone,
And they were both the truest friends
    That any man could own.
The gamekeeper he caught them,
    And from old England's strand
They were seven years transported
    To plough Van Diemen's Land.

We had a lady fair on board,
    Mary Johnson was her name,
And she was sent from Liverpool
    For a-chasing of the game.
She took the captain's fancy
    And he married her off-hand,
And she gave us all good usage
    Going to Van Diemen's Land.

The minute that they landed us
    Upon that dreadful shore,
The planters they inspected us,
    Full twenty score or more.
They led us round like horses
    And sold us out of hand,
And yoked us to the plough my boys
    To plough Van Diemen's Land.

As I lay in the hold one night
    A-dreaming all alone,
I dreamed I was in Liverpool,
    Way back in my old home
With my true love beside me
    And a jug of ale in hand,
When I awoke quite broken-hearted
    Lying off Van Diemen's Land.

AUTHOR UNKNOWN

Prince Albert opens the Albert Dock, 30 July 1846

His Royal Highness Prince Albert visited the town, having cruised up and down the river (in the Royal Yacht *Fairy*), steamed into and opened the Albert Dock amid the rejoicing of many thousands, who crowded the quays and the windows of the warehouse; cheering and music being heard at intervals between the deafening discharge of cannon. The Prince Consort afterwards laid the foundation stone of the Sailors' Home. The sun shone brightly throughout the day.

BENJAMIN BLOWER
The Mersey, Ancient and Modern (1878)

Prince Albert opens the Albert Dock

I have heard of the greatness of Liverpool but the reality far surpasses the expectation.
PRINCE ALBERT, in his speech, 30th July, 1846

*... Walked round the new Albert Dock Warehouses - most lavish expense everywhere;
the construction is for eternity, not time; it appears prodigally extravagent.*
Diary of GEORGE HOLT ESQ.

Heathcliff
from *Wuthering Heights*

One fine summer morning - it was the beginning of harvest, I remember - Mr Earnshaw, the old master, came down stairs, dressed for a journey; and, after he had told Joseph what was to be done during the day, he turned to Hindley and Cathy, and me - for I sat eating my porridge, with them - and he said, speaking to his son,

'Now, my bonny man, I'm going to Liverpool to-day . . . What shall I bring you? You may choose what you like; only let it be little, for I shall walk there and back; sixty miles each way, that is a long spell!'

Hindley named a fiddle, and then he asked Miss Cathy; she was hardly six years old, but she could ride any horse in the stable, and she chose a whip.

He did not forget me; for he had a kind heart, though he was rather severe, sometimes. He promised to bring me a pocketful of apples and pears, and then he kissed his children good-bye, and set off.

It seemed a long while to us all - the three days of his absence and often did little Cathy ask when he would be home. Mrs Earnshaw expected him by supper-time, on the third evening; and she put off the meal hour after hour; there were no signs of his coming, however, and at last the children got tired of running down to the gate to look. Then it grew dark, she would have had them to bed, but they begged sadly to be allowed to stay up; and, just about eleven o'clock, the door-latch was raised quietly and in stept the master. He threw himself into a chair, laughing and groaning, and bid them all stand off, for he was nearly killed - he would not have another such walk for the three kingdoms.

'And at the end of it, to be flighted to death!' he said, opening his great coat, which he held bundled up in his arms. 'See here, wife; I was never so beaten with anything in my life; but you must e'en take it as a gift of God; though it's as dark almost as if it came from the devil.'

We crowded round, and, over Miss Cathy's head, I had a peep at a dirty, ragged, black-haired child; big enough both to walk and talk - indeed, its face looked older than Catherine's - yet, when it was set on its feet, it only stared round, and repeated over and over again some gibberish that nobody could understand. I was frightened, and Mrs Earnshaw was ready to fling it out of doors: she did fly up - asking how he could fashion to bring that gipsy brat into the house, when they had their own bairns to feed, and fend for? What he meant to do with it, and whether he were mad?

The master tried to explain the matter; but he was really half dead with fatigue, and all that I could make out, amongst her scolding, was a tale of his seeing it starving, and houseless, and as good as dumb in the streets of Liverpool where he picked it up and inquired for its owner - Not a soul knew to whom it belonged, he said, and his money and time, being both limited, he thought it better to take it home with him, at once, than run into vain expenses there; because he was determined he would not leave it as he found it.

Well, the conclusion was that my mistress grumbled herself calm; and Mr Earnshaw told me to wash it, and give it clean things, and let it sleep with the children.

Hindley and Cathy contented themselves with looking and listening till peace was restored; then, both began searching their father's pockets for the presents he had promised them. The former was a boy of fourteen, but when he drew out what had been a fiddle, crushed to morsels in the greatcoat, he blubbered aloud, and Cathy, when she learnt the master had lost her whip in attending on the stranger, showed her humour by grinning and spitting at the stupid little thing, earning for her pains a sound blow from her father to teach her cleaner manners.

They entirely refused to have it in bed with them, or even in their room, and I had no more sense, so, I put it on the landing of the stairs, hoping it might be gone on the morrow. By chance, or else attracted by hearing his voice, it crept to Mr Earnshaw's door, and there he found it on quitting his chamber. Inquiries were made as to how it got there; I was obliged to confess, and in recompense for my cowardice and inhumanity was sent out of the house.

This was Heathcliff's first introduction to the family; on coming back a few days afterwards, for I did not consider my banishment perpetual, I found they had christened him 'Heathcliff'; it was the name of a son who died in childhood, and it has served him ever since, both for Christian and surname.

EMILY BRONTË
Wuthering Heights (1847)

Branwell Brontë and the origin of Heathcliff

... in August 1845 Branwell was sent to Liverpool in the care of John Brown after his dismissal by the Robinsons. It was the time when the first shiploads of Irish immigrants were landing at Liverpool and dying in the cellars of the warehouses on the quays. Their images, and especially those of the children, were unforgettably depicted in the *Illustrated London News* - starving scarecrows with a few rags on them and an animal growth of black hair almost obscuring their features. The relevance of such happenings within a day's journey of Haworth (collections were made in Haworth Church for the victims of the Irish Famine) cannot be overlooked in explaining Emily's choice of Liverpool for the scene of Mr. Earnshaw's encounter with 'the gipsy brat' Heathcliff, 'dirty, ragged, black-haired' ... who can say that he was not first given a being and a body by Branwell's report of starving immigrant children in the Liverpool streets? Branwell's visit to Liverpool was in August 1845; the writing of *Wuthering Heights* belongs to the autumn and winter of that year.

WINIFRED GÉRIN
Emily Brontë (1971)

Liverpool's part in the origins of George Bernard Shaw

... It was at this moment that some devil, perhaps commissioned by the Life Force to bring me into the world, prompted my father to propose marriage to Miss Bessie Gurly. She caught at the straw. ...

Finding it impossible to make her see the gravity of the pecuniary situation, or to induce her to cancel her engagement on such a ground, her people ... told her that George Carr Shaw was a drunkard. She indignantly refused to believe them ... He assured her most solemnly that he was a convinced and lifelong teetotaller. And she believed him and married him. But it was true. He drank...

... I can only imagine the hell into which my mother descended when she found out what shabby-genteel poverty with a drunken husband is like. She told me once that when they were honeymooning in Liverpool (of all places) she opened her bridegroom's wardrobe and found it full of empty bottles. In the first shock of discovery she ran away to the docks to get employed as a stewardess and be taken out of the country. But on the way she was molested by some rough docklanders and had to run back again.

GEORGE BERNARD SHAW
Sixteen Self-Sketches (1949)

Maggie May

Come all ye sailors bold
And when my tale is told
I'm sure you'll all have cause to pity me.
For I was a goddam fool
In the port of Liverpool
When I met up with a girl called Maggie May.

Chorus: Oooh, dirty Maggie May
They have taken you away
And you'll never walk down Lime Street any more, any more,
For you robbed full many a sailor
also a couple of whalers
And now you're doing time in Bot'ny Bay, oooh! ...

Oh, I'll not forget the day
When I first met Maggie May,
She was strolling up and down old Canning Place
In a full-sized crinoline
Like a frigate of the line,
As she saw I was a sailor I gave chase.

Traditional

74

From *The Journal of a Spinster, aged 17, on her tour to North Wales*
Augusta Pearson, 1853

... we proceeded by the 5 o'clock train to Birkenhead. A large hotel adjoins the station and we there found a sitting room looking out upon the Mersey and reminding one strongly of a dining room at Blackwell. A thick mist concealed Liverpool which is just across the river. Charles sallied forth to see the Docks. Cara took a nap and I did my best to follow her example.

August 13th

Up, dressed, breakfasted, bonnetted and down on the pier at half ten, where we were told we should find the porter who had preceded us with our luggage, but 'sorry' no porter could we see, or anything approaching to a box or carpet bag and, leaving us there, Charles sped back to the Hotel, in search of the missing articles. Minutes passed away, and so did a quarter of an hour, and so did half an hour, and no Charles, and no porter made their appearance. We began to think about missing the steamer altogether, and were discussing the probabilities thereof, when a man came up and touching his forelock informed us we were to return to the Hotel, that our luggage had been taken by mistake to the 'Amerikay' ship which was lying in the river, and was to sail at one o'clock, that 'the gentleman has gone after it', that we were too late for the steamer, that no other steamer went that day, and having delivered himself of that pleasing intelligence he turned upon his heel leaving us in a state of dismay.

We walked up and down in the Hotel Garden for some considerable time waiting for Charles' return and at last he came and reported the success of his mission, though it was with much difficulty that he had been able to recapture our property, which the porter had taken with other luggage. Charles was not allowed to go on board and was required to describe most accurately the different packages, their direction etc. He never stopped to think that mine could have been directed with my own name but vowed they all had 'Thomas' on them, and accordingly everything was produced but my unlucky bag, for which they searched far and wide and they said it could not be there, and that the only carpet bag which *had* been there had been sent off in some tender as it belonged to Lady Greenock of 4 Chester Square. It suddenly flashed across Charles' mind that I might have used one of Lady G's cards for my direction, which was just the case and what was more, I had most stupidly forgotten to scratch out her name. The card had turned, I suppose, and my modest little 'A.P. Birkenhead' had been completely overlooked. A lesson to all travelling spinsters to direct their boxes fully and carefully. It was much more than I deserved to see my brown bag reappear emulating the far famed 'black box'.

The Hotel keeper was so penitent and so extremely civil, offering to pay the difference of the railway fare, to give us a dinner *gratis* and I know not what besides and they ended by sending a man over to Liverpool to ascertain whether there would be any other steamer later in the day or whether we should be obliged to rail back to Chester.

He brought us back a favourable answer in half an hour and reported that the *Menai* would leave Liverpool at 1/2 after 4. Dinner was ordered at 2, and *pour passer le temps* we got a fly and drove to the docks or rather the would-be docks, upon which upwards of a million has already been spent, and they are not half completed, for want of further funds. In prospect of these docks a large town has been laid out, squares and streets without end, churches and shops all closed, and a large park with a very handsome piece of water. It has the appearance of a city of the dead and made one quite melancholy to look upon.

From thence we went to the Emigrant's House and went all over the *New Zealander* an emigrant ship which was to sail in a few days. Nothing could exceed the order and cleanliness which reigned everywhere, and all the arrangements for their comfort were most admirable. They have a very nice little church in the precincts, or rather I should say, a Hall fitted up as a church. The ship was to contain 400 emigrants, and certainly they had not much room to spare, their little berths were like so many little narrow coffins closely wedged together and I could not but fancy the poor wretches in a storm. There were all manner of ingenious devices for making a great deal of room out of a very little, the tables being made to push up and down from the ceiling etc.

There were two huge chests from 'Apothecaries Hall' in the cabin, called the Hospital. A doctor was examining them all when we were there, to ascertain whether they had all been vaccinated. We spoke to a very attractive looking girl who told us she came from Oban. She said she had a husband, but no children, and she did not seem to have quite made up her mind whether she was going to Australia *con amore* or not. She had such pretty eyes and such a sweet smile and countenance that we quite lost our hearts to her. At 4 p.m. we went on board the *Menai* Steamer which was to take us to Beaumaris; we had prepared our minds for a cold and rough passage, but it proved quite the contrary ...

AUGUSTA PEARSON, 1853
from *A Spinster's Tour Through North Wales* (1988)

Johnny Todd

Johnny Todd he took a notion
For to cross the raging sea,
And he left his true-love behind him
Weeping by the Liverpool quay.

For a week she wept full sorely,
Tore her hair and wrung her hands;
Till she met with another sailor
Walking on the Liverpool sands.

'Why, fair maid, are you a-weeping
For your Johnny gone to sea ?
If you'll wed with me tomorrow
I will kind and constant be.

'I will buy you sheets and blankets,
I'll buy you a wedding ring;
You shall have a gilded cradle,
For to rock your baby in.'

Johnny Todd came back from sailing,
Sailing o'er the ocean wide;
But he found that his fair and false one
Was another sailor's bride.

All young men who go a-sailing
For to fight the foreign foe;
Don't you leave your love like Johnny,
Marry her before you go.

AUTHOR UNKNOWN

Nathaniel Hawthorne, the American Ambassador in Liverpool, records his impressions 1853-6

The Mersey and Rock Ferry

August 8th, 1853: Day before yesterday, I escorted my family to Rock Ferry, two miles either up or down the Mersey (and I really don't know which) by steamer, which runs every half-hour. There are other steamers going continually to Birkenhead and other landings, and almost always a great many passengers on the transit. On this occasion the boat was crowded so as to afford scanty standing-room; it being Saturday, and therefore a kind of gala day....Some girls danced upon the crowded deck, to the miserable music of a little fragment of a band, which goes up and down the river on each trip of the boat. Just before the termination of the voyage, a man goes round with a bugle turned wide and upward, to receive the ... half-pence of the passengers. I gave one of them, the other day, a silver four-pence; which fell into the vitals of the instrument, and compelled the man to take it to pieces.

At Rock Ferry there was a great throng, forming a scene not unlike one of our muster-days or Fourth of July; and there were bands of music, and banners with small processions after them; and there was a school of charity-children, I believe, enjoying a festival; and there was a club of respectable persons playing at bowls on the bowling-green of the hotel; and there were children, infants riding on donkeys, at a penny a ride, while their mothers walked alongside, to prevent a fall.

August 9th: A pretty comfortable day, as to warmth; and I believe there is sunshine overhead; but a cloud composed of fog and coal-smoke, envelops Liverpool. At Rock Ferry, when I left it at half past nine, there was promise of a cheerful day. A good many gentlemen ... came in the steamer; and it is not unpleasant, on these fine mornings, to take the breezy atmosphere of the river. The huge steamer *Great Britain,* bound for Australia, lies right off the Rock Ferry landing; and at a little distance, too, are two old hulks of ships of war ... homes for old seamen ... There are a great many steamers...also, many boats, most of which have dark red or tan-coloured sails, being oiled to resist the wet; also, here and there, a yacht or pleasure boat; also, a few ships riding stately at their anchors, and probably on the point of sailing. The river, however, is by no means crowded; because the immense multitude of ships are ensconced in the docks; where their masts make an intricate forest for miles up and down the Liverpool shore. The small black steamers, whizzing industriously along ... make up the chief life of the scene. The Mersey has the color of a mud-puddle; and no atmospheric effect, so far as I have seen, ever gives it a more agreeable hue....

August 20th: This being Saturday, there early commenced a throng of visitants to Rock Ferry. The boat, in which I came over, brought from the city a multitude of factory-people, male and female ... pale-looking people ... They are brought on reduced terms by the railways and steamers and come from considerable distances in the interior. These, I believe, are from Preston ...

... At the dock, the other day, the steamer arrived from Rock Ferry with a countless mulititude of female children in coarse blue-gowns, who, as they landed, formed in procession and walked up the dock. These girls had been taken from the work-houses, and educated at a charity-school, and would by-and-by be apprenticed...as servants. I should not have conceived it possible that so many children could have been collected together, without a single trace of beauty, or scarcely of intelligence, in so much as one individual ... All America could not show the like.

September lst: Today, we leave the Rock Ferry Hotel, where we have spent nearly four weeks. It is a comfortable place; and we have been well-victualled, and kindly treated. We have occupied a large parlor, extending through the whole breadth of the house, and with a projecting window looking towards Liverpool, and adown the intervening river, and to Birkenhead on the hither side ... the parlor-window has given us a pretty good idea of the nautical business of Liverpool... Now and then, after a blow at sea, a vessel comes in with her masts broken short off in the midst, and marks of rough handling about the hull. Once a week comes a Cunard steamer, with its red funnel pipe whitened by the salt-spray; and firing off some cannon to announce her arrival, she moors to a large iron-buoy in the middle of the river, and a few hundred yards from the stone-pier of our ferry. Immediately comes puffing towards her a little mail-steamer, to take away her mail-bags and such of the passengers as choose to land; and for several hours afterwards, the Cunarder lies with the smoke and steam coming out of her, as if she were smoking her pipe after her toilsome passage across the Atlantic ... the Chinese Junk, which lies by our pier ... looks as if it were copied from some picture on an old tea-cup. Beyond all these objects we see the other side of the Mersey, with the delectably green fields opposite to us; while the shore becomes more and more thickly populated, until two miles off, or thereabouts, we see the dense centre of the city, with the dome of the Custom House, and steeples and towers, and close to the water, the spire of St Nicholas; and above and intermingled with the whole city-scene the duskiness of the coal-smoke, gushing upward. Along the bank, we see the warehouses of the Albert Dock, and the Queen's Tobacco Warehouses, and other docks; and, nigher to us, a ship-yard or two. In the evening, all this sombre picture gradually darkens out of sight; and we see only the lights of the city kindling...and the bright red gleam of a furnace, like the 'red planet Mars'; and, once in a while, the bright wandering star gliding along the river, as a steamer comes or goes between us and Liverpool.

September 2nd: We got into our new house in Rock Park, yesterday. It is quite a good house, with three apartments, besides kitchen and pantry, on the lower floor; and three storeys high, with four good chambers in each story .... The rent ... furnished, £160. Rock Park ... is private property, and is now nearly covered with residences for professional people, merchants, and others of the upper middling class ... It is the quietest place imaginable; there being a police station at the entrance; and the officer on duty admits no ragged or ill looking person to pass. There being a toll, it precludes all unnecessary passage of carriages ... On either side there is thick shrubbery ... trim gardens, with smooth shaven lawns ...

The snow Trinculo, c. 1838 (Samuel Walters)
This two-masted snow (or brig) seen off New Brighton, voyaged from Liverpool to India.
Fort Perch Rock, the Lighthouse and Rock Channel are in the background.

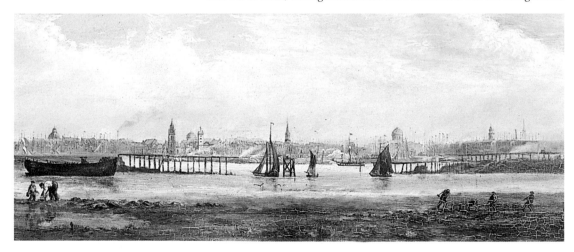

Liverpool from Wallasey Pool, c. 1850 (William J. J. C. Bond)
Wallasey Pool, a large natural inlet of the Mersey, was enclosed by break waters
from Seacombe to Wallasey when Birkenhead Docks were built.

December 10th: I don't know any place that brings all classes into contiguity, on equal ground, so completely as the waiting-room at Rock Ferry, on these frosty days. The room is not more than eight feet square...and wooden benches ranged round; and an open stove in one corner, generally well-furnished with coal. It is almost always crowded; and I rather suspect that many persons, who have no fireside elsewhere, creep in here and spend the most comfortable part of their day.

Street Life

At one o' clock or thereabouts, I walked out into the city, down through Lord Street, Church Street, drank a glass of porter, and back to the Consulate through various untraceable crookednesses. Coming to Chapel-street, I crossed the church-yard of the old church of St Nicholas ... much the oldest sacred site in Liverpool; a church having stood there since the Conquest ...

Almost every day I take walks about Liverpool; preferring the darker and dingier streets, inhabited by the poorer classes ... at every two or three steps, a gin-shop...women, nursing their babies at dirty bosoms; men haggard, drunken, care-worn, hopeless, but with a kind of patience, as if all this were the rule of their life; groups stand or sit talking together, around the door-steps, or in the descent of a cellar; often a quarrel is going on in one group ... Sometimes a decent woman may be seen sewing or knitting at the entrance of her poor dwelling ... I never walk through these streets without feeling as if I should catch some disease; but yet there is a strong interest in such walks; and moreover there is a bustle, a sense of being in the midst of life, and of having got hold of something real, which I do not find in the better streets ... Doubtless, this noon-day and open life of theirs is entirely the best aspect of their existence; and if I were to see them within doors, at their meals, or in bed, it would be unspeakably worse. They appear to wash their clothes occasionally; for I have seen them hanging out to dry in the street.

Further items of street-rambles: - little gray donkies, dragging along disproportionately large carts ... the apparition, now and then, of a bright, merry, child's face, with dark, knowing eyes, gleaming through the dirt like sunshine through a dusty window-pane; at provision-shops the little bits of meat, ready for poor customers, and little heaps of selvages and corners, snipt off from points and steaks; - the kindliness with which a little boy leads and lugs along his little sister...a milkwoman, with a wooden yoke over her shoulder, and a large pail on each side; - in a more reputable street, respectably dressed women going into an ale and spirit-vault, evidently to drink there.

From 1 o' clock till 2 today, I have spent in rambling along ... Tithe Barn Street, Scotland Road, and that vicinity. I never ... imagined from any description, what squalor there is ... Women, with young figures, but old and wrinkled countenances; young girls...barefooted, with dirty legs. Women, of all ages, even elderly, go along with great, bare, ugly feet; many have baskets and other burthens on their heads ....

Dinner at the Town Hall

On Friday, at 7 p.m. I went to dine with the Mayor. It was a dinner given to the Judges and the Grand Jury ... at the Town-Hall; and the rooms, and the whole affair, were all in the most splendid style. Nothing struck me more than the footmen in the city-livery; they really looked more magnificent, in their gold-lace, and breeches, and white silk stockings, than any officers of state whom I have seen. The rooms were beautiful; gorgeously painted and gilded, gorgeously lighted, gorgeously hung with paintings ... the dinner gorgeous, in the English fashion. As to the company, they had a kind of roughness, that seems to be the characteristic of all Englishmen so far as I have yet seen them; - elderly John Bulls ... large body, protruding paunch, short legs, and mottled, double-chinned, irregular-featured aspect. They are men of the world, at home in society, easy in their manners, but without refinement; nor are they especially what one thinks of, under the appellation of gentleman.

Bebington, Eastham and Poulton Hall

August 29th: Yesterday (Sunday), wife, the children, and I, took a walk into the country ... a clear atmosphere, bright sunshine, and altogether a Septemberish feeling. The ramble was very pleasant, along the hedge-lined roads, in which there were flowers blooming and the varnished holly ... We passed through a village (Higher Bebington, I believe) with narrow streets, and mean houses, all of brick or stone, and not standing wide apart from each other, as in American country villages, but conjoined. There was an immense alms-house in the midst ... The bell of the old church (St Andrews in Lower Bebington) was ringing ... and many respectable looking people, and cleanly dressed children were moving towards the sound. Soon, we reached the church; and I have seen nothing in England that so completely answered my idea of what such a thing was, as this old village-church of Bebington. It is quite a large edifice, built in the form of a cross, with a low peaked-porch in the side, over which...is the date 1300 and something. The steeple has ivy on it, and looks old, old, old ...

April 3rd, 1854. I walked with Julian to Eastham...the finest old English village I have seen, with many ancient houses, and altogether a picturesque and rural aspect ... several crooked streets, gathering the whole village into a pretty small compass. In the midst of it stood an old church ... with a most venerable air, considerably smaller than Bebington church, but more beautiful, and looking quite as old ... In the center of the church-yard stood an old yew tree of immense trunk, which was all decayed within, so that it is a wonder how the tree retained any life - which nevertheless it did. (This tree was noted as the Old Yew of Eastham, 600 years ago) ....

This village is too far from Liverpool to have been much injured, as yet, by the novelty of cockney residences which have grown up almost everywhere else...About a mile from it, however, is the landing-place of a steamer, which runs regularly except in the winter-months, and where a large, new hotel is built. The grounds about it are extensive and well-wooded. We got some biscuits and another glass of ale at the hotel; and I gave the waiter - a splendid gentleman in black - four half-pence, being the surplus of a shilling. He bowed and thanked me very humbly. An American does not easily bring his mind to the small measure of English liberality to servants.

We took the steamer at two o' clock for Liverpool, and arrived in half an hour; and after waiting half an hour on the landing-stage, steamed back to Rock Ferry.

August 8th: Yesterday...Mr Barber came in his carriage to take us to his place at Poulton Hall... about three miles from Rock Ferry; the road passing through some pleasant rural scenery...

We passed through a considerable extent of private road, and finally drove through a lawn, shaded with trees...and reached the door of Poulton Hall. Part of the mansion is three or four hundred years old...Mr Barber is only the tenant of it...a merchant of Liverpool, formerly resident in New Orleans, a bachelor, with two sisters keeping house for him...They say that there are many legends and ghost stories connected with the house ....

NATHANIEL HAWTHORNE
English Notebooks, ed. Randall Stewart (1941)

The Legend of Poulton Hall

'On a dark and stormy winter's night many centuries ago, a Nun was passing from St Werburgh's Abbey in Chester to Birkenhead Priory and finding herself night-bound in the vicinity of the Mere Ford (the crossing of the Dibbin nearest to the Mersey side of the Wirral Peninsula) she sought shelter at Poulton just off the road above the ford. Now the lord of Poulton of that day took what he wanted and did not much care how he came by it; he made the Nun welcome in his house, but he also made her advances which could not be tolerated by one of her pure and saintly vocation.

Indignantly she repulsed his overtures, declaring that she would rather die than acquiesce in them and so he shut her up in the Martyr's Chamber, declaring (with suitable oaths) that there she would remain without food or drink until she should decide to grant him what he desired. And there she remained steadfastly withstanding him, until she died of starvation and ever since that day the room in which she met her end has been haunted by her ghost.'

ROGER LANCELYN GREEN
Poulton-Lancelyn (1948)

Harriet Beecher Stowe's first visit
to Liverpool, 1853, staying at Dingle Bank

... Our carriage at last drove on taking us through Liverpool and a mile or two out, and at length wound its way along the paths of a beautiful little retreat on the banks of the Mersey, called Dingle. It opened my eyes like a paradise, all wearied as I was with the tossing of the sea.

Shipping in the Mersey, c. 1840 (Frederick Calvert)
"Liverpool, the young giant just springing into vigorous life ...
... The man of 1801 can scarcely believe his eyes in 1862." JAMES STONEHOUSE

from *The Tour of Dr Syntax in Search of the Picturesque (1865)*

... Liverpool, that splendid mart,
Imperial London's counterpart,
Where wand'ring Mersey's rapid streams
Rival the honours of the Thames,
And bear, on each returning tide,
Whate'er by commerce is supplied,
Whate'er the winds can hurry o'er
From ev'ry clime and distant shore.

WILLIAM COMBE

The young Henry M. Stanley leaves his native Vale of Clwyd to stay for the first time in Liverpool with relatives; from here he travelled to America, 1856

... When about half-way across the Dee estuary, I was astonished at seeing many great and grand ships sailing, under towers of bellying canvas, over the far-reaching sea, towards some world not our own. Not long after there appeared on the horizon clouds of smoke, out of which, presently, wound a large city. There I saw distinctly masses of houses, immensely tall chimneys, towers, lengths of walls, and groves of ships'-masts.

My rustic intelligence was diverted by the attempt to comprehend what this sight could mean. Was this Liverpool, this monstrous aggregation of buildings, and gloomy home of ships? Before I could answer the question satisfactorily, Liverpool was all around me: it had grown, unperceived by me, into a land covered by numberless structures of surpassing vastness and height, and spread on either side of our course. We sped along a huge sea-wall, which raised its grim front as high as a castle, and before us was a mighty river; on either side there was an immeasurable length of shore, crowded with houses of all sorts; and when I looked astern, the two lines with their wonders of buildings ran far out towards the sea, whence we had so swiftly come.

Before my distracted mind could arrange the multitude of impressions which were thronging on me, my aunt, who had sat through all unmoved and silent, touched me on the shoulder and bade me follow her ashore. Mechanically, I obeyed, and stepped out on a floating stage which was sufficiently spacious to accommodate a whole town-full of people and, walking over an iron bridge, we gained the top of the colossal wall, among such a number of human beings that I became speechless with fear and amazement.

Entering a carriage, we drove along past high walls that imprisoned the shipping, through an atmosphere impregnated with fumes of pitch and tar, and streets whose roar of traffic was deafening. My ears could distinguish clinks of iron, grinding roll of wheels, tramp of iron-shod hoofs, but there was a hubbub around them all which was loud and strenuous, of which I could make nothing, save that it was awful and absorbing. Fresh from the slumbering existence of a quiet country home, my nerves tingled under the influence of the ceaseless crash and clamour. The universal restlessness visible out of the carriage windows, and the medley of noises, were so overwhelming that from pure distraction and an impressive sense of littleness in the midst of such a mighty Babel, every intelligent faculty was suspended.

The tremendous power of this aggregate force so fiercely astir, made me feel so limp and helpless that again I was tempted to implore my aunt to return with me to the peace of Tremeirchion. But I refused the cowardly impulse, and, before my total collapse, the carriage stopped at an hotel. We were received by such smiling and obliging strangers that my confidence was restored. The comfort visible everywhere, and the composed demeanour of my aunt and her friends, were most soothing. In the evening Aunt Maria appeared, and her warm greetings served to dissipate all traces of my late panic ....

SIR HENRY MORTON STANLEY
Autobiography (1909)

Impressions of a German Traveller, Julius Rodenberg,1856

On the Banks of the Mersey

I spent three days in Liverpool, happy in the company of dear relations...
Liverpool held very much of interest to me; it was the first English city which I
had seen, and moreover it was close to the sea. I love the sea more than is usual
among people born in the mountains.

On the very day after my arrival in Liverpool, we set out for the banks of the
Mersey and the docks. The Liverpool docks, larger and more important than those
of London or any other port in the world, extend for miles, along the whole length
of the city, from the sea far up the Mersey, a broad majestic mirror which seems to
be a continuation of the sea. Liverpool and its port is the go-between for the Old
World and the New. This lighthouse and these quays greet the home-comer from
Australia, when he first sets foot on dear land again after months of voyaging;
here Brazil sends its dye-woods and Havana its tobacco, here Central America
sends its sugar and its coffee, and North America the hides and horns of the
buffalo. And to stand on one of these three-deckers, with the wind flapping in the
rigging and a brown sailor hanging on the bowsprit revarnishing the spray-
ravaged figure-head - 'Lord Canning' or 'St. George' or the 'Amazon' - for a new
voyage ... or to saunter along the quay and see the forest of masts and the strange
life ruling within it; the monstrous movement on the water, caused by the constant
coming and going of the ferry steamers; the work of the gangs in the warehouse,
wondrously enlivened by underground railways; the rattle and rumble of the
wagons moving up and down through the impenetrable throng on the shore road
- to hear all this, to see all this was a joy and a delight.

The scene was pictured more poetically when we came back in the evening to
cross over to New Brighton on the steamer. At first all the banks grew dark and
that bluish haze, which can only be seen in an English evening landscape, adorned
the hills and woods which rose inland. Towards the sea the view was clear, and
the water glistened in the last evening light. The lighthouse too with its alternating
flames - now golden and now reddish purple - was already shining out in the
twilight. On the ship there was music, harmoniously accompanying the beat of the
waves. The darker the sky became, the more the lights shone, one after another-
from both banks, in the water on the ships, and on the boats sailing through the
night with a lantern hung on the mast. More and more - and finally we saw
ourselves in endless avenues of lights on both sides, their mightiest point being the
dome of the lighthouse at the end. Beyond began the enormous blackness of the
ocean. Not far from that, at the quay of New Brighton harbour, our ship tied up
and we got off for a while. Leaning on the wooden planks, we saw the waves
losing themselves in the white sand; we heard the dull roaring of the water and
the wind from the misty distance ...

As we returned home through the illuminated alleys along the shore, music
sounded, especially the shrill bagpipe, from the taverns where the sailors were
drinking, singing and dancing. ... Nowhere can one get a better picture of the
incessant bustle of a port than here. One street is inhabited entirely by negroes and
half-castes, three or four others by perpetually drunken prostitutes, a whole
district consists of shop after shop, supplying the departing seaman and his ship

St. George's Hall, 1854 (John Eastty Goodchild)
Designed by Harvey Lonsdale Elmes. An impression of the interior before completion.

The fifth Custom House, built 1839 on the site of the Old Dock. It was bomb damaged in the 2nd World War and had to be demolished. (W. Herdman)

for the journey round the world, or providing long-missed delights for the home-comer. Out of this tangle of mostly narrow and dirty alleys rise two imposing buildings, the Custom House - a toll-house I believe even more important than the one in London - and the Sailor's Home, a barracks-like institution established by Prince Albert, in which sailors can find accommodation safe against theft and other accidents for the duration of their stay ashore.

Further on, at the opposite end of town, lies St. George's Hall: 'Artibus, Judiciis, Consiliis' - dedicated to Art, Justice, and Counsel; a building that was shown to me in pride ... a shining demonstration of the wealth of the city; the concert hall with its columns of blue and walls of red marble, its gigantic dimensions and its profligate splendour down to the smallest detail, is perhaps unequalled. Hard by are the assizes. Many listeners of both sexes were present; interest in public affairs is quite different in England than in Germany. ... Finally I want to mention the free libraries for the common people, which would be worth closer appreciation and even imitation in Germany.

As far as I could discover, establishments of this sort, in which the working class can entertain and instruct themselves free of charge by reading in a well lit room, heated in winter, have been in existence for only three years, and as yet besides Liverpool are found only in the cities of Hull, Manchester and Birmingham. The crowd is very great, and the reading room is never empty from eight in the morning to ten at night; every hour which the working man has free, he betakes himself here in order to read, and besides technical works, excluding the novel, it is the works of the English poets which are most sought after, according to the very accurate lists maintained by the librarians. This poetic sensitivity of the English is surprising, alongside their so very practical approach to life; but it is a fact, and if necessary can be demonstrated statistically by the consumption of the relevant books. The catalogue is more comprehensive than is usual in many learned institutions in Germany; regal munificence has adorned the rows of books with fine and costly works, every company and every publishing house counts it an honour to present their editions to the library. In other respects, the city bears the cost of maintenance and administration. It gave me great pleasure to survey the reading public. There on the wooden benches sits the sooty-faced apprentice in leather apron beside the grizzled master craftsman; each diligently bent over his book, one smiling, another serious and attentive, as the subject takes him. There is no question that noble aims are promoted more lastingly in this way than by many other previous efforts to counteract corruption in the common people; however, it is debatable whether there would be the same lively interest in Germany among that section of the populace for which this arrangement is precisely created.

The last afternoon, as indeed my whole memory of Liverpool, was embellished by my friends who had arranged an excursion to show me the neighbourhood. We went out through high vaulted avenues of chestnut trees, the foliage already slightly brown with the approach of autumn and here and there a leaf sinking to the ground in the evening breeze. From my youth I have cherished a strong feeling for the beauty of autumn, so the view of this landscape, after I had seen nothing but the sea for several days, was particularly pleasant. Finally, we came back to the sea shore and saw the sun go down over the boundless shining mirror of water. The shore was bare and desolate here; some of the company had taken themselves off to a scaffold-cradle in which a sloop had been hoisted up for repairs. I stood alone near a young lady who was happy to converse with me, for she was a German and for a long time had had no opportunity to talk with a fellow countryman. ...

With the dusk, which had suddenly made itself perceptible by the cooler breeze after sunset, we went back into the country and came to a quiet village which my friends called Childwall. Here we were suddenly in the midst of greenery and peacefulness again, and to accentuate this in an ominous way, the restaurant into which we had gone to take tea, stood opposite a cemetery on a gentle slope, on the top of which was a church with a clocktower. On the other side, embowered in dark trees, we saw a half-ruined mansion, the lower parts of which seemed to be inhabited by needy people. Between these two venerable objects, forming a boundary to it, the view extended to the sea which appeared as a mere light streak through the mist, over the landscape to the broad Mersey, and in the very distant background to the mountains, a jagged violet mass cutting the softer night sky. They were the mountains of Wales which I was seeing this evening for the first time. ...

The next day I betook myself down to the docks to start my journey to Wales. It was sunny clear autumn weather, the sky cloudless and blue, the water shining gold and the landscape beyond tinged with the faintest haze. On the river brisk activity again prevailed, seeming even more lively at this early hour. At the shore lay three or four steamboats so tightly together that one could have stepped comfortably from one to the other; they were all filled with a gay and lively crowd, most of whom were making only the short journey to one point or another on the opposite bank. In the middle of the river, however, a sailing ship was raising anchor, and the wind carried the farewell song of the sailors over to us. These half sorrowful, half hopeful sounds were suddenly drowned again by a steamer going merrily upstream with a brass band on board, and now, as one boat after another, and finally too the one on which I found myself, gradually left the shore, then suddenly the picture that had occupied my mind with such varied impressions had disappeared, and the next moment saw new ships and new people coming and going. Then I was sailing in mid river, and I enjoyed what the picturesque banks had to offer me on both sides. On the right Liverpool and in its endless docks, the tangle of masts, ropes and spars, in which the white sails fluttered - everything dry and stiff like a forest in winter with strips of snow and sunshine; in the middle, far out over the Mersey and out to sea were the ships and their sails on the blue horizon, while on the left pleasant hills with gardens, woods, and cottages adorned the shore from New Brighton to Egremont and Birkenhead, forming an effective natural contrast of tranquility and movement, charmingly harmonized by the river.

In Birkenhead I left the ship and boarded the railway which runs from here to Chester. The train went through green meadows and luxuriant woods, and only occasionally did the Mersey and its pennanted ships appear afar off.

JULIUS RODENBERG
An Autumn in Wales (1856)
(trans and ed. by William Linnard 1985)

Cotton Rhymes, mid 19th Century

1. They bought themselves new traps and drags,
   They smoked the best cigars;
   And as they walked the Exchange Flags,
   They thanked their lucky stars.

2. Yes, Great King Cotton's been and gone,
   And cleaned his subjects out,
   And those who trusted him the most,
   Have vanished up the spout.

from *King Cotton*

The Emily Laurens sails into Liverpool after her Atlantic voyage in 1859...

The seascape was beginning to fill and, listening to Quince's professional observations on the mass of deeply-laden shipping they were meeting, the outward-bound fleet which had left Liverpool at the top of high-water, Kit Ormerod had sufficient to distract him otherwise.

It was an animated scene, with ships of every kind, in steam and in sail or in a combination of both. Snow-white canvased clippers, some of whom were in competition for the fastest passage to Melbourne, and others in keen rivalry on the China run, flew past squat coasters which waddled along under tanned sails; and farther astern, steadily overhauling the most speedy, a fine Atlantic packet pushed along, her bow-wave high and heavy smoke pouring from a black funnel picked out with a white band, that distinguishing mark of the famous Inman Line.

There were schooners, brigs and paddle-steamers belonging to John Bibby and Sons and James Moss and Company, whose principal business was in the Mediterranean; sailing ships of the White Star Line, whose trade was in Australian waters; West Coast and East India ships flying the house flags of Jas. Beazley and Co., McDiarmid and Greenshields, and Imrie and Tomlinson: a couple of ships whose man-of-war smartness bespoke the Liverpool House of Brocklebanks.

From a punt dropped by a schooner-rigged pilot-boat cruising for custom with numbers painted large on a sail, the pilot had climbed aboard, and by now the *Emily Laurens* had left behind that confused and choppy patch of water which marks the place where the stream of the Mersey encounters the cross-set of the Irish Sea. The Snowdonian mountains, the Welsh coast, and the estuary of the Dee were dropping astern and, with other vessels whose patched sails and weather-beaten appearance showed that they, also, were returning from a bout with the elements, the ship was moving along the Rock Channel, close inshore to avoid the

Burbo Bank. To the right, no more than a stone's throw away it seemed and empty save for a few fisherman's huts crudely built from the timbers of lost craft, was the beach which extended from Hoylake to New Brighton; ahead, the long sweep of sandhills between Crosby and Formby.

Quite forgetful that his American companion knew them far better than himself, Kit Ormerod was eyeing these navigational hazards. "Aye, it's a dangerous coast, this," he said oracularly. The Second Engineer was smiling at Kit's homecoming excitement. He had changed into a working suit which shone with oil within a few minutes; when the ship's bell rang for the last dog-watch he would be on duty once more.

"Waal," he observed, "I guess the Chief won't have that cup o' coffee for me if I'm not below in a brace of shakes."

Kit was scanning the New Brighton beach from which most of the bathing-machines of summer had gone, watching a single donkey-carriage sedately proceed along the foot of a grass slope at the top of which were a few highly ornate villas. From this quiet prospect his glance next went to the lighthouse, thence to the fort at Rock Point with its menacing 32-pounders on travelling platforms, its barracks with splinterproof roofs and furnaces for heating shot.

Filled with the shipping of every seafaring nation, the vast docks of Liverpool stretched for miles into the distance. Open to traffic that same month, the Canada Dock was abeam, its new and massive granite walls likely to wear better than the more southerly and more ancient line of docks reaching up-river nearly as far as the old pottery at Herculaneum, whose local red sandstone was a Joseph's coat of repair work. Great warehouses rose behind the forest of tapering masts and spars which towered along the waterfront and, as the evening sun emerged from behind a low cloud the Gothic lantern adorning the tower of the "Old Church" of St. Nicholas, the immense seated figure of Britannia surmounting the dome of the Town Hall, the over-ponderous cupola of the Custom House, the Telegraph Tower and the arches of the Goree Piazza were all golden-shaded by the slanting beam.

Some farther distance behind, seen through the smoke which had gradually soiled the fine buildings of the city, the land rose steeply until it reached its highest point on the site of the old beacon at Everton, the ridge on which St George's Church stood. And steadily up the hill, their remorseless progress marked by lines of narrow streets, crept row after row of small terrace houses, an ever-advancing army of brickwork and Welsh tile which, one by one, were engulfing the venerable mansions of former Liverpool worthies, merchants and shipowners who had taken pride in well-laid-out gardens and pleasure grounds.

The boatswain's pipe was twittering and there was a whine from the powerful peak purchases and patent blocks which made easy the stowage of the *Emily Laurens'* canvas. As she swung to her temporary anchorage the view of the Cheshire side of the river now appeared, a sight which, because he lodged and earned his living in Liverpool, was one far better known to Kit than that at which he had been staring hitherto. Nestling at the water's edge there was the charming little village of Seacombe, and slightly to the left, almost in line with the signalposts on the skyline of Bidston Hill, the foliage on tall trees, still green, hid the delights of pretty Poulton; farther up-stream, beyond the cheerless Emigrants' Shed, erected upon one of the modern docks whose building had aroused so much resentment in the great port across the river, a spired tower in the small but rising town of Birkenhead pointed towards the evening sky, its sweet lines sometimes hidden by the dark smoke which, etched against the reddening afterglow, belched out purposefully from both the tall and the short chimneys of Mr John Laird's busy shipbuilding yard.

THOMAS ARMSTRONG
King Cotton (1962)

Mr Laird's Ship-Building Yard

Extract from the Pantomime performed at the Amphitheatre, 1861:
The Old Woman who lived in a shoe or The Harlequin Child of Childwall
from Scene V, Everton Village; Molly Bushell's Toffy Shop

Enter the Old Woman and her children.

Dame: They've turned me out of my old shoe, to roam,
And play at 'hunt the slipper' for a home.
So far my search is *bootless* - Hard it is!
For rents run high and water rates is riz.
O, if I catch that farmer, I declares,
I'll knock his head off.
Boy: Aye, and Suriganswares!
Dame: Their hearts are hard, if they have hearts at all,
As those four lions at St George's Hall.
Boy: Keep up your pecker, Mother, never fret;
2nd Boy: Here's Farmer Nightshade,
1st Boy: We'll cook *his goose* yet.

The Amphitheatre

Two Years of Terror

When the American Civil War broke out, Georgia-born Captain James Dunwoody Bulloch, European naval representative of the Confederate States, was despatched to Liverpool to organise the building of warships for the Confederate Navy. In those days Liverpool's livelihood was wrapped up in Southern cotton and Bulloch was made welcome, so much so that after the war ended he remained in Liverpool for the rest of his life. His office at 10 Rumford Place is still there and his grave can be found in Toxteth Cemetery.

Over the Mersey in John Laird's Birkenhead shipyard it was soon obvious that the 'fast merchantman' being built there was in fact a Johnny Reb' raider. The North was up in arms over this 'violation of neutrality' and demanded that the ship should be seized, forgetting perhaps that they themselves had asked John Laird to

The Alabama

build them a warship the previous year! By the time the British Foreign Secretary's order to incarcerate the ship eventually reached Liverpool she had sailed out of the Mersey earlier that very afternoon. A classic case of 'missing the boat'!

When John Laird's ship, numbered the *290*, slid gracefully into the River Mersey on that beautiful summer morning on the 28th July, 1862, the invited guests on board innocently thought they were to enjoy a trial run. After lunch, however, they were asked with typical Southern courtesy to leave in the tug that somehow had been standing by for the purpose. The *290* did not return to Liverpool. She sailed out of the Mersey and headed for the Azores where, now known as the *Alabama*, she was fitted out as a Confederate blockade runner. With Alabama-born Raphael Semmes as her captain and a largely Liverpool crew (their Northern enemies described them as 'the scum of Liverpool'!) the *Alabama* proceeded to inflict a terrible carnage on the pride and glory of Lincoln's North. In a short but glorious two-year career, she sank or captured no less than 68 Yankee ships. Her day of retribution came off Cherbourg when she was sunk by the Federal cruiser *Kearsage*, the gallant Captain Semmes being plucked from the sea and the grip of the Yankees, by another of John Laird's ships, the *Deerhound*. This act of rescue itself caused an international incident between Britain and the U.S. Ironically, whilst the *Alabama* was plundering her way across the oceans, the Northern barque *Achilles* arrived in Liverpool in 1863 with a gift from the Philadelphia Committee for the relief of Lancashire Distress - 5,000 barrels of flour. The Civil War was having a disastrous effect on Liverpool's lifeblood, her trade with the Southern States.

Almost a decade after the *Alabama* rode the waters of the Mersey like a swan, the final chapter in the story was written when an arbitration tribunal in Geneva, set up under the Treaty of Washington, awarded the United States $15,500,000 for the mischief caused by the *Alabama*, the *Banshee* and other Confederate raiders built on Merseyside.

The building of the *Alabama* on the banks of the Mersey, her escape from Liverpool, the havoc she caused to American shipping all over the world and the final insult of the rescue of her captain by another Liverpool ship aroused extraordinary bitterness. For many years the 'Alabama Incident' continued to rankle in Northern hearts and remained a running sore in Anglo-American relations.

RON JONES
The American Connection (1986)

How to make Scouse

Workhouse Scouse
As provided for the inmates of Birkenhead Workhouse in 1864:

> 1 oz beef. 15 oz potatoes.
> 1 gallon water.
> Cut up and boil.
> Serve 2lbs to men
> and $1^{1}/_{2}$ lbs to women.

Luxury Scouse

> Piece of breast or neck of lamb.
> $^{1}/_{2}$lb stewing steak.
> 4lbs potatoes.
> $^{1}/_{2}$lb carrots.
> Large onion.
> Any other root vegetables available.
> Salt, pepper, herbs, black pudding to taste.
> Cut up and bring to boil.
> Simmer for at least 2 hours.

Blind Scouse
As above but leave out the meat.

Monsters of the Mersey

Visualize yourself on the Mersey shores at Speke, as dawn was breaking on a clear summer's day, with the tide fast receding from the Devil's Bank. The whole aspect before you is dominated by one huge monster, over thirty feet in length, that is writhing and tossing about, flinging a great tail, over ten feet in width, up into the air higher than a man's height to bring it down with a terrific whack upon the soft sand, with a noise that re-echoes out over the Cheshire plain beyond Stanlow Point. Suddenly, with a terrible snorting, the great monster heaves itself right over in the air to land upon its back, its shining white furrowed belly gleaming in the morning sun.

This was the sight that met the Mersey fishermen on the morning of July 17th, 1863.... The monster made such struggles on the sand-bank where the tide had stranded it that the fishermen were too terrified to venture out. Finally the beast died with its great weight crushing its chest, and then, their courage returned, the Mersey fishermen crowded round it and securely fixed it with ropes. The monster proved to be the second British record of the humpbacked whale. Its total length was 31 feet 4 inches, and the width of its tail 11 feet; its eye measured 3 feet in length.

Nor was this the only monster to prove a thrill for Mersey fishermen, for on September 1st, 1881, two fishermen, named William Dunbobin and Adam Ireland, observed a great Beaked Whale 23 feet long, struggling on a sandbank off the Dungeon Point below Speke. Remembering the former monster, they decided to show no fear, and venturing out, commenced to battle with the beast, finally, after a severe struggle, succeeding in capturing it.

A whale 24 feet long, whose skeleton used to adorn the Liverpool Royal Institution, was captured at the same spot in October, 1865. The beaked or bottle-nosed whale has been found over ten times between the Mersey and the Dee, and one stranded on the East Hoyle Bank in 1858 was exhibited on Tranmere Slip, and 140 gallons of oil were obtained from its blubber. Another, 21 feet in length, was taken off Hoylake in 1853, and contained hundreds of cuttle fish. Very large specimens of the basking shark are common in the Irish Sea, and one 30 feet in length was stranded on Egremont Beach...

Eric Hardy
in *Mersey* (Mersey Dock Board Magazine)
Vol. VII (1934)

Kilvert comes to Liverpool

Thursday, 20 June, 1872

At ten o'clock Mr, Mrs, Miss Gwatkin and I went down to the Landing Stage and embarked on board a steamboat for New Brighton on the Cheshire side of the Mersey, a suburb of Birkenhead. The morning was lovely, all was fresh and new, the salt air and the wind exhilarating and I was in dancing spirits. The Mersey was gay and almost crowded with vessels of all sorts moving up and down the river, ships, barques, brigs, brigantines, schooners, cutters, colliers, tugs, steamboats, lighters, 'flats', everything from the huge emigrant liner steamship with four masts to the tiny sailing and rowing boat. From the river one sees to advantage the miles of docks which line the Mersey side, and the forests of masts which crowd the quays, ' the pine forest of the sea, mast and spar'.

At New Brighton there are beautiful sands stretching for miles along the coast and the woods wave green down to the salt water's edge. The sands were covered with middle class Liverpool folks and children out for a holiday, digging in the sand, riding on horses and donkeys, having their photographs taken, and enjoying themselves generally. Some of the lady and gentlemen riders upon the hired horses were pitiable objects, bumping up and down upon their saddles like flour sacks, and even requiring their horses to be led for them. The ladies as a rule rode without riding habits and with crinolines. The effect was striking.

As we came down the river this morning several large emigrant ships lay in the river getting up steam and the Blue Peter, the signal for sailing, flying at the fore. They were going down the river this afternoon. They seemed crowded with Irish and German emigrants and small steam-boats kept bringing fresh loads of passengers alongside the big ships. One could not help thinking of the hundreds of sorrowful hearts on board and ashore and the farewells and partings for ever, so many of them, on this side of the grave. ...

Eventually we came back to Liverpool, got luncheon and went to see the Docks. Nothing gives one so vivid an idea of the vast commerce of the country as these docks, quays and immense warehouses, piled and cumbered with hides, cotton, tallow, corn, oilcake, wood and wine, oranges and other fruit and merchandise of all

Going on board the Tender

kinds from all corners of the world. I admired the dray horses very much, huge creatures 17 or 18 hands high, more like elephants than horses. Liverpool boasts the finest breed of Flemish draught horses in the world.

Mrs Gwatkin said that 15, 10 and even 5 years ago there was much more trade and wealth in Liverpool and much larger fortunes more rapidly made than now. There has been of late and there still is a stagnation of trade, a depression and deterioration of credit. Formerly the streets were blocked by the enormous business and the mountains of merchandise passing about, but there is plenty of room now.

Friday, 21 June

Liverpool left upon my mind an impression of ragged Irish barefooted women and children. Enormous wealth and squalid poverty, wildernesses of offices and palatial counting houses and warehouses, bustling pushing vulgar men, pretty women and lovely children.

Saturday, 22 June

I was very sorry to leave Liverpool this morning. Theodore went with me in the cab to the Lime St Station at 9.15. The cab was driven by an old gentleman named Gwynne who was once a man of good estate and county magistrate. He married a woman of family, but he dissipated his fortune and now he has sunk to be a common cabman and his wife makes him an allowance.

THE REV. FRANCIS KILVERT
Kilvert's Diary, ed. William Plomer (1944)

Phileas Fogg disembarks

... Queenstown is the Irish port at which the transatlantic steamers stop to put off the mails. These mails are carried to Dublin by the Express trains always held in readiness to start; from Dublin they are sent to Liverpool by the most rapid boats, and thus gain twelve hours on the Atlantic steamers.

Phileas Fogg counted on gaining twelve hours in the same way. Instead of arriving at Liverpool the next evening by the *Henrietta*, he would be there by noon, and would therefore have time to reach London before a quarter before nine in the evening...

Phileas Fogg at last disembarked on the Liverpool quay, at twenty minutes before twelve, December 21st. He was only six hours distant from London.

But at this moment Fix came up, put his hand upon Mr. Fogg's shoulder, and showing his warrant, said, "You are really Phileas Fogg?"

"I am."

"I arrest you in the Queen's name!"

JULES VERNE
Around the World in Eighty Days (1873)

Visit to Liverpool by a young lady from Chester

October 11th, 1875

Went to Liverpool to see the docks & shipping. Went by train to Birkenhead & crossed over the Mersey in a steamer. Frank met us on the landing stage, & we went at once to some rooms near the Exchange & had lunch. We then walked up Bold St. & Lord St. the Oxford & Regent St. of Liverpool. We here took a cab & drove through all the dirty ware-house parts of the town to the Docks. We went to see over the *Algeria,* Betsy's swain's ship, one of the Cunard line, but they were so busy unloading her & cleaning that we could not get a good idea of what she really looked like when at sea. So we went on to the *City of Berlin,* the next largest ship in the world next to the *Great Eastern.* She is one of the Inman line, & is 525 feet long, and has five decks. It was marvellous to see all the arrangements for stormy weather. In the pantry all the things fitted into each other so that they should not shake about & get broken. The egg cups were all strung onto a piece of wood fitted into the dresser, & everything else in the same way. The dining saloon was immense & very prettily fitted up, & there were drawing & smoking rooms besides, lucky for those who can enjoy them. We spent a long time here, & then took the tramway bus back to the landing stage, going close to the docks all the way. They are a wonderful sight, extending for more than five miles. It is a regular forest of ships masts. The landing stage is partly rebuilt & will extend for a quarter of a mile when finished. We came home in the same way as we went after a very enjoyable day. The *City of Berlin* has just made the quickest passage ever known, coming from New York, in 7 days 18 hours.

SARAH ALICE SCOTT *(later Sarah Alice Meredith)* from the Diary, 1875

The White Star liner **S. S. Celtic** *at anchor off the Pier Head 1873.*

The impressions of a French visitor, H. Taine

We started for Liverpool. Its name denotes an old pond, and, in truth, the flat damp country, bathed in sea-mist and covered with stagnant water, seems less adapted for men than for wild-duck....The inhabitants number 500,000, and the port is the most frequented after that of London.

Along the docks the cotton warehouses form a kind of cyclopian, endless and monotonous rampart; nearly all the cotton of the world is housed here....Yet the spacious and numerous docks do not suffice to contain the multitude of ships; they are crowded together in rows and masses at the entrances, awaiting their turn to pass in; at Birkenhead, on the opposite bank, new docks are being built for their accommodation.

Emigrants going on board.

I believe this spectacle to be one of the grandest in the world. Some of the vessels are 3,500 others 4,000 tons burden. A steamer is upwards of 300 feet in length. A vessel at anchor, the *Great Britain*, is about to carry 1,200 emigrants to Australia....

The view from Birkenhead commands the harbour, and the vast reach of the river; it is rather agitated, and gleams with yellow lustre, amid a slight haze. The steamboats ascend and descend, cross and re-cross, with stiff mechanical movements, like black crabs. Sailing ships, lightly heeling over, skim along like beautiful swans. *The George*, a man-of-war carrying 86 guns, arrives in lordly style, all the others making way for her. On the other side the boundless row of masts and rigging lines the sky, while the huge city is massed behind.

We visit several workshops, among others, the establishment of Messrs. Laird, the builders of iron ships. It is said that within the last thirty years they have built two hundred and fifty; they employ fifteen hundred workpeople, have gigantic furnaces and machines, and have stocks, to which water is brought through canals. At present the hull of a paddle steamer is on the stocks...

I was shown a spot where four or five preachers - Methodists for the most part - come to address a crowd on Sunday in the open air; the idea of the Kingdom of God...is one refuge for distressed minds. Another refuge is intoxication. The authoress of a "Life for a Life" writes: 'This Liverpool is an awful town for drinking. Other towns may be as bad; statistics prove it; but I know no place where intoxication is so open and shameless. Not only in bye streets and foul courts, where one expects to see it, but everywhere'...

It is now six o' clock, and we return through the poorer quarter. What a sight! In the vicinity of Leeds Street there are fifteen or twenty streets across which cords are stretched and covered with rags and linen, hung up to dry. Bands of children swarm on every flight of steps, five or six children are clustered on each step, the eldest holding the smallest...in tatters, they have neither shoes nor stockings, and they are all shockingly dirty; their faces and hands appearing to be encrusted with dust and soot. Perhaps two hundred children romp and wallow in a single street. On nearer approach one sees one of the mothers and a grown-up sister, with little more covering than their chemises, crouching in the dusky passage. What interiors!...The smell resembles that of an old rag shop. The ground-floor of nearly every dwelling is a flagged and damp basement... Some of the younger children are still fresh and rosy, but their large blue eyes are painful to behold...many of their faces are scrofulous, being marked with small sores covered with plaister. As we proceed the crowd is more dense. Tall youths seated or half-crouching at the side of the pavement play with black cards. Old, bearded hags come out of the gin-shops; their legs totter; their dull looks and besotted smile are indescribable: it appears as if their features had been slowly eaten away by vitriol. The rags which they wear are falling to pieces, displaying their filthy skins...Rembrandt's beggars were far better off in their picturesque holes. And I have not yet seen the Irish quarter! The Irish abound here; it is supposed they number 100,000; their quarter is the lowest circle of Hell.

H.TAINE
Notes on England, trans. W.F.RAE (1873)

Irish Hair

Coming over from Ireland, the boat
lurching its way in snapping wind,
the decks wet and slippery with spume,
the girl, Christiana Breary,
is leaving behind the stench
of rotting potatoes, the abandoned
household gods, the shallow trench
where they left her brother
wrapped hastily in straw,
the baby dead of road fever,
seeming at the last to cry
bread or blood, and then silence.

She is nearly six years old.

When she was four it was
a fine hot summer until August
rain and biting sleet
wetted her bare feet.
She does not know that the boat
will dock at Liverpool and not Quebec,
that they will throw her mother
into the sea, free from the misty confusion
of typhus, free from the unfounded illusion
of a better life. She does not know
that she will marry into pure Norman stock,
a man gaunt as a gibbet, melancholy
as an undertaker, and that from her
will be extracted a life of labour,
but not smell of famine or abandoning
of home and children.

They brought with them the two
brass candlesticks, wrapped
in a camisole and a pair of corsets,
the youngest riding on his shoulder.
Her father will find a new wife,
now scrubbing steps in Watling Street,
the roads the Romans made, as he
will make English roads with his pick.
She is tired of serving the gentry,
but not crying of the hunger,
the basement kitchen warmed
by well-stoked ovens.

Buying my bag of potatoes I hurry
to the hairdressers. Cutting
my coarse hair the girl says:
'We call this Irish hair',
and nearly a century later I now
think of her, Christiana Breary,
my father's mother, who made
her own pilgrim's progress
to an alien land, her bible in her hand,
and in her body her unseen corn seed
which will never exorcise the devil
of hunger, or my own anger.

Elizabeth Bartlett

Brother and Sister

It was getting dark, though the Town Hall clock had only just struck four. But a fog had hung all over Liverpool since morning, and everything was as damp and dismal as it well could be; and now, as evening came on, the fog had settled into a downright drizzle, converting the streets into what seemed to Nelly Bates (who was crouched in the shadow of St. George's Church) to be endless puddles.

"I wish Benny would come," said she to herself. "I wonder what has kept him? He said he'd be here when the clock struck four."

And she wrapped her tattered clothes more closely around her, and looked eagerly down Lord Street and up and down Castle Street. But no Benny appeared in sight.

"I'm glad as how they're lighting the lamps, anyhow. It'll make it feel a bit warmer, I reckon," she went on, "for it's terrible cold. But Benny won't be long now, nohow. I hope he's sold all his fusees."

And she looked wistfully at the unsold matches lying in her lap. Then, after a pause, she went on again.

"I's had desp'rate bad luck today. I reckon the gen'lmen thinks it too much trouble to take off their gloves to get at the coppers. I wonder if they know what it is to be cold and hungry like me ?"

And the child moved a little farther into the shadow of the church, to escape the keen cold blast that swept up from the river.

Little Nelly Bates was a delicate-looking child, with a pale, thoughtful face, and big, round dreamy-looking eyes. She had none of that wolfish expression that so often characterizes the street Arabs of our large towns and cities; but, on the contrary, there was an air of refinement about her that was difficult to account for. Poor little waif! Her own mother she could not remember. She had only known a stepmother—a cruel, drunken woman; and, alas! her father was no better. Almost as soon as she could walk she had been sent into the streets with her brother Benny, who was a year older, to get her living as best she could. Never knowing a parent's love, the affections of these two children had gone out to each other. Each to each was more than all the world beside. At the time our story opens Nelly was nine years of age, and Benny, as we said, a year older.

Still the minutes dragged along, and Benny came not. The buses were crowded with people outside and in, wrapped in huge warm overcoats, and all down Lord Street she watched the hurrying crowds bending their steps homewards. And she tried to picture their cheerful homes, with great blazing fires, and happy children running to greet them, and wondered how none of them ever paused to notice her, shivering there in the shadow of the church.

At length the great clocks all around began to strike five, and Benny had not come; a sense of unutterable loneliness crept over the child, and she began to cry. Besides, she was hungry and cold, and there was a great fear in her heart that something had befallen her brother. The first stroke of the Town Hall clock, however, had scarcely died away when she heard the patter of bare feet around the corner, and the next moment her brother, panting and breathless, stood before her.

"Oh, Nell!" he burst out, "I's just soft, I is. I's missed a hour in the time. I never did think I was such a fool. But can't be helped now, nohow."

"I was afraid you'd got hurt, Benny; but I don't care now you're all right," said Nelly, looking proudly at the fiushed face of her sturdy young brother.

"Me hurt? Oh, never fear! I knows how to take care of myself. But what luck, Nell ?"

"Bad, Benny, very bad. Nobody wanted matches today."

For a moment Benny was silent, then he burst out,

"By golly, Nell ! What's us to do ? You know what the guv'nor said when we came away this morning ?"

"Ay," said Nelly. "But 'ave you 'ad bad luck too?"

"Horful, Nell—simply horful !"

And for a moment the children looked at each other in blank dismay. Just then a gentleman was seen crossing the street carrying a portmanteau.

"Here's a gent with a portmantle," whispered Benny to his sister. "I'll try my luck! Foller me, Nell, as quick as you can." And off he darted across the street.

"Carry yer bag, sir?" said he, stepping in front of the gentleman; and there was something very appealing in his tone as he spoke.

The gentleman looked kindly down into the two honestlooking eyes that flashed in the gaslight.

"What will you take the bag to the fcrry for?" he inquired.

"For what you please to give," said Benny sturdily. "Times is bad at present, and little chaps like us is glad to 'ave what we catches."

"Oh, that's it, is it? But I'm afraid this bag is too heavy for you."

"Oh, never fear," said Benny, as he got hold of the portmanteau. "I'se 'mazing strong, and I ken carry this like winkin'." And he trotted down the street before the gentleman in a way that showed he was in earnest about the matter.

The gentleman looked after the little fellow with an amused smile, but volunteered no further remark.

Meanwhile little Nelly, who had become stiff and cramped with cold, followed at a little distance, taking care, however, that Benny did not get out of her sight. On reaching the bridge that led down to the landing-stage, Benny turned round, and, seeing his sister behind, shouted back,

"Stay here, Nell, till I come back—I'll be no time sca'ce." And down the bridge he trotted, evidently glad that he was so near laying down his burden.

"Woodside boat, sir?" said he, turning round to the gentleman.

"Yes, my lad."

* * *

"Where is we going?" said Nelly, as she stepped along by Joe's side, her eyes sparkling with delight.

"Into the woods somewhere on t'other side o' the water," said Joe, looking fondly down into the child's beaming eyes.

Benny had nearly stood on his head again when he heard that; but thought better of it, and contented himself with a shrill whistle expressive of delight.

"Better an' better," he thought, flinging his cap into the air and catching it on his toe; "won't I enjoy myself, just, that's all?"

103

The grouping of the characters that figure in the story is purely fictitious, but not the characters themselves. Benny and little Nell, Perks and Joe Wrag, Granny and Eva Lawrence, are drawn from life.

SILAS K. HOCKING

By ten o'clock they were on the landing-stage, and soon after they were gliding up the river towards Eastham. Oh, how the wavelets sparkled in the summer's sunshine, and how the paddle-wheels tossed the water into foam. How happy everything seemed today! The ferries were crowded with passengers, all of whom seemed in the best of spirits; and the rush of water and the beat of the engine seemed to Nelly the happiest sounds she had ever heard.

Benny was rushing here and there and everywhere, and asking Joe questions about everything. But Nelly sat still. Her thoughts were too big for utterance, and her little heart was full to overflowing.

At length they reach New Ferry, where several passengers get off and several others get on; then on they glide again. The river here seems like a sheet of glass, so broad and smooth. Now they are nearing the river's bank, and Nelly is delighted to watch the trees gliding past. How wonderful everything seems! Surely her dreams are becoming a reality at last.

For a while after they land they sit on the river's bank in the shade of the trees, and Nelly rubs her eyes and pinches herself, to be certain that she is not asleep. How grandly the mile-wide river at their feet flows downward to the sea! And what a beautiful background to the picture the wooded landscape makes that stretches away beyond Garston and Aigburth! And Nelly wonders to herself if it is possible that heaven can be more beautiful than this.

SILAS K. HOCKING
Her Benny (1879)

"Thoughts on Revisiting a Centre of Commerce Where a Vast Cathedral Church is being Erected" (c. 1880)

City of festering streets by Misery trod
Where half-fed, half clad children swarm unshod
While thou dost rear that splendid fane to God.
O rich in fruit and grains and oils and ores,
And all things that the feastful Earth outpours,
Yet lacking leechcraft for those leprous sores ...
Let nave and transept rest awhile; but when
Thou hast done His work who lived and died for men,
Then build His temple on high - not, not till then ...

SIR WILLIAM WATSON

'I am brought face to face with the deepest poverty and misery in my district': Gerard Manley Hopkins, the poet and Jesuit priest, at St Francis Xavier's, 1880-81

From Hopkins' letters to his friend, Robert Bridges:
St. Francis Xavier's, 8 Salisbury Street, Liverpool.

15 February 1880: I hope Mr. Woolrych will call as he proposed. I will do all that Jenkinson Street and Gomer Street and Back Queen Ann Street and Torbock Street and Bidder Street and Birchfield Street and Bickerstaffe Street and the rest of my purlieus will spare of me to entertain him.

22 May 1880: ...my Liverpool work is very harassing and makes it hard to write. Tonight I am sitting in my confessional, but the faithful are fewer than usual and I am unexpectedly delivered from a sermon which otherwise I should have had to be delivered of. Here comes someone.

26 October 1880: Rose Hall, Lydiate, Lancashire (I am often here for a night).

I daresay you have long expected as you have long deserved an answer to your last kind and cheering— let us say, number or issue. But I never could write; time and spirits were wanting; one is so fagged, so harried and gallied up and down. And the drunkards go on drinking, the filthy, as the scripture says, are filthy still: human nature is so inveterate. Would that I had seen the last of it.

23 January 1881: I am, by this niggling pen, at Gill Moss, having just walked out of town by frost and starlight; I saw deep drifts frozen as hard as ice, and yet I think this part of the country has felt as little of the storm as any. I lost my way, but two children fetching milk led me, said 'you must follow ooz'.

26 January 1881: . . . I am shortly going down to see the ice in the Mersey and the infinite flocks of sea-gulls of which I hear .

27 January 1881: Well, I went. The river was coated with dirty yellow ice from shore to shore; where the edges could be seen it seemed very thick; it was not smooth but many broken pieces framed or pasted together again; it was floating down stream with the ebb tide; it everywhere covered the water, but was not of a piece, being continually broken, ploughed up, by the plying of the steam ferryboats, which I believe sometimes can scarcely make their way across. The gulls were pampered; throngs of people were chucking them bread; they were not at all quick to sight it and when they did they dipped towards it with infinite lightness, touched the ice, and rose again, *but generally missed the bread:* they seem to fancy they cannot or ought not to rest on ground.—However I hear the Thames is frozen and an ox roasted whole. Today there is a thaw, and the frostings, which have been a lovely fairyland on the publicans' windows, are vanished from the panes.

30 April 1881: Today in lieu of tomorrow, May day, is fixed for the Liverpool yearly procession of horses, which I am in a few minutes going out to see something of. But the procession should begin properly at 2, at which hour I must be in my own loose box; I mean my confessional.

1 May 1881: The procession was not so very good: some people had thought it shd. be on Monday and so everybody and every horse did not come. A busman or cabman consoled me by declaiming in a voice hoarse with professional passion that he could not get on for this damned show. While I admired the handsome horses I remarked for the thousandth time with sorrow and loathing the base and bespotted figures and features of the Liverpool crowd. When I see the fine and manly Norwegians that flock hither to embark for America walk our streets and look about them it fills me with shame and wretchedness. I am told Sheffield is worse though.

23rd February 1889: ...as I went up Brunswick Road (or any street) at Liverpool on a frosty morning it used to disgust me to see the pavement regularly starred with the spit of workmen going to their work; and they do not turn aside, but spit straight before them as you approach.

GERARD MANLEY HOPKINS
Letters to Robert Bridges, ed. C. C. Abbott (1935)

Felix Randal

Felix Randal the farrier, O he is dead then? my duty all ended,
Who have watched his mould of man, big-boned and hardy-handsome
Pining, pining, till time when reason rambled in it and some
Fatal four disorders, fleshed there, all contended?

Sickness broke him. Impatient he cursed at first, but mended
Being anointed and all; though a heavenlier heart began some
Months earlier, since I had our sweet reprieve and ransom
Tendered to him. Ah well, God rest him all road ever he offended !

This seeing the sick endears them to us, us too it endears.
My tongue had taught thee comfort, touch had quenched thy tears,
Thy tears that touched my heart, child, Felix, poor Felix Randal;

How far from then forethought of, all thy more boisterous years,
When thou at the random grim forge, powerful amidst peers,
Didst fettle for the great grey drayhorse his bright and battering sandal!

GERARD MANLEY HOPKINS
(written at Liverpool, 1880)

Felix Randal
From the radio play by Jimmy McGovern.

Felix was a farrier who died in Birchfield Street, the street in which my father was born some forty years later. The street is in St Francis Xavier's parish where I grew up and was educated. Felix's real name was Felix Spencer. I could not trace any record of his birth or baptism, which led me to thinking he was possibly an Irishman who came to Liverpool to escape starvation. And that led me to this play.

In this extract from Act One, Hopkins has been 'having a go' at Felix for making his wife serve him meat on a Friday; and here is Felix's response. The play also reflects something of Liverpool's Irish history.

JIMMY McGOVERN

FELIX: I never had any faith. And hate! It's Englishmen and priests who put that in my heart like a spear in my side. Six months inside me mammy's womb before she knew I was there - for wasn't every Irish belly swollen with the hunger and the blood of women long sucked dry. Me father I never knew: he was a man who'd had a belly-full of mud-cabins and the hanging-gale and English landlords spending Irish money in England and Wales and anywhere else so long as it wasn't Ireland. A man who'd had enough of eating potatoes so black and foul he had to leave the door open and the gale blowin' through when he ate. Of seeing the young and the old and the sick dragged out of their homes by the agents with their soldiers; and the roof torn down as the women shrieked and their men cursed with English muskets at their throat. Then huddling in the ruins out of the wind till the agents came again and pulled down the walls to the very foundations. Then scratching a scalpeen in the ground, huddling in it, praying that it won't fill up with water, while the blood of Irishmen was being spilt in India for the sake of the Great British Empire. Cabbage leaves and blackberries, nettles and weeds, children like monkeys dyin' in your arms and not so much as a peep out of them.

The soup kitchens in Dublin where they fed you like cattle and all the time the ships loaded with food - food that should be going in Irish bellies - streaming along the Liffey to the English landlords. My father went for that food. My father went for that food and they shot him like a farmer shoots a dog. And the blood poured out of his chest as the soldiers held back the crowd and "render to Caesar the things that are Caesar's" poured out of the mouths of the Catholic priests.

HOPKINS: I don't deny Ireland has suffered.

FELIX: Don't talk to me, father. Don't talk to me 'cos, by Christ, I can't hear your English voice without the screams of women and children ringing in me ears.

HOPKINS: You criticise my country yet you live here.

FELIX: 'Cos England is an ever-open mouth sucking Ireland dry. Is it any wonder now that you've sucked her people over too? Sure, it's a great big sieve you want so that only Ireland's blood comes through and the corpses of her people drop in the sea to feed the fishes. Stay away from my home, priest and Englishman. Stay away from my wife.

JIMMY McGOVERN
from *Felix Randal,* broadcast on BBC Radio Four (1985)

Collectors and Collections - Liverpool's development as an important Art centre

The Walker Art Gallery

In 1877 the Walker Art Gallery was opened to the public, paid for by a retiring Lord Mayor, Sir Andrew Barclay Walker, a member of the famous Warrington brewing family. The Gallery housed the great autumn exhibitions held annually from 1871 which were modelled upon the summer exhibitions at the Royal Academy in London. Out of the profits generated by entrance fees and catalogue sales, pictures were bought for the permanent collection. Examples were purchased of the most successful British artists. Millais' early 'Lorenzo and Isabella', Hunt's 'Triumph of the Innocents' and Rossetti's 'Dante's Dream' were all bought within fifteen years of the gallery opening and these three large canvases still form the core of the Walker's Pre-Raphaelite holdings.

FRANK MILNER
The Pre-Raphaelites (1988)

Gerard Manley Hopkins sees George Rae's Collection, including some pictures by Rossetti
15 May, 1881... I have been to see Mr Rae's pictures: I wrote to Mr Rae himself. He has built himself a handsome house and it is full of beautiful objects wherever your eye can rest. Mrs Rae was at home and spent hours in taking me about and shewing me everything, then gave me lunch, and asked me to come again. She was simple and homely and at the same time lively, with a real enthusiasm for art and understanding of it and had nothing whatever of the 'cultshah' manner: I suppose she dates from before it came in. She was very kind, I liked her very much. The pictures were beautiful of course. They still buy: there was that queer landscape of the Beloved in the Canticles by Spencer Stanhope which I saw at the Grosvenor last year. She said by the by that he too had nothing of the modern nonsense.

GERARD MANLEY HOPKINS
Letters to Robert Bridges, ed. C.C. Abbott (1935)

Merseyside and Pre-Raphaelitism

Merseyside has been closely associated with Pre-Raphaelitism almost since the birth of the movement. While London critics were hostile and potential patrons chary of novelty, the Liverpool Academy in 1851 boldly awarded Holman Hunt the £50 non-member prize for his 'Valentine rescuing Sylvia from Proteus'....Between 1851-57 Hunt, Millais and Madox Brown each won two annual prizes at the Liverpool Academy. Hunt in particular desperately needed the money won. When he came to Liverpool sixty years later in 1907 as an old and established artist to view an exhibition of his paintings at the Walker Art Gallery, he paid tribute to the support that the Academy had given to the Brotherhood and donated two fine portrait drawings to the Walker collection.

Liverpool was unique among provincial towns in having its own Pre-Raphaelite school led by artists within the Liverpool Academy who supported and imitated the London group. The chief amongst them were William Windus, John Lee, James Campbell and William Davis.

In addition to imitation and artistic prizes, the Brotherhood was fortunate in obtaining Merseyside patronage. Most important for the group was the Scottish tobacco merchant John Miller of Everton who augmented his already wide collection of British art with Pre-Raphaelite works in the early 1850s. He encouraged the group and helped them make sales to other newly-rich northern industrialists and traders. Unfortunately, Miller tended to buy in order to sell again and most of his pictures did not stay on Merseyside....George Rae, a Birkenhead banker, bought directly from both Rossetti and Ford Madox Brown. The shipping magnate, Frederick Leyland, who rented Speke Hall from 1869-77, was one of Rossetti's best patrons. On a more modest scale, George Holt of the Holt Shipping Line, a generation later, collected eighteenth and nineteenth century British paintings which included a group of Pre-Raphaelite works for his home at Sudley House...

FRANK MILNER
The Pre-Raphaelites (1988)

J.M.W. Turner - his paintings well-represented in Merseyside Collections
Turner's personal links with Merseyside were slight. In 1799, en route from Whalley Abbey near Blackburn to North Wales he passed through Liverpool. Whether he travelled on via Chester the same day or stayed the night is not known. Not a single surviving pencil sketch or study shows the city, the Mersey or the immediate surrounding countryside. Turner never painted the city in oil or ever received a commission for a watercolour view of Liverpool as an illustrative engraving for the many publications with which he was involved.

The principal reason was probably the continued demand by publishers for picturesque topography rooted in the traditional shire and county capitals and more ancient ports and cities. Also Liverpool was off Turner's normal northern route that took him up into Yorkshire and then either on to Scotland or across into Lancashire and the Lake District.

Turner was not without patrons on Merseyside. Early collectors included John Miller, the Everton tobacco merchant who had nine oils, and John Naylor of the banking firm of Leyland and Bullin who had eight oils. Both were keen on maritime and port subjects. However, they did not commission new work but bought pictures, late in Turner's life, that he had painted some time previously. Moreover, both their collections were soon dispersed...and the presence of Turner's work on Merseyside today reflects the interest of a later generation of collectors, particularly of the period 1870-1920 when Turner was richly represented in Liverpool.

FRANK MILNER
Turner: Paintings in Merseyside Collections (1990)

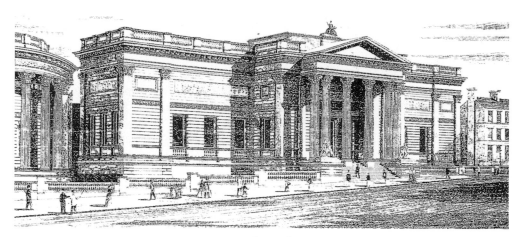

The Walker Art Gallery, architect Cornelius Sherlock.

The Liverpool Welsh

By 1813 one out of every ten people in Liverpool was Welsh; a Cymrodorian Society began in 1819; within the next 40 years the Welsh population increased to 40,000, many of whom spoke no English; National Eisteddfodau were held in Liverpool in 1840,1851, 1884 and 1900 and in Birkenhead in 1878.

Some of the Welsh immigrants to Liverpool, like those to London, became extremely wealthy men. Owen Owen, born in Machynlleth, presided over the growth of one of the largest department stores in the country, whereas Sir Alfred Lewis Jones, born in Carmarthen in 1845, rose to become one of nineteenth century imperial Britain's most famous and powerful entrepreneurs.... The larger of the Welsh builders in Liverpool, like David Hughes (1820-1909) and Owen Elias (1806-80), both from Anglesey, were amongst the wealthiest men in a city much of which they had been responsible for building. In Walton there was a complete series of streets so named that the consecutive initials of the streets spelt 'Owen and William Owen Elias' and 'E. Alfred', the name of his eldest son....When, in 1884, the National Eisteddfod came to Liverpool, the middle class turned out in force; according to J. Glyn Davies, first Professor of Celtic at Liverpool University...'all the affluent Welsh turned up at the ...concerts in evening dress...Even the English were impressed'. The Welsh themselves certainly were. 'Cymry Lerpwl' (the Liverpool Welsh) became forever associated in Welsh minds with the rustle of silk...

Many of the Liverpool chapels were guilty of rampant snobbery....One new arrival from a Caernarvonshire slate quarry in 1890 was overwhelmed by the luxury of Stanley Road chapel and found the whole atmosphere suffocatingly formal and over-polite. There were, he thought, three social classes represented in the chapel and they took no notice of one another.

R. MERFYN JONES & D. BEN REES
Liverpool Welsh and their Religion (1984)

110

from *Liverpool, St David's Day, 1882*

Dear mam a dad...
O mam, this is a strange place,
you would never believe.
It is not possible
not even to see the sky
without lying on your back
on these sharp streets
and looking straight up.
I saw some poor people from Ireland doing this
in longing I thought,
an old policeman took them to jêl
saying they were drunk.
There were the marks of crying on them
their eyes all red
like someone had opened them with a bread-knife.
The sun isn't here
as much as it is in Anglesey;
a little red bead
seen through the big smoke.
Yes, smoke so thick some days
that people put their clothes out
to dry on it,
like you do a blackthorn hedge...
But they will steal things off you
at any minute:
I put my umbrella out to dry in this entry, one day,
I never saw it since...
The chapel is near, lucky.
There are good preachers.
The one last Sunday
gave us that have come here to work
a lot of advice.
O, I was thinking of you, mam,
hearing him tell us,
the dear thing,
as if he knew us all.
There is a strange Sunday School here
read in Welsh,
then questions and answers in English.
There was four girls in my class
all Jonsus...
O, if I could only set off home now
this minute.
I am short and untidy
my warmest feelings to you.
                    your dearest daughter, Jen Ifans

                    GWYN PARRY

Letter written by Jen Ifans, who went to work in Liverpool in 1882. Gwyn Parry found the letter recorded in
Mynydd Parys by O. Griffiths (a book written at the turn of the century) and translated the letter from Welsh.

111

By The Mersey (1883)

I watched the sunlight on the river Mersey - all
  glorious with sailing clouds and shadows - and sailing
craft and steamers on the tide - a stirring sight!
  And heard the clang and clamor of Liverpool behind me;
And saw in front the crowded ferry-boats crossing, and
  gulls in clusters swooping down for garbage;
(Two steps on the green water with webbed feet - and up
  again, their full beaks raised in air!)

And the great Atlantic liner lay at the landing-stage,
  towering up, a mighty wall of iron, full thirty feet, over the
little people who rushed to and fro below, completing the
  last shipments and farewells.
For even now the gong sounded in the ship's interior;
  and all was ready - every rope in place;
The shrouds and stays were taut on mast and spar;
Two slender wires, Marconi's, at the stern, ran sloping
  down from mizen-truck to wheel-house,
Ready to catch (far out at sea) a faint thrill from the
  home-land.
The little tug's towing-cable strained too at the monster,
  but still four mighty hawsers held her fast;
And still she delayed to move, and still the folk, on ship
  and shore, with jokes and quips beguiled the hour of parting.

Then sudden rang a bugle from the deck. Down came
  blue peter; and the foghorn sounded.
The hawsers fell, and she was free. A moment more,
  magnificent, she glided down the river.

And instantly from all the decks (from some of the port -
  holes too) there burst a flutter of waving hands and scarves -
  a fringe of white, answered by such another fringe on shore;
And instantly I saw - what I had missed before -
(Stronger, it seemed, than even cable and hawser, more
  numerous and tense than shrouds and stays, finer and subtler
  than Marconi wires,)
A thousand invisible threads which bound the ship, and
  would not be cast off or loosed or snapt,
But tugged and strained at living human hearts - and
  strained and tugged and tore -
Till hearts were sore and broken:
Threads of some unseen world - that stretched and
  stretched, and floated like fair gossamers in the evening light -
So fine and strong, so stronger even than steel;
And followed lengthening as the great ship faded - lost
  in the glory of the sunset -
Far out to the Atlantic.

EDWARD CARPENTER

Matthew Arnold and Liverpool - some associations

From his opening address for the University College, 30 September 1882: if, by means of this College, intellectual culture becomes a power among you, without doubt it will gradually affect and transform the amusements, pleasures, society, even the aspect and architecture of Liverpool.

His voyage to America, 1886: a letter to his daughter.

Cunard Royal Mail Steamship Umbria, May 22, 1886, 9.45 p.m.

My Dearest Fan - One line to tell you I have made a good start in this splendid ship. The sea is quite calm and we are not crowded. 180 passengers, and they reckon they have room for 400. We left the Mersey at one today. Dear old Dick saw me on board, but had to leave almost immediately, as the *Umbria* was going to start. I shall settle down into some regular reading presently, but at present I have done little except walk the decks....   (from *The Letters of Matthew Arnold*)

* * *

His death at the Dingle, Sunday April 15, 1888.

Arnold and his wife, Frances Lucy ('Flu') were staying with his sister, Susanna, and her husband, the Rev. John Cropper, at their home, Dingle Bank. On Sunday morning, after hearing Dr Watson preach at the Sefton Park Presbyterian Church, when Arnold declared that he had "rarely been so affected by a preacher", they returned to Dingle Bank. Later, Matthew and Frances set off to take the horse-tram from the Dingle to the Pier Head to meet their daughter and her husband, Frederick W. Whitridge of New York, due at Liverpool from America in the liner, *Aurania*. Arnold collapsed just opposite the Ancient Chapel of Toxteth, at the bottom of Park Road. He was carried into a doctor's house.   DEREK WHALE

The Majestic *at the Landing Stage 1889.*

Two little girls and Matthew Arnold

Gone Slack's fishing-boat off green Dingle Head
          and the flagpole
from which a gardener broke the Union Jack
for the state visit of Queen Victoria
          to Liverpool.

Gone the gardener, Victoria,
          even the century—
the good years and bad alike
          gone flesh and fell.

Gone the gardener's cottage in the grounds
          of Dingle Bank—
where, to the delight of his two little daughters,
the sea-spray dashed the window-panes.

Gone the little daughters.
          Gone their pinafores
that were so beautifully sewed
          by Mr Arnold's sewing-maid.
Gone too the poet who in the lost long-ago
gave the little girls pennies, and blessed them.

RICHARD POOLE

Liverpool, 1890

Gray sea dim, smoke-blowing, hammer-racket, sirens
Calling from ships, ear-breaking riveting, the calthrops
Of great gray drays, fire-smiting on the cobbles, dragging
The bales of cotton.

The warehouse roofs, wet-gleaming, the ships bedraggled
Awry-swung yards, backt on the main, the jib booms
Run in, the winches clanking, the slings of cargo
Running up, jolt.

There lie the ships, paint-rusted, each as a person
In rake or sheer or rig, coulters or counters,
Sea-shearing bows, those swords of beauty that thrust
The heart with rapture.

All fair ships, man-killers some, sea-eagles, sluggards.
Tall, too, many: lofty, a dread to look at, dizzy thus:
Among them always one more sky-aspiring, queen,
Remembered always.

JOHN MASEFIELD

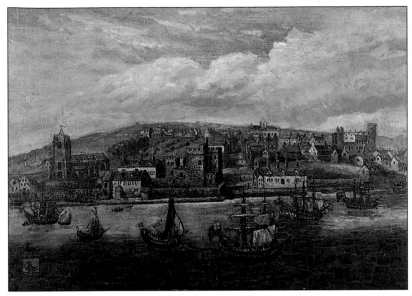

Plate 1: *(left)*
Liverpool in 1682 (unsigned)
One of the earliest known
representations of Liverpool. The Arms
of the borough are shown, with the
initials of the Mayor, Richard Windell.

Plate 2: *(below)*
*Liverpool from
the Bowling Green c. 1768
(Michael Angelo Rooker)*
The Bowling Green was in the Upper
Duke Street area.

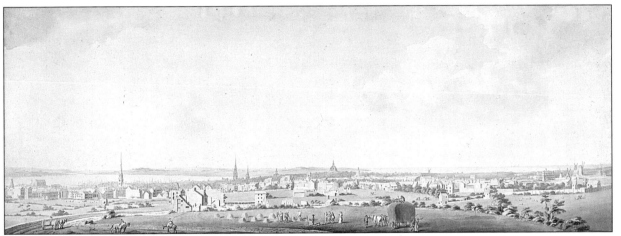

'The Liverpoolians, Free and Open as the Ocean on which They Get their Riches' - Catherine Hutton, 1788

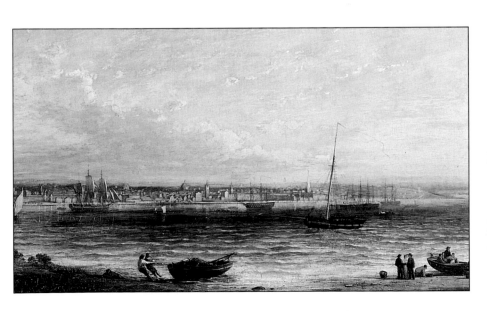

Plate 3: *(bottom)*
*View of Liverpool c. 1811
(Henry Freeman James)*
The Liverpool waterfront is
depicted, with a revenue cutter
in the right foreground
and a man o'war in
the middle distance.

Plate 4: *Liverpool from Seacombe, c. 1815 (John Jenkinson)*
A summer scene, with shrimpers. Landmarks on the Liverpool skyline include The Exchange, the Old Fort, the spires of St. George's and St. Nicholas'.

Plate 5: *Bidston Old Lighthouse and Flagpoles, 1825 (Robert Salmon)*
The fine view from Bidston Hill of the Wirral Coast and approach to the Mersey is captured here. The Lighthouse was erected in 1771 by Liverpool Corporation. Cylinders hoisted on 3 poles on the roof conveyed details of vessels approaching. The flagpoles belonged to Liverpool merchants whose flags were raised to indicate that their ships were nearing the port. This system was replaced by semaphore after 1826.

Plate 6: *(left)*
*Sir John Moore, c. 1834
(Samuel Walters,
attributed).*

The paddle steamer ferry is
heading for New Brighton,
which a smaller ferry has
just left. Perch Rock
Lighthouse and Battery are
on the right. The New
Brighton ferry service was
founded by James
Atherton, the regular
service opening up Wirral
for residential
development.

Plate 7:
American Ships in the Mersey off Liverpool, c. 1840 (Robert Salmon)

Plate 8: *(left)*
Sweethearts and Wives, 1860
(John J. Lee)
The sailors are setting off for duty on HMS Majestic, engaged in port defences. The view from Liverpool looks across to Birkenhead, showing Bidston Windmill and St. Mary's Church.

Plate 9: *(below)*
Liverpool from Tranmere, 1863
(William Collingwood)
Seen from the cornfields in the foreground, Liverpool is an impressively expanded port.

Plate 10:
St. George's Hall, 1854 (J. Penn, Lithograph Raphael Isaacs)
Worthy of Ancient Athens', Queen Victoria said of this neo-Classical building, designed by Harvey Lonsdale Elmes,
comprising concert hall and assize court. Inaugurated 18 September 1854.

Plate 11:
The Port of Liverpool, c. 1873 (Samuel Walters)

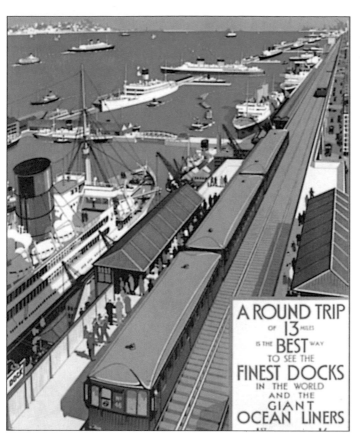

Plate 12: *(left)*
Liverpool Overhead Railway
(from the original poster)
with the docks and giant Ocean Liners.

Plate 13: *(below)*
The Enemy Raid, May 3rd 1941
(George Grainger Smith)
*Liverpool burning during the May Blitz,
seen from Wallasey, where the artist lived.*

Plate 14: *The Soviet training ship 'Kruzenshtern' arriving in the Mersey (John Calderbunk)*
Tall Ships Cutty Sark Races, August 1984

Plate 15: *The Two Cathedrals (John Calderbank)*

Plate 16:
The anchor of HMS 'Conway' in front of the
Merseyside Maritime Museum (Gladys Mary Coles)
The Liver Building, The Port of Liverpool Building and
Mersey Tunnel Ventilator Shaft in the background.

Plate 17:
Canning Dock with the Pier Head Buildings, 1992
(Gladys Mary Coles)

Plate 18: *Floodlit splendour of the Tall Ships in the Vittoria Dock, Birkenhead (Stephen Shakeshaft)*
The Grand Regatta Columbus, August 1992.

The Levers and the beginnings of Port Sunlight, 1888

...The guests to be present had assembled on the Liverpool landing stage at one o' clock and were conveyed to New Ferry in the steamer *Firefly*. From the landing stage at New Ferry they were taken to the steam barge *Warrington*, which was made to have a smart appearance by the covering of crimson cloth. The barge steamed towards Bromborough Pool, and entered an estuary of the Mersey seldom explored by any except those connected with a nearby candle-works. The barge then proceeded under a bridge that spans the pool, and which forms part of the Birkenhead and Chester turnpike road. Steaming a short distance higher up the creek they came to Port Sunlight, named after Mr Lever's already well-known household soap....

Mr W. Owen, architect, who had negotiated the purchase of the land, presented Mrs Lever with a silver spade and asked her to peform the ceremony of cutting the first sod ... The silver spade digging gently into the earth subtly implied the building of a community as well as an industrial enterprise.

The promise thus implicit in this gesture was amply confirmed this evening ...a banquet was held in the Bear's Paw Restaurant in Liverpool....Mr Lever said, 'It is my hope and my brother James' hope, some day to build houses in which our workpeople will be able to live and be comfortable - semi-detached houses with gardens back and front, in which they will be able to know more about the science of life than they can in a back slum, and in which they will learn that there is more enjoyment in life than in the mere going to and returning from work and looking forward to Saturday night to draw their wages.'...He had made an exhaustive search along both banks of the River Mersey before deciding on the purchase of the land to be called Port Sunlight....he was confident that he could soon transform the barren landscape.

The Liverpool Echo, Saturday 3 March, 1888.

"T'will make your brow a snowy white,
As free from grief and care,
As when with youth your eyes were bright,
And cheeks beyond compare ...
This article, if you but try,
Will realise each hope,
Go send your maid at once, and buy
A box of Sunlight Soap".

The City in Moonlight

Dear city in the moonlight dreaming,
    How changed and lovely is your face;
Where is the sordid busy scheming
    That filled all day the market-place ?

Was it but fancy that a rabble
    Of money-changers bought and sold,
Filling with sacrilegious babble
    This temple-court of solemn gold ?

Ah no, poor captive-slave of Crœsus,
    His bond-maid all the toiling day,
You, like some hunted child of Jesus,
    Steal out beneath the moon to pray.

RICHARD LE GALLIENNE

from *How I Began*

...O Time! surely it was only yesterday that I was a boy in Liverpool, with a book under my arm, dreaming that the only thing worth doing in the world was the writing of a book, the only success worth achieving, its being published... Liverpool, while not exactly element to the muses, was not quite without literary traditions and associations, of which I made the most. The shade of Roscoe haunted one of its libraries; the great Matthew Arnold came sometimes to stay with friends in the suburbs; at Mr Walmsley's book-shop in Lord Street, Mr William Watson's "Epigrams" had been published a few years before; and occasionally, like wings of prophecy, the locks and cloak of Mr Hall Caine passed over the city. Men who occasionally wrote for magazines and reviews did actually walk its streets, bright beings...

...I rented a great old loft in an ancient office building near the docks, turned it into a study with the co-operation of an ever-helpful mother - and seriously, as they used to say, "commenced author"....in that old loft I dreamed the dream - shared with others of my generation - of writing prose that should include the qualities of poetry...To that old loft came my first commission from Mr Lane: to write a book on George Meredith. I would hardly venture upon the task now, but one is afraid of nothing at twenty-one. So I wrote the book for Mr Lane, and, as a result of it went up to London...

RICHARD LE GALLIENE
from the unpublished essay 'How I Began'

The Coming in of Ancestors

Here are the strangers with shabby holdalls
and pale enigmatic smiles:
they disembark, looking around uncertainly
as cloud shadows move
on the moving Mersey;
and what they bring
is partly left at terminals;
and what they say
is scarcely comprehended.

Here are the docks, alive with arrivals,
cargoes of Irish, Germans, Poles.
Are they prepared
for what this land will give?
Will they, the foreigners,
ever feel they belong?
Perhaps not until their blood is passing
in the veins of English grandchildren.

My grandfather merges now
in the whisper of their lives:
his Scandinavian father
that whiskered man at chess
in the old, newly discovered photograph,
naturalised and with suitably altered name—
did he, as he slowly moved the chess pieces,
recall the forests, the fiords, the frozen winters?

My grandmother remembers her own:
Italian, in black toque hat,
wearing bright carnelian beads.

Here is their Liverpool—
the landfall in the west,
waterfront, heartland, home.

GLADYS MARY COLES
from *Liverpool Folio* (1984)

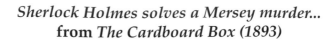

Sherlock Holmes solves a Mersey murder...
from *The Cardboard Box* (1893)

"..my dear Watson...I have in my hands here a little problem...Have you observed in the paper a short paragraph referring to the remarkable contents of a packet sent through the post to Miss Cushing, of Cross Street, Croydon?"...

I picked up the paper which he had thrown back to me, and read the paragraph indicated. It was headed 'A Gruesome Packet'...'A cardboard box...filled with coarse salt...two human ears, apparently quite freshly severed...no indication as to the sender...the matter is being actively investigated. Mr Lestrade...in charge of the case.'

"So much for the *Daily Chronicle*," said Holmes, as I finished reading. "Now for our friend Lestrade. I had a note from him this morning, in which he says: 'I think that this case is very much in your line.'

As a medical man, you are aware, Watson, that there is no part of the body which varies so much as the human ear. Each ear is as a rule quite distinctive... Imagine my surprise then, when looking at Miss Cushing, I perceived that her ear corresponded exactly with the female ear which I had just inspected....It was evident that the victim was a blood relation, and probably a very close one....Then we heard of this steward, married to her sister, and learned that he had at one time been so intimate with Miss Sarah that she had actually gone up to Liverpool to be near the Browners, but a quarrel had afterwards divided them... I therefore sent off a telegram to my friend Algar, of the Liverpool Force, and asked him to find out if Mrs Browner were at home, and if Browner had departed in the *May Day*...."

Browner's confession on board the May Day *in the Albert Dock*

"Have I anything to say? Yes, I have a deal to say...I tell you I've not shut an eye in sleep since I did it...Sometimes it's his face, but most generally it's hers. I'm never without one or the other before me....But it was Sarah's fault...she loved me, until all her love turned to poisonous hate when she knew that I thought more of my wife's foot-mark in the mud than I did of her whole body and soul....in all Liverpool there was no better woman than my Mary....Sarah hated me... I was a fool to let her go on biding with us...I can see now how she was plotting and scheming and poisoning my wife's mind against me...

We had gone on the *May Day* for a round voyage of seven days, but a hogshead got loose and started one of our plates, so that we had to put back into port for twelve hours. I left the ship and came home, thinking what a surprise it would be for my wife, and hoping that maybe she would be glad to see me so soon...as I turned into my own street...a cab passed me, and there she was, sitting by the side of Fairburn, the two chatting and laughing, with never a thought for me as I stood watching them from the footpath....

Well, I took to my heels, and I ran after the cab. I had a heavy oak stick in my hand, and I tell you I saw red from the first...They pulled up soon at the railway station...They took tickets for New Brighton. So did I, but I got in three carriages behind them. When we reached it they walk along the Parade, and I was never more than a hundred yards from them. At last I saw them hire a boat and start for a row, for it was a very hot day, and they thought no doubt that it would be cooler on the water.

It was just as if they had been given into my hands. There was a bit of a haze, and you could not see more than a few hundred yards. I hired a boat for myself, and I pulled after them. I could see the blurr of their craft, but they were going nearly as fast as I, and they must have been a long mile from the shore before I caught them up. The haze was like a curtain all round us, and there were we three in the middle of it. My God, shall I ever forget their faces when they saw who was in the boat that was closing in upon them? She screamed out. He swore like a madman and jabbed at me with an oar, for he must have seen death in my eyes. I got past it and got one in with my stick, that crushed his head like an egg. I would have spared her, perhaps, for all my madness, but she threw her arms round him, crying out to him...I struck again, and she lay stretched beside him...If Sarah had been there, by the Lord, she should have joined them. I pulled out my knife, and - well, there! I've said enough. It gave me a kind of savage joy when I thought how Sarah would feel when she had such signs as these of what her meddling had brought about. Then I tied the bodies into the boat, stove a plank, and stood by until they had sunk. I knew very well that the owner would think that they had lost their bearings in the haze, and had drifted off out to sea...."

ARTHUR CONAN DOYLE
'The Cardboard Box' in
*The Annotated
Sherlock Holmes,*
ed. William S. Baring-
Gould, Vol.II (1965)

*Illustration by Sidney Paget
for the Strand Magazine, January, 1893.*

New Brighton c. 1893

John Masefield, a cadet on H.M.S. Conway in the 1890s, finds the Mersey's 'gift of beauty'

... the flower of all England's shipping belonged in Liverpool: the river and docks were always busy with the best ships of the time. The Cunard moorings were just downstream from us; the White Star and Inman moorings beyond them; and the P.S.N. and Alfred Holt moorings still further on, but in sight. The Elder Dempster ships were near us in the Sloyne. The steamers of many famous lines were weekly visitors to the river, we knew them all, their funnels, their houseflags and their tenders: even the foreign steamers and what they brought were known to us.

But in those days the bulk of the world's freight was carried in sailing ships, which had then reached their last, strange, beautiful perfection. At all times we could see in the river or in the docks the queens of that last construction, the superb four-masted ships and barques, of from two to three thousand tons, which went with general cargoes to San Francisco and came back with grain. They are now gone, but then they were many; and many of the many were strange with new device of build or rig, of intense interest to us, whose talk and thought was of ships.

Often, perhaps every week, sometimes for weeks together, every day one such queen would come with her tugs into the Sloyne and anchor near us all trim from

H.M.S. Conway

her last month's work, her sails in harbour-stows, her blocks gleaming, her mainyards still aback, just as they had braced them on taking the towline, and her house-flag at her main truck. Then at the next flood her crowd would man the capstan, her anchor would come in to "Rolling Home" or "Good-bye, fare you well," and she would pass to dock.

At flood tide in any case the river would waken into bustle and beauty of ships coming in and going out, till it would seem like a street with ships for people. The dock-gates would open to the sound of cheers to let pass some ship with her blue peter flying; barges would tack by under their red sails; schooners, brigantines, yawls and ketches went out or returned, under all sail. Greek and Italian polaccas of all sizes came in under sail. Norwegian barques sometimes sailed in, tack and tack, to anchor near us. No such display of living ships could be seen in any other port in the world at that time.

The display did not cease with the living ships, far from it. On both sides of the river there were the slips and gantries of the building firms, and all the racket and clatter of new construction, always going on in sight and sound of us. We watched ships being built and launched and floated. We saw them going forth in splendour and coming back shattered by the sea, listed, shored up, dismasted, red with sea-rust, white with sea-salt, holed, dinted, ruined, all pumps still spouting, just limping into dock with three tugs, or just crawling to the mud and lying down.

And with these, we saw the ships of the river services; not only the tugs, famous all over the world, such as the *Helen Dagmar,* the *Blazer,* the *Kings* and the *Cocks,* but the ferries and the bar-dredgers, the salvage and diving craft; all the fleet of a great port.

For beauty, interest and variety no scene on earth could compare with the river in which we lived. We were in the seaworld and of it, initiated into the mystery and free of the guild, and there at its busiest heart. Of all the many joys that youth and the ship offered, that gift of beauty was the greatest.

JOHN MASEFIELD
The Conway (1933)

The Forest of Masts

Blow The Man Down

As I was walking down Paradise Street
Whey, hey, blow the man down
A flash-looking Packet I chanced for to meet
O-oh, give me some time to blow the man down

Chorus:
Blow the man down, bullies, blow the man down
Whey, hey, blow the man down
Blow him right back into Liverpool Town
O-oh, give me some time to blow the man down

Liverpool Sea Shanty (17th Century)

PART THREE

I am the English sea-queen; I am she
Who made the English wealthy by the sea.

The street of this my city is the tide
Where the world's ships, that bring my glory, ride.

Far as the tide along my highway swings,
The iron of my shipwrights clangs and rings.

Far inland as the gulls go are my stores,
Where the world's wealth is lockt with iron doors.

And these my merchants gather day by day
The wealth I bring, the wealth I send away.

JOHN MASEFIELD
from *A Masque of Liverpool*

'...there were fires still burning, there was a heavy pall of smoke lying
over the northern part of the city, there were gaps, whole streets
missing, rows of houses mis-shapen and torn.'

NICHOLAS MONSARRAT
from *The Cruel Sea (1951)*

Morpeth Dock, Birkenhead

The squalls that blew the cattle boat from Dublin
Dashed themselves out with impotent fury on the Mersey Bar
And all is calm.

In Morpeth Dock, the flaring gas-light draws
Steam from a thousand sunken flanks.
Sick yellow eyes roll mournfully and vermin hop and creep
In filthy straw about their hooves.

Along the quay, a power-house belches flame,
Goods-wagons clank and groan
And engines shriek into the station roof,
Looming like Lucifer over everlasting fire.

The ramps are lowered now and drovers swarm the decks,
Belabouring the cattle viciously with knotted sticks.
They swing their massive heads in sad bewilderment,
Thinking their torments had been at an end — and one by one
They stumble down the ramps,
Now crashing to their bony knees, now struggling upright,
Lowing in misery, shying from the whips.

Dry land at last — but then another ramp —
A tortuous tunnel, swooping black above the docks,
Smelling of fear and trampled excrement of bygone herds,
Who made their long journey from the hills of Ireland
To death.

HEATHER WILSON

(Above right) Liverpool Landing Stage, with ferries, 1903

(Below right) Pier Head and St. Nicholas' Church at the turn of the century.
Liverpool Overhead Railway (from Seaforth to Dingle), opened 4th February 1893,
the world's first electric elevated railway and the first to have electric automatic signals.

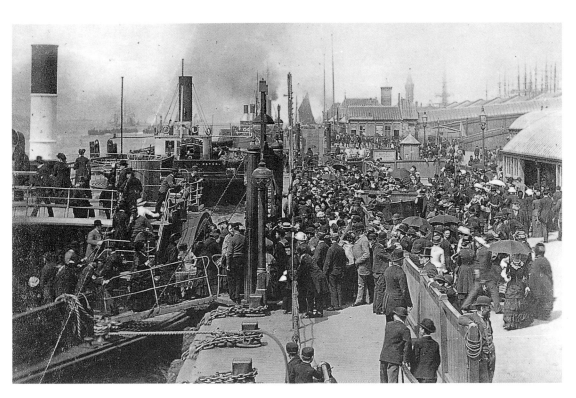

Wilfred Owen — His Childhood in Birkenhead

The family of Wilfred Owen moved from Oswestry to
Birkenhead in 1900, when Wilfred was seven years old.
He attended the Birkenhead Institute, which he liked.

Wilfred was the only close friend that I made while at the Birkenhead Institute, so that I have many memories of him, chiefly of a trivial and unimportant kind which happened to impress themselves on the mind of a schoolboy. I was at the Institute from 1903 till 1907, that is, from the age of eleven to fifteen, and during my later years there Wilfred and I were rivals — always friendly — for the position of first in the form. In the schoolboy language at the time we were both " swots ", and were subjected to a certain amount of " ragging" by many of the boys, who took as their heroes the ones who excelled at games and tended to look down on the bookish prize-winners. Wilfred was small and neat in personal appearance, with a round, serious, little face. As a contrast I was tall and lanky, so that the masters jokingly called us " the long and the short of it ".

Games were not part of the school curriculum in those days and neither of us played football or cricket, but we used to join in with others in the old game of "tag" or "tic", as we called it, in the school asphalt playground during morning break or at other free times. On Saturday mornings our form had a regular period at the Argyle Street Swimming Baths where we both learned to swim, and also, out of school time, we often went to Livingstone Street Baths where Wilfred became quite an efficient swimmer. During the various outings we had together I discovered, too, that he was very good at horse-riding. This was when we had a gallop on New Brighton sands. I was hanging on like grim death to any part of the horse available while he was quite at his ease and enjoying the invigorating activity.

My classroom memories centre especially on the English lessons which he and I much enjoyed. Mr Bennett's lessons are the ones which come vividly to mind and pieces like Shakespeare's "Seven Ages of Man", and Scott's "Marmion", and especially Dickens's ''Christmas Carol" which we read and studied with him. Wilfred and I evolved a word game which consisted in reading downwards the words on the extreme right hand end of the lines of print on a page and making some ridiculous sense or nonsense out of them. This "pastime" caused us much unauthorised merriment and occasionally a reprimand or punishment from the master. Another similar game was the invention of names for people we met on our way home from school. One such was a young man with large dark eyes whom we nicknamed "Nigoc" from the Latin "niger oculus". On one occasion we were enjoying our joke as he was passing and, assuming we were laughing at him, he stopped and boxed Wilfred's ears.

Words interested Wilfred very much and later, when he paid me a visit from Shrewsbury, he and I got into a discussion on figures of speech such as "hyperbole, tautology, zeugma" etc. This interest developed at quite an early age, as is shown by a postcard sent to me from Cornwall when he was aged thirteen in which he writes as a postscript "There are plenty of 'we's' in this".

around women's suffrage. In 1916 Sylvia Pankhurst, in Liverpool to speak at a conference on women and sweated labour, stayed in her house.

In November 1916 Dr. Ker moved to London, where she spent the rest of a long and active life. She died in 1943, aged 90.

MARIJ VAN HELMOND
Votes For Women: The Events On Merseyside 1870-1928 (1992)

Adrian Boult's early years on Merseyside

Adrian's father was in oil, in those early days. A curious thing called Valvoline Oil in Liverpool and when I first knew him they were living at Blundell Sands. It was rather fascinating, because you could see all the boats going along the Mersey as they came in - and the sands were wonderful .... The sands were so hard you could bicycle on them quite happily ... Then they moved to a beautiful house - the Abbey Manor in West Kirby ... owing to the lie of the land West Kirby was entirely blotted out and you looked right across to the Welsh Hills and the Dee.

LAWRENCE TANNER

Adrian Boult as a young man

Arthur Nikisch (1855-1922) was Boult's god. Nikisch exercised a precise control of ensemble, dynamics, rubato, and phrasing which even today leaps out of the grooves of his primitive gramophone recordings. He did this by revolutionising the conductor's stick technique, making its pivot the fingers and wrist rather than the elbow .... Boult was determined to go to Leipzig and study ... By the time he arrived there in 1912, Nikisch had retired from teaching. But he still conducted the Gewandhaus Orchestra: young Boult obtained a card to attend Nikisch's rehearsals - and thereby to study the technique at first hand.

He would have gone on to Vienna, but an overstrained heart forced him home. Within a few months he was conducting his first professional concert: the date was 27th February 1914, the place the Public Hall at West Kirby, the orchestra part of the Liverpool Philharmonic. The programme ranged from a Bach Brandenburg Concerto to one of the earliest performances of George Butterworth's 'The Banks of Green Willow'. When the war came in August, Boult was declared unfit for service: he drilled recruits from the Lancashire mines, and organised a series of concerts to employ local musicians whom the war had deprived of their livelihood.

JERROLD NORTHROP MOORE
in *Sir Adrian Boult, Companion of Honour -*
A Tribute edited by NIGEL SIMEONE *and* SIMON MUNDY (1980)

Small Beginnings

from *Arthur Askey's Autobiography*

I was born in a basket of dirty tights
In a broken-down theatre in Crewe,
My Dad was a red-nosed comedian,
My Mother was Danny La Rue.

It doesn't get a laugh on the stage either! And, of course, it's not true - I was actually born in The Holy Land! This was the name given to a small area in the dockland of Liverpool, which consisted of streets named David, Jacob, Isaac, and Moses. In the front bedroom of 29 Moses Street, on 6 June 1900, was born to Samuel and Betsy (née Bowden) Askey the gift of a son. There is no plaque on the wall of the house to commemorate this great event - yet !

When I was six months old, either on account of complaints from the neighbours, or because the family wished to better themselves, we moved to a rather nicer district. Naturally, I did not give them any help with the handcart, but we moved into 90 Rosslyn Street: three-up, two-down, bathroom, and two loos (one outside).

I cannot remember too much about my very early years. After all, it was a long time ago. But I do remember my paternal grandfather and grandmother. Grandad was a typical Liverpool docker: I think I saw him only once when he was sober, and obviously not himself. My grandma used to call occasionally for a 'touch', but got short shrift from my mother. My mother had two brothers: Arthur (whom I am named after - Arthur Bowden Askey), and Edward, known as Ned. Ned was quite a character and lived with us for a short time. He had a habit of reading aloud from the newspaper, but as he was not much of a scholar he would just pause when he came to a long word and say 'Manchester'. For example, 'The coroner brought in a verdict of . . . "Manchester",' sort of thing.

Uncle Arthur married Auntie Barbara, who came from Oswaldthwistle, and it was she who first taught me little songs and nursery rhymes, which probably laid the foundations of the genius to come! In addition to the nursery rhymes, I also learned what I term my father's 'Bathroom Ballads'. Every morning while washing and shaving he would sing songs from a large repertoire ranging from 'When I survey the Wondrous Cross' to 'Boiled Beef and Carrots'.

Rosslyn Street was in the Parish of St Michael's-in-the-Hamlet, and it was the feeling and the changing moods of this area that became engraved on my imagination. The River Mersey flowed past at the end of the street, and in the distance were the Welsh mountains, which could be clearly seen when it was going to rain. Another certain sign of rain was the croaky whistle of the trains on the Great Central Railway which ran between Liverpool and Manchester. The

Dr Alice Ker - from Suffragist to Suffragette

Dr Alice Ker c. 1912

Alice Jane Shannon Ker was born in 1853, the eldest of nine children of William Stewart Ker, Free Church Minister in Deskford, a tiny parish in Banffshire, Scotland. By the time she emerged as a member of the Birkenhead Women's Suffrage Society (BWSS) she was a practising G.P., the thirteenth woman to have had her name placed on the British Medical Register....In 1888 she married her cousin, Edward Ker, a shipping merchant in Liverpool and settled with him in Birkenhead....She became a Honorary Medical Officer to the Wirral Hospital for Sick Children, and to Birkenhead Lying-In Hospital. Alice kept a fairly accurate record of her social engagements, the more splendid of which included receptions at the Town Hall and garden parties given by families such as the Brocklebanks and Bibbys.

Soon she widened her range of 'good works'...(and) in 1891 she published a book called *Motherhood: A Book For Every Woman,* in which she dealt with female adolescence, marriage, pregnancy and childcare in a manner considerably more open, forthright and progressive than similar texts of the period....

Judging by the notes in her diary, by 1908 things began to change for Alice. In May 1907 her husband had died unexpectedly. She had shared a lot of activities with him - sport, socializing, travel - and his death must have left her with a gap to fill. It may also have left her freer to make the kind of contacts she was really interested in. In addition to existing activities Alice visited the Clarion Club in Liverpool, attending lectures by George Bernard Shaw....She was not present at the first public meeting of Christabel Pankhurst in Liverpool in 1909 but in February of that year she noted that the Temperance Society had a suffrage meeting and that Patricia Woodlock, 'from Liverpool', was the speaker....on 21 June she noted: 'Did up all necessary work in morning, and in afternoon Margaret and I went over to Liverpool to meet Miss Patricia Woodlock. Margaret helped to draw her carriage and I to carry the banner. Speaking from a lorry in front of St. George's Hall.' And the next day: 'Margaret and I went to Miss Woodlock's reception at the Yamen Cafe (Bold St.). Late of getting home'. In the course of a year Alice and her daughter Margaret, now seventeen, had changed from suffragists into suffragettes....

Cartoon in 'Votes For Women' portraying Patricia Woodlock's Holloway imprisonment

For the WSPU she undertook a lot of hard, often menial work like selling the newspaper *Votes for Women* twice a week on train stations and on her own 'pitch', chalking pavements to announce meetings and events, minding the shop, accommodating visiting speakers in her home or speaking at the weekly open air meetings in Liverpool. She also enjoyed taking part in the more colourful WSPU events and travelled to London for the monster procession in June 1911. Her diary entry: 'Up early, breakfast very punctually. A little before 9 went by (tram)car to Ferry and by 10 a.m. train from Lime Street to London. Meal at Eustace Miles Restaurant, then took place for procession. Wonderful meeting in Albert Hall. Train back to L'pool at 12.45, rather cold, and did not sleep much'.

Militancy: window-smashing and the consequences for Dr. Ker

The point at which Alice Ker became militant was when the Government introduced a Reform Bill, which put the Conciliation Bill on which the movement had pinned so much hope on a backburner....On 27 February (1912) she had caught the 9.20 train from Lime Street to London, seen off by her daughter Margaret....she was arrested smashing windows at Harrod's Stores, Knightsbridge..At the Magistrates Court she was offered bail which she refused and was removed to Holloway Prison to await trial....

Dr. Ker was sentenced to three months imprisonment and was allowed to write and receive only one letter per fortnight. However she managed to have a few letters smuggled out. In one of these she mentioned a letter she had from the Secretary of the Birkenhead Rescue Home asking her to resign her position as Hon. Physician of the Home 'owing to a recent episode'. She felt very upset about this as she worked for the Rescue Home for several years. She decided not to resign - 'if they want to get rid of me, they must have the scandal of dismissing me...I should think it is quite possible that I may find I have to leave Birkenhead, even if it were only to go over to Liverpool. I was prepared for this possibility before I left home, knowing that it might be the price I would have to pay'.

It has often been said that it was much easier for middle class women actively to take part in the suffrage campaign, and risk arrest and imprisonment. This may be so, but for some, such as Dr. Ker, a widow and parent, it was at considerable personal and financial cost....the struggle for the vote meant much more to her than gaining another right. For her it meant changing the world, for women as well as for men, and was not to be won without personal sacrifice....After her release from prison on 10 May 1912 she continued to work for the organisation. In August 1914 she moved to Liverpool where she took a house in the new Wavertree Garden Suburb development, became involved with the war work (Welfare of Sailors' and Soldiers' Wives) but remained active

Liverpool WSPU election poster (David Jenkins).

Looking out to sea where a great liner slowly took the sun like a queen, I vowed that I would be a novelist, good or bad, for the remainder of my earthly days.

HUGH WALPOLE
The Crystal Box (1924)

Boys at the Steble Fountain, Liverpool, July 1901

Grange Road, Birkenhead.

131

Augustus John, the Gypsies and Liverpool

Now married and installed as art-master at a school of Art in Liverpool which was affiliated to the University College, I became acquainted with John Sampson, its Librarian and our foremost Gypsy scholar. We immediately struck up a close friendship, which with occasional disturbances lasted till his death. He introduced me to his Gypsy friends, and we made a practice of visiting the tents together. Under his tutelage and by personal contact with the Gypsies, I soon picked up the English dialect of Romani, and during our expeditions to North Wales began to cultivate the inflected or 'deep' speech of the descendants of Abraham Wood which Sampson has recorded in his magnum opus, *The Dialect of the Gypsies of Wales*...

Our visits to Cabbage Hall and other camping grounds were rich in incident. 'Cabbage Hall' for us denoted a large patch of waste ground, where the Boswells were in the habit of encamping during the winter months. Under Sampson's aegis I was made welcome in the tents and got to know their occupants, who bore such exotic names as Noah, Kenza, Eros, Bohemia, Sinfai, Athaliah, Counseletta, Alabaina, Tihanna, Simpronius, Saiforella ... By showing a sympathetic interest in their speech and customs, and without neglecting the lubricative medium of liquor, the collusion of the men was assured: they admitted us into their confidence and disclosed their tribal secrets unreservedly. ...

Liverpool, commonly considered a dull, ugly and commercial city, for me abounded in interest and surprise. With what wonderment I explored the sombre district of the Mersey side! This was largely populated by Scandinavian migrants on their way to the New World.

John Sampson (Augustus John)

The Goree Piazza, with such a name, for ever reeking of the slave-trade, might still harbour a few superannuated buccaneers musing over their rum: in the Chinese quarter, while visiting certain tenebrous dens, I attempted, but failed, to attain the blissful *Kif* in the company of dishevelled and muttering devotees of the Laughing God: off Scotland Road I penetrated, not without trepidation, into the lodging houses of the Tinkers, where a rough nomadic crew gathered round the communal fire in a spirit of precarious good-fellowship.

With a few notable exceptions, I had little to do with the University people. Oliver Elton and Kuno Meyer, the Celtic scholar, I knew well; I painted their portraits, and also Chaloner Dowdall's. The latter picture, on being exhibited, nearly led to a riot; why, I don't know.

AUGUSTUS JOHN
Chiaroscuro (1952)

'The Book of Pictures'

They turned on, chatting casually, till George suddenly exclaimed, 'There ! '
It was Maurice Greiffenhagen's 'Idyll'.

'What of it?' she asked, gradually flushing. She remembered her own enthusiasm over the picture.

'Wouldn't it be fine? ' he exclaimed, looking at her with glowing eyes, his teeth showing white in a smile that was not amusement.

'What?' she asked, dropping her head in confusion.

'That - a girl like that - half afraid - and passion!' He lit up curiously.

'She may well be half afraid, when the barbarian comes out in his glory, skins and all.'

' But don't you like it?' he asked.

She shrugged her shoulders, saying, 'Make love to the next girl you meet, and by the time the poppies redden the field, she'll hang in your arms. She'll have need to be more than half afraid, won't she?'

She played with the leaves of the book, and did not look at him. ...

'Didn't you know the picture before?' she said, in a low toneless voice.

He shut his eyes and shrank with shame.

' No, I've never seen it before,' he said.

'I'm surprised,' she said. 'It is a very common one.'

An Idyll (Maurice Greiffenhagen)

'Is it?' he answered, and this make-belief conversation fell. She looked up, and found his eyes. They gazed at each other for a moment before they hid their faces again. It was a torture to each of them to look thus nakedly at the other ... She sought almost in panic, for something to say.

'I believe it's in Liverpool, the picture,' she contrived to say.

He dared not kill this conversation, he was too self-conscious. He forced himself to reply, 'I didn't know there was a gallery in Liverpool.'

'Oh, yes, a very good one,' she said.

Their eyes met in the briefest flash of a glance, then both turned their faces aside.

D . H . LAWRENCE
The White Peacock (1911)

133

Ode for the opening of the
Liverpool Repertory Theatre, First Night 1911

Here in this house, to-night, our city makes
Something which must not fail for our sakes,
For we begin what men have been too blind
To build elsewhere, a temple for the mind.
So many Englishmen give wealth to build
The great museums with which our towns are filled,
Our millionaires compete with so much rage
That all things get endowed except the stage.
Men will not spend, it seems, on that one Art
Which is life's inmost soul and passionate heart;
They count the theatre a place for fun
Where men can laugh at nights when work is done.
If it were only that t'would be worth while
To subsidise a thing which makes men smile;
But it is more: it is that splendid thing,
A place where man's soul shakes triumphant wing,
A place of Art made living, where men may see
What human life is and has seemed to be
To the world's greatest brains; it is the place
Where Shakespeare held the glass to Nature's face;
The place the wise Greeks built by public toll
To keep austere and pure the city's soul;
And now we make it here.
O, you who hark,
Fan to a flame through England this first spark,
Till in this land there's none of so poor purse
But he may see high deeds and hear high verse,
And feel his folly lashed, and think him great
In this world's tragedy of Life and Fate.

To-night our city leads. All you who care
For her fair fame in England keep it fair,
Make this foundation firm, work till it be
Part of her praise on men's lips over sea
That when they name her they will say of her,
"Famous for ships and this her theatre."

JOHN MASEFIELD

(Above) Red Sunday, 13 August 1911.
At St George's Hall Plateau, a strikers' demonstration in which more than 30,000 men and women gathered, led to a violent clash with soldiers and police. In three days of riots, two men were shot dead and hundreds hurt.

(Left) Memorial to the Engine Room Heroes (W. Goscome John), 1916.
Intended to commemorate the Liverpool men lost in the Titanic, 1912, but became dedicated to all the heroes of the Engine Room lost at sea... It is the only memorial of its kind in the world. The White Star liner Titanic was registered in Liverpool and many of the crew came from Merseyside. News of the loss of the Titanic was telegraphed to the White Star building - thousands of people waited outside to hear news of relatives and friends

> In a solitude of the sea
> Deep from human vanity,
> And the Pride of Life that planned her,
> stilly couches she.

THOMAS HARDY
(from 'The Convergence of the Twain')

Photograph by Gladys Mary Coles

135

from *Young Adolf*

Always Meyer took Adolf to the Pier Head. They stood, buffeted by wind, facing the mile-wide strip of river separating Liverpool from New Brighton. The ferry boats, encircled by screaming gulls, ploughed the muddy stretch of water towards the bulbous domes of the pleasure gardens and back again. Shouting to make himself heard, Meyer stabbed his finger at the skyline and named the docks, the Battery and the distant Welsh hills. He spoke of sailing ships forced to wait a dozen tides before floating into the Mersey, of the construction of the docks, of cholera, of how the monopolies of the great trading companies - the Hudson Bay, the Royal Africa, the East India - had eventually been broken. Finally, placing his arm enthusiastically about Adolf's shoulder he would swing him round and point at St Nicholas's church, the offices of the Docks and Harbour Board, and the vast bulk of the Royal Liver Building, its twin towers set with clocks like full moons and those giant birds, green wings spread, crouched under the sky. 'Consider,' he would bellow, 'the advantages of cast iron.'

His lectures, delivered in the teeth of the wind, entire sentences blown away, excited and silenced Adolf. Adolf didn't wish to appear stupid. He stood with his hands thrust deep into the pockets of his fluttering coat, an expression of eager concentration on his gaunt face. All he wanted, deep down, was for Meyer to compare him favourably with the buildings, the people, the past. At times like these Meyer considered him a good listener.

Shortly after midday, footsore and exhausted by the sound of his own voice, Meyer would suggest they go to the Kardomah Café or to a public house. Adolf invariably refused. 'Ah,' Meyer would exclaim. 'I had forgotten you were a lone wolf. ' Thanking him profusely, Adolf would shake him by the hand and return to the house in Stanhope Street. He didn't want Meyer to tire of him, and besides he hadn't a halfpenny to his name.

BERYL BAINBRIDGE
Young Adolf (1978)

Suffragette Demonstration on Lime Street, 5 September 1908. The Liverpool banner is behind the speaker.

That Long Ago Army

Imagine a Britain brought up on rigid ideas of social class, where a lady hardly showed an ankle, and most women who were not ladies were dressed in the shoddy best they could muster. What then, did everyone make of the upper-crust suffragettes, who waded into open air meetings, whose crystal accents cut through the rabble, all dressed to kill with flowing skirts and Ascot hats and then, who were unceremoniously carried, writhing and struggling away to the local nick? The suffragettes arrested in Liverpool usually languished in Walton Jail until they were released or bailed out by their well-to-do husbands. They were fighting for something many of us today take for granted: the right to vote.

There were two arms of the Suffragette movement; the first established was the National Union of Women's Suffragette Societies, under whose banner came the Liverpool Women's Suffrage Society. It was run almost solely by upper and middle class women with Liverpool's social campaigner Eleanor Rathbone at the helm. LWSS confined its activities largely to polite and mannered lobbying, petitioning and writing letters to newspapers. But although members badgered away energetically behind the scenes, they never once forgot they were first and foremost Ladies. However, although progressives in both political parties made appreciative noises, nothing happened. The ladies kept writing letters and complaining.

Then in 1903, the Women's Social and Political Union was formed. WSPU decided the polite approach had been given a fair run without many, if any, concessions being made. Votes for women went militant. Under their fierce and inspiring leader Emily Pankhurst, WSPU decided to take a leaf from well thumbed books of male campaigners down the ages. They would get physical. In 1906 they moved into Liverpool, initially without much success, but then under the direction of Ada Flatman, the movement took off. Ada was imported from out of town to organise WSPU on Merseyside and she was an extraordinarily shrewd lady.

Meanwhile, the supporters of the older organisation were appalled. They sent letters to the papers, disassociating themselves from what was going on. Eleanor Rathbone and her fellow members of the Liverpool Women's Suffrage Society continued their own peaceful campaign. WSPU's activities began with a very upfront approach. They took a shop on Berry Street, plastered the windows with posters and organised campaigns outside St George's Hall. They interrupted public meetings, the bigger the better. When Prime Minister Campbell Bannerman addressed 6,000 supporters in the Sun Hall, Kensington in 1906, ten suffragettes in succession stood up, heckled him and were thrown out, one by one.

One of the highest profile local stalwarts was Birkenhead widow Dr Alice Ker. She actively encouraged women to avoid Government census officials by hiding in her cellars. On the premise that if they didn't have the vote, they didn't exist, the suffragettes saw no reason why they should take part in the Government's ten yearly national head count. They simply were not in their homes to be counted, but in Dr Ker's cellars, having a party.

But this kind of anarchy was not to be permitted. The law began to come down strongly on the Suffragettes, and militant WSPU campaigners found themselves in Walton Jail. There, several of them attempted hunger strikes. They were restrained, gagged, rubber tubes were forced down their mouths or noses and pumped full of liquid 'sustenance'.

An interesting example of how the prison authorities treated different types of women was proved by the aristocratic Lady Constance Lytton. Lady Constance, an avid WSPU member had been arrested before but because of her social standing, was released almost immediately. On this occasion, on a Suffragette protest rally outside Walton Jail in support of their incarcerated comrades, Lady Constance dressed herself as a member of the working classes. Not only was she arrested but she was force fed and only released when her identity became known. The scandal shook society. Lady Constance became a heroine.

Many of the women were married, with supportive husbands and although, like the LWSS, most were middle or upper class, membership included wives of trade unionists notably Mrs Bessie Morris and Mrs Annie Meyer. But probably the most active local woman was the indefatigable Dr Ker who led a shop window raid on Harrods and received three months in London's Holloway Prison as a result. Trips to London were a large part of the Liverpool WSPU's activities.

The movement tailed off, both locally and nationally after 1912 - Europe was darkening for war. Strangely enough, or maybe not, the militant WSPUs threw their resources behind the Government's war effort. The National Union of Womens' Suffrage Societies and Eleanor Rathbone's Liverpool Women's Suffrage Society continued their campaign throughout, still lobbying, still pressing quietly behind the scenes. And still writing letters to newspapers. The *Liverpool Echo* and *Post* were sympathetic, the rival *Mercury,* now defunct, was not.

In 1918, the vote was given to all female householders and all women over 30. In contrast, the age of franchise for men was 21. Still, a victory of sorts had been achieved. All women finally got the vote in 1928. It is difficult to imagine, just 60 years later, a certain three-year-old toddler daughter of Mr and Mrs Roberts, Grantham grocers, would grow up to be prime minister.

DIANE MASSEY in *Daily Post,* November 1989

Merseyside Museum of Labour History Exhibition:
'Votes for Women - The Liverpool Story', Nov 1989 - June 1990

A Suffragette's letter

6 James Street,
Thursday, March 7th, 1912

My dear Aunt Meta
...Mother was arrested on Monday at 10.30 a.m. She and Miss Davies, the Liverpool organiser, and Mrs Healiss, broke some windows at Harrod's Stores, Knightsbridge, and they were all arrested together and taken first to Walton St. Police Station and then to Westminster Police Station where they were all tried together on Monday afternoon....

Margaret

Letter from Margaret Ker, daughter of Dr Alice Ker. Margaret was a student at Liverpool University. She set fire to a letter box in James Street in November 1912 and was imprisoned in Walton Jail for three months. The Vice-Chancellor Dr Alfred Dale was sympathetic towards the Kers and the Suffrage Movement.

Virginia Woolf sails from Liverpool on a Voyage Out to France, 1905

Wednesday 29 March

Our start was early, so we had to rush our last packings after breakfast - indeed we left before my last blouse came home, & only had about 5 minutes for train. Gerald met us at Euston - & thus we left at 10.45. Reached Liverpool about 2.30 & went in a Bus to the pier, where a great many people were walking up and down, saying good-bye, & preparing to go. A huge steamer, the *Oceanic,* 2nd largest afloat was black with passengers, just leaving for America. The *Anselm* came alongside in time, & we embarked. It is all white & clean & luxurious; we each have a cabin to ourself, in wh. I now write on my knees, & the sea is beginning to rise: We walked on the deck & saw all the lights along the Coast of Wales, steamers passing, & our own foam spread like white lace on the dark waters - a very lovely thing is a ship at sea.

VIRGINIA WOOLF

A Passionate Apprentice - The Early Journals of Virginia Woolf, ed. Mitchell A Leaska (1990)

The Lusitania, at the Landing Stage.
The Royal Liver Insurance Building, one of the world's first multi-storey buildings with a reinforced concrete structure, is being built to W. Aubrey Thomas' design, completed 1911. The Cunard liner Lusitania, sailed from Liverpool to New York on her maiden voyage, September 1907. She was torpedoed on May 7, 1915 and sank with the loss of 1,192 passengers and crew.

Extracts from the diary of Dirk and Else Van den Bergh, emigrants from Holland to Canada, via Liverpool in 1906.

Between 1830 and 1930 more than 9 million emigrants sailed from Liverpool. The Van den Bergh family stayed at a Dominion Line boarding house in Upper Frederick Street, awaiting their ship.

March 29th, 1906: After giving the boarding house a good and careful look of inspection the place looked really cleaner than we thought the moment we entered. At the back of the dining room was a long shed in which the Poles and Russians were served - they were all single men. For these people admittance to our dining room was absolutely denied. The evening meal consisted of white bread, corned beef and tea. When supper time was finished they gave us a big room with 4 beds, the sheets looked fesh and clean. We decided to stay together, although 4 beds for fourteen people was no luxury....

March 30th: ...After breakfast was over we went down town, we went into the centre of Liverpool, what a busy place and what traffic. If we could imagine Liverpool and imagine it without fog and smoke it really would be an impressive city. After mid-day dinner we took a wandering walk again. Now we go to the harbour, thousands of heavy loaded freight wagons roll with ear-deafening noise over cobbled streets. It swarms with many emigrants.

Friday, 6 April: Just after midnight someone from the Steamship Office came storming in and announces that we all must be ready to leave at 4 a.m. Great joy among the travellers... At 11 a.m. finally there appeared big carriages, the street is crowded with emigrants. Passengers are packed as herrings in a barrel into the carriages, baggage and all. After a ride of 15 minutes we arrive at the harbour, we step out and take our place on the pier.

Van Den Bergh Diary- transcript from tape in the Merseyside Maritime Museum 'Emigrants to a New World' Exhibition (National Museums & Galleries on Merseyside)

The Mersey helps Hugh Walpole, age 22, to decide against becoming a clergyman *(in 1907 he was working for the Mersey Seamen's Mission)*

I went out and down to the Mersey, and there, looking at the river, I had one of the most important hours of my life. That foaming flood tossing in grey froth and spume out to the sea was invincibly strong and mighty. Ships of all sizes were passing; gulls were wheeling with hoarse screams above my head - the sun broke the clouds and suddenly the river was violet with silver lines and circles.

At that moment I knew. The ferry arrived from the other side; people pushed out and past me. The life and bustle and beauty of the world was everywhere about me. I loved it; I adored it; but not for me to try and change it.

He was a sensitive, quiet little boy and, like all shy people, was easily abashed by any incident which involved him in a clumsy or ridiculous situation. I recall a visit we made to our Sunday school teacher—a Miss McHutcheon. We had knocked on her front door and were waiting for her to open it. When she did so, Wilfred, in his eagerness to greet her, took a quick step forward, tripped and fell full-length on the mat in front of her! Such was his confusion that a deep blush spread all over his face and for the remainder of our visit he stammered out his replies with difficulty and could hardly find words to express himself clearly. I speak of our Sunday school teacher here because I attended the same Sunday school (the one held in Christ Church, Claughton) for some time with him. We belonged to a Bible-reading

Wilfred Owen, 1893 - 1918

group in the Church. Each member of the group had a small printed card on which certain chapters from the Bible were marked for reading each day. Wilfred was very conscientious over this and during a holiday in Wales which he spent with me and my family he never once missed taking out his Bible when we were both in bed at night and reading the marked passage by candle-light. ... It says much for Wilfred's sense of duty and will-power that, in spite of all these pleasurable distractions and the healthy tiredness induced by them, he still persisted in his Bible-reading each night. This strong religious background to his character was mainly due to his mother, and undoubtedly she was the one who had most influence in the moulding of his personality throughout his childhood days...

The effects of war and of the awful and horrible sights and sounds of battle on a sensitive, imaginative mind such as his, can well be appreciated. His mother told me that when he came home on sick leave in 1917 his hair had turned quite white. His decision to rejoin his regiment at the front again in spite of these experiences speaks much of courage and determination.

ALEC S. PATON
in *A Tribute to Wilfred Owen,* compiled by T.J. WALSH (1964)

from *Wilfred Owen's boyhood letters to his mother and brother Harold*

Birkenhead, October 1905

Dear Mother, It is Saturday night; struck half past seven this moment, and I have work to do. There is arithmetic to be done, which is out of those 'harder' examples....During tea this afternoon a porter arrived with a brace of pheasants, shot Oct.7th (from Mr Melly). It has been very wet here so we could not go out this afternoon. We went to the Seamen's Institute & saw Mr Grindon. He was very nice and took us round the docks....

Birkenhead, Spring 1906

Dear Mother, We went to the Bible party on Saturday afternoon and were not a bit late! In fact we were there at the exact time....Mr. Thomson was a very nice gentleman...He has two fine gardens, one in B'head Park which is almost wild. In it is what he calls his rock-garden. I am sure you would be delighted with it. There are banks of ferns & foxgloves, and it has a little pool in the middle. When we ...had passed through the garden we came to his bowling-green. The big boys then had a game of bowls, while Harold with the little boys played golf! (in the other garden). We only had a very short meeting just after tea, & before the games. I only wish you were there to have seen the gardens.

Dorfold, Meols, Cheshire, September 1908

My dear Harold...I went to Anfield on Friday you know, but I did not go to the Park. I spent most of the afternoon looking for Miss Taylor's house...I liked Anfield very much but it is not like Meols. It is really lovely here. There are miles of fields in front of the house & it is not far from the sea....Tell Colin I shall be so glad to have him to come walks with me after Kenneth. He always comes with me to the shore, but he doesn't seem to understand anything I tell him & he says nothing but 'Is this water deep? Eh? Is it vewy deep in de miggle of de sea?', and whenever he sees a piece of rope or cord or chain he asks 'Could a steamer bweak this? Eh?' But he is not so rude as he used to be. Margaret began to howl when she first saw me, but now she is all right. I must get ready now to go to Birkenhead. Goodbye!

Dorfold, Great Meols, Cheshire, 10 April 1910 (postcard to his mother)

...Cecil took me in the evening to the Parish Church at West Kirby.

Dorfold, Great Meols, Cheshire, circa 9 August 1910

Dearest Mother...The air is *perfect* in temperature and humidity: and that for every single hour of the 24; The skies unclouded; the Rain waits till 11 o' clock, p.m. as it should do.... Yes: I went with Kenneth to bathe at 8 o' clock this mng. and it is always between 10.30 and 11 when we come in at night. I should not be so energetic if fresh air were obtainable in the house. But it is *not*. The drawing room now is as stuffy as a Severn Tunnel. Hence the hasty brevity of this letter.... I have not been away from Meols; except on the Lake (W. Kirby). The family are going on Friday to Connah's Head so I am staying till Thursday.

WILFRED OWEN

Collected Letters of Wilfred Owen, ed. Harold Owen and John Bell (1967)

railway line was almost on the banks of the Mersey, running along the Cast Iron Shore, and I was to use our local station, St Michael's, constantly when, in 1911, I went to the Liverpool Institute High School for Boys, and later when I was a clerk in the Education Office.

Between the railway and the river was a private recreation ground, known affectionately as 'The Crick' - short for cricket field. I was to spend many happy hours there during my first twenty years. For an annual fee of five bob (twenty-five pence to younger readers) you were given a key which entitled you to enter the ground where there were bowling greens, half a dozen tennis courts, and a cricket pitch. Even grassy slopes were provided for us kids to play roly-poly down to the wall that kept the 'buckoes' out. We often had the odd stone thrown at us from the rough types on the shore, not that we didn't reply, or even start it, on occasion. Shades of Belfast. With its strong Catholic population and the prejudices, there was always a slight undercurrent of unrest in Liverpool. My mother, a staunch Wesleyan, would clip my ear if she found me playing with 'that Catholic boy from next door'. Ironically I am certain that my ancestors on my father's side came from Ireland. The quick temper, the love of music, and the fiery-red hair (I was always Rusty, Ginger, or Coppernob at school) were distinct characteristics in both my father and me. My mother was more sedate, coming from Knutsford in Cheshire.

When I started at St Michael's Council School I was five and already finding my aunt's nursery rhymes and my father's ballads helping me towards success. I was soon quite a teacher's pet, singing and showing off in front of the class. However, all my young social life was really centred around the church: morning and evening services on Sunday, with Sunday School in the afternoon; Band of Hope on Monday; Scripture Union on Tuesday; choir practice on Wednesday; rehearsals for the church concert on Thursday; more choir practice on Friday. Even on Saturday there would usually be a garden fête, or a bazaar connected with the church. No wonder that for a long time I wanted to take Holy Orders - and I don't mean darning socks!

I started in the choir as a probationer at threepence a month. You had to wait for one of the choristers' voices to break before you got your chance. Mine came and it was the tallest boy in the choir who had to leave, so I got his cassock and surplice. To fit 'Titch' Askey they had to be turned up, and the tuck in the cassock came right up to my armpits. It was like wearing a heavy overcoat, and the first time I led the choir up the chancel steps I tripped and fell on my face, followed by the two boys directly behind me. To add to my indignities, my mother had given me a tin of small liquorice pellets to suck (she was determined I would be best), and these shot out of my waistcoat pocket and spread over the chancel. When the procession resumed, the crunching sounded like a squad of soldiers marching up a gravel path.

ARTHUR ASKEY
Before Your Very Eyes (1975)

Olaf Stapledon writes about the War to his future bride, Agnes Miller. Extracts from his letters.

(Olaf Stapledon, then a Liverpool WEA tutor, joined the Friends' Ambulance Unit, serving at the Western Front. Agnes Miller was in Australia)

2 August 1914 ...Germany and Russia definitely at war...Military preparations are going on about us and the coast is guarded...If the war spreads and England fights, of course everything will be dislocated...I believe it will all be over in a fortnight, but it may be the beginning of unheard-of horrors, and goodness knows what may become of European civilisation.

16 August 1914 ...Yesterday I had a good little sea voyage from Bangor. When we reached the Mersey we saw all kinds of ships going in and out, several in government service with their funnels painted black, which made them quite unrecognisable. At the entrance of the river we were stopped by the guard boats, and told what signal lights to hoist as a pass word. Then we passed through the beam of a searchlight which sweeps the river right across....Liverpool is a turmoil of holiday makers and war.

29 August 1914 ...The chance of my having to volunteer seemed at first very small, but with the advance of German troops it grows daily a more serious possibility. The war, one is beginning to see, is a more tremendous thing than has been upon the earth for many ages. For good or ill we have all to play some part or other in it, and our own affairs must sink before it.

8 November 1914 ...I do want my commission...we certainly can't sit still and watch our friends die for us. So here is one more for His Majesty, and Kitchener, but more especially for England... and also for Humanity. Alas! poor Humanity, like a mad thing tearing its own flesh.

23 June 1915 ...You speak about casualty lists. There are so many now that I never look at them, but one keeps hearing of "casualties" one knows. The other day the Liverpool Scottish did a great charge, and suffered terribly. Liverpool is in mourning. The Scottish are a crack territorial regiment, & are used much for dangerous work. They are all sons of Liverpool gentlemen. Don't you keep wondering what it is really all for? I cannot rake up any enthusiasm at all for the issues at stake, but for the fighters indeed I can. We think we are fighting for certain things, but we fight simply because a myriad tiny causes all have worked that way - great historical causes and multitudinous tiny personal causes.

OLAF STAPLEDON

Talking Across the World - The Love Letters of Olaf Stapledon and Agnes Miller, 1913-1919, ed. Robert Crossley (1987)

Liverpool Pals - the 17th, 18th, l9th and 20th (Service) Battalions The King's (Liverpool Regiment).

On 24th August 1914 Lord Derby received Kitchener's permission to raise a battalion of men from the business houses of Merseyside.

Lord Derby's basic idea was that men who worked together in the close confines of a business, and who met together socially as 'pals', might well respond to a call to serve together, and if necessary fight together, so long as they were not separated...If the original idea was not Derby's, then he was the perfect innovator, and it was certainly he who coined the title 'Pals', which, though purely unofficial, was to stick thereafter, in the minds of the soldiers themselves, and the public in general....

Long before 7.30, on the evening of August 28th, St. Anne's Street was crowded with young eager men trying to get into the drill hall. Those inside found that the hall itself was packed to capacity, and men were standing in the aisles, the doorways, and even on the stairs. So great was the crush, that another room below also had to be opened to take all those who wanted to enlist. When Lord Derby arrived and stepped onto the platform to address the multitude, his welcome was tumultuous... "This should be a Battalion of Pals, a battalion in which friends from the same office will fight shoulder to shoulder for the honour of Britain and the credit of Liverpool....You have given a noble example in coming forward. You are certain to give a noble example in the field of battle."

Would-be Pals recruits marching up Dale Street, Liverpool on 31 August 1914 to enlist at St George's Hall

By 8.00 am, on August 31st the area outside St. George's Hall was even more packed than St. Anne's Street had been, with men waiting patiently to enlist...Some concerns, like Cunard and the Stock Exchange, actually formed up their men first, and then marched them to St. George's Hall en masse to enlist. A similar gesture was made in Wallasey, across the Mersey, so that men wishing to enlist from the Wirral Peninsula could all arrive together at what was to become Liverpool's largest recruiting office...Lord Derby had over 3,000 recruits, enough in fact to raise three battalions of Pals....By mid-October, Lord Kitchener gave Derby permission to raise a fourth battalion of Pals, to bring the men so far recruited up to Brigade strength.

GRAHAM MADDOCKS
Liverpool Pals (1991)

Poem for the Liverpool Repertory Theatre, during the First World War.

September 1914

Friends, we are opening at this solemn time
Because, as we believe the stage reveals
Not simply play, but all that is sublime,
Living, and wise in what the nation feels.

Because (as we believe) a nation needs
A temper and support in times of strain,
Beauty for solace when the spirit bleeds,
Laughter for respite to the weary brain.

Because, like you, we wish to play a part
In helping England in the months of stress
To bear the battle with a steady heart,
And by our efforts make her troubles less.

JOHN MASEFIELD

Lines from Malta, 1915

There's bright sunshine here in Malta, while at home are fog and rain,
With the wet wind on the uplands and the floods down in the plain.
But in spite of winter's weather I would far, far rather be
In the wide, sweet, open country 'twixt the Mersey and the Dee.

Though the woods are bare and leafless and the song-birds all are fled;
Though the flowers in the gardens and the hedgerows all are dead;
And the wet west wind comes sweeping in across the Irish Sea,
To wake the foam on Mersey Bar and flood the Sands o' Dee;

Yet, spite of wintry storm or rain or fog, I love it all,
And long to be on Thurstaston as evening shadows fall;
For no sight is half so beautiful or half so dear to me,
As the stormy, golden sunsets o'er the gleaming Sands o' Dee.

And when the war is over, with what joy shall I return,
To the fields and paths and commons and the woods for which I yearn;
To the moors and the uplands, and the salt kiss of the sea,
In the Hundred of the Wirral 'twixt the Mersey and the Dee.

FRANK JOCELYN PRIEST

in *The Illustrated Portrait of Wirral* by
KENNETH BURNLEY (1987)

Siegfried Sassoon, subaltern, at his Depot on Merseyside, prior to returning to the Western Front, late 1916

Clitherland Camp had acquired a look of coercive stability; but this was only natural, since for more than eighteen months it had been manufacturing Flintshire Fusiliers, many of whom it was now sending back to the Front for the second and third time. The Camp was as much an essential co-operator in the national effort as Brotherhood & Co.'s explosive factory, which flared and seethed and reeked with poisonous vapours a few hundred yards away. The third winter of the war had settled down on the lines of huts with calamitous drabness; fog-bleared sunsets were succeeded by cavernous and dispiriting nights when there was nothing to do and nowhere to do it.

Crouching as close as I could to the smoky stove in my hut I heard the wind moaning around the roof, feet clumping cheerlessly along the boards of the passage, and all the systematized noises and clatterings and bugle-blowings of the Camp. Factory-hooters and ships' fog-horns out on the Mersey sometimes

147

combined in huge unhappy dissonances; their sound seemed one with the smoke-drifted munition-works, the rubble of industrial suburbs, and the canal that crawled squalidly out into blighted and forbidding farmlands which were only waiting to be built over...The war had become undisguisedly mechanical and inhuman. What in earlier days had been drafts of volunteers wcrc now droves of victims. I was just beginning to be aware of this.

*   *   *

But Clitherland had accessible compensations. One of them was the Golf Course at Formby. The electric train took only twenty minutes to get there, and Formby was famous for its bracing air, comfortable Club House, and superlatively good war-time food. I went there at least one afternoon a week; usually I played alone, and often I had the links to myself, which was no disadvantage, since I have always been considerably addicted to my own company....

Going into Liverpool was, for most of us, the only antidote to the daily tedium of the Depot. Liverpool usually meant the Olympic Hotel. This palatial contrast to the Camp was the chief cause of the overdrafts of Ormand and other young officers. Never having crossed the Atlantic, I did not realize that the Hotel was an American importation, but I know now that the whole thing might have been brought over from New York in the mind of a first-class passenger. Once inside the Olympic, one trod on black and white squares of synthetic rubber, and the warm interior smelt of this pseudo-luxurious flooring. Everything was white and gilt and smooth; it was, so to speak, an air-tight Paradise made of imitation marble. Its loftiness made resonance languid; one of its attractions was a swimming-bath, and the whole place seemed to have the acoustics of a swimming-bath; noise was muffled and diluted to an aqueous undertone, and even the languishing intermezzos of the string band throbbed and dilated as though a degree removed from ordinary audibility...

*   *   *

Sassoon, after returning from the Front in 1917, makes a formal protest against the war.

... on Saturday afternoon I decided that I really must go and get some fresh air, and I took the electric train to Formby. How much longer would this ghastly show go on, I wondered, as the train pulled up at Clitherland Station. All I wanted now was that the thing should be taken out of my own control, as well as the Colonel's. I didn't care how they treated me as long as I wasn't forced to argue about it any more...

At Formby I avoided the Golf Course... Wandering along the sand dunes I felt

148

outlawed, bitter, and baited. I wanted something to smash and trample on, and in a paroxysm of exasperation I performed the time-honoured gesture of shaking my clenched fists at the sky. Feeling no better for that, I ripped the M.C. ribbon off my tunic and threw it into the mouth of the Mersey. Weighted with significance though this action was, it would have felt more conclusive had the ribbon been heavier. As it was, the poor little thing fell weakly onto the water and floated away as though aware of its own futility. One of my point-to-point cups would have served my purpose more satisfyingly, and they'd meant much the same to me as my Military Cross.

Watching a big boat which was steaming along the horizon, I realized that protesting against the prolongation of the War was about as much use as shouting at the people on board that ship.

SIEGRIED SASSOON
Memoirs of an Infantry Officer (1930)

Captain Noel Chavasse, V. C. (P. J. Connolly)

Captain Noel Chavasse (died 4 August 1917), awarded two V.C.s and the M.C., one of the most decorated men in British history, was the son of the Bishop of Liverpool. Educated at Liverpool College and Cambridge, Noel competed in the 1908 Olympics. He was a Medical Officer at the Royal Southern Hospital, Liverpool, and in 1914 joined the Liverpool Scottish Regiment as Second Medical Officer. In October 1916 he was awarded the M.C. and his first V.C. 'for conspicuous bravery and devotion to duty. During an attack he attended the wounded in the open all day under heavy fire and in view of the enemy ... Altogether he saved the lives of some twenty badly wounded men, besides the ordinary cases which passed through his hands.' Chavasse, though severely injured in July 1917, saved the lives of several men before dying of his wounds. A posthumous (second) V.C. was awarded to this 'hero of heroes'.

149

Mines and Torpedoes, 1917

I sailed for New York in the *Celtic* on February 14, but only got as far as the Isle of Man when we ran into a newly laid minefield, and were unfortunate enough to hit something at about 9 a.m. next day. We did not know at first whether it was a mine or torpedo we had struck, but as no second explosion occurred, and no submarine was seen, concluded it was a mine. I looked over the side to see when to stop the engines, and then as I turned to walk amidships again I bumped into Griffiths, who was holding an old shore overcoat and a bucko cap for me to put on instead of my uniform in case we had to take to the boats—most thoughtful of him. Not only he, but everyone else, was prepared to say that the Captain had gone down in the ship, providing she had sunk and the submarine wanted to take me prisoner.

On sounding the ship we found twenty-eight feet of water in the fore-peak and in No. I hold, which showed the explosion had taken place somewhere near the bulkhead that separated them. No. 2 hold was practically dry, so we, after shoring the bulkhead between Nos. I and 2 holds, decided to return at reduced speed to Liverpool and informed the authorities on shore by wireless to that effect.

We reached the Mersey safely, accompanied by an armed trawler which had turned up in answer to our message, and on letting go the port anchor, found that the cable did not run out, so we brought up with the starboard one.

A day or two later, when we put into dry-dock, we found that a hole 30 feet long by 20 feet deep had been blown in her side, and the cable in the port chain-locker had been shattered into many pieces by the force of the explosion.

A fortnight later, I sailed in the *Adriatic* for New York, and managed to make that voyage successfully, though on our return we were ordered into Milford Haven as mines had been found at the entrance to the Mersey.

SIR BERTRAM HAYES (Commodore of the White Star Line)
Hull Down, Reminiscences of Windjammers, Troops and Travellers (1925)

Ferry boats Iris & Daffodil returning from the Zeebrugge raid, 1918

Unemployed Demonstrations at St. George's Plateau and Police batonings at the Walker Art Gallery, 1921. George Garrett's account.

Monday, 12 September, 1921.

...Monday afternoon, droves of unemployed hurried along Liverpool's widest street to St. George's Hall plateau. The oblong-shaped Hall is like a huge Greek Temple with its Corinthian columns standing sixty feet high. Several rows of stone steps raise the Hall itself above the street level. In front is the city's largest open space. Across the wide busy street on the left are a group of other big impressive buildings: the Museum; the Picton Reference Library; the well-filled Walker Art Gallery; and the Sessions court.

This was the setting for the largest meeting yet held. Men and women kept crossing the surrounding tram-lines from all sides to join the mass of people already assembled on the plateau. These in turn attracted the interest of casual passers-by who dawdled awhile before coming across to increase the numbers further.

This large crowd lacked the cohesion of the two previous ones. Unemployment cards were not in evidence. No arms were being linked together. There were plenty of gaps. It might have been because of the plateau's reputation for batonings, and the advisability of being free enough to run if necessary. Very few uniformed police were to be seen, although there were plenty of plain-clothes detectives moving about in pairs.

From the top of the stone steps, the committee stared over the heads of the vast crowd, and then at each other. They were in a difficult position. This was the third demonstration. No offer of work schemes had been made by the City Council, and no offer of suitable relief had come from the Board of Guardians. There was nothing fresh to tell the crowd excepting what most of them already knew, that prominent members of both ruling bodies and of all political shades were using the newspapers and party platforms to discredit the unemployed leaders. The stories included the dollops of gold supposed to be coming from Moscow.

Some of the committee had to dash away early to sign on at the Labour Exchange. Those remaining co-opted a woman trades union organiser just back in town from the Labour Party's annual conference, and disgusted with its dilatory treatment of the unemployment problem. She was now surveying the restive crowd below. So was the old police-striker and the others. All were undecided on what to do next...

The young man in the dungarees, ever suspicious of the old police-striker, suddenly blurted out: "Come on. We're wasting our time standing here like a gang of dummies. Let's take them around the shops again."

The clergyman swung on him immediately. "Oh damn the shops," he yelled.

The police-striker's glance conveyed the same. To prevent further argument, he again stepped forward to address the crowd, too vast to hear much of what he was saying.

"I think we'll go for a walk," he suggested. "A short walk. It's too late for anything else. We'll all be art critics this afternoon. We'll go across and have a look at the pictures in the Art Gallery. Those places are as much for us as anybody else. They belong to the public."

He moved off down the steps, leaving the rest of the committee free to follow if they chose. Only the clergyman and woman organiser went after him. The remainder stood fuming as sections of the huge crowd flocked across the tram-lines.

The suspicious young man turned to the others. "Well," he said, "Isn't that proof enough? What did I tell you. He's leading them into a trap; him, and that bloody devil-dodging parson."

The others kept staring across the gradually emptying plateau to the crowded street beyond, their eyes fixed on the short flight of steps fronting the Art Gallery entrance. The clergyman and the old police-striker were slowly ascending, surrounded by a pack of followers.

The clergyman's fuzzy head disappeared through the door-way. Impatient men and women streamed in behind. The gallery steps, the side-walk, and the wide roadway was a mass of eager pushing people.

Suddenly hundreds of foot-police rushed out of the Sessions Court and adjacent buildings, batoning heads right and left. The frightening confusion of the crowd was worsened as the mounted police galloped up and rode full charge into them, trampling and scattering in all directions. Many of the unemployed lay stretched in the roadway. Others were led away to hospital to have their wounds dressed.

From the plateau, the few remaining committee men ran across the street to try and rally the crowd together. But the police attack had been too well planned. Unlike the half-nourished unemployed they were privileged to carry truncheons and sticks and were cracking everybody they could lay hands on.

Inside the Art Gallery, more police caused pandemonium. Men yelled aloud as they were batoned down. Others dashed around panic-stricken. A few desperate ones dropped from an open window into the side-street and got away. Those attempting to follow were struck down from behind. The police closed all windows and doors. There were no further escapes. Batons split skull after skull. Men fell where they were hit. The floor streamed with blood. Those lying in it were trampled on by others who were soon flattened out alongside them. Gallery workmen were battered too. The police had gone wild. The old police-striker, appealing to their decency, had his arm broken and his head smashed. The young parson, protesting, was knocked bleeding to the floor, and as he lay unconscious was batoned again. An ambulance took both of them to hospital. Fourteen of those most seriously injured followed later. Others were bandaged on the spot. The hundred and forty who remained, including the woman organiser, were bundled into black marias and driven to the lock-up.

GEORGE GARRETT
Unemployed Struggles: Liverpool 1921-22

By way of apology

Some people today seem to think that modern English poetic drama began with Mr T. S. Eliot. I was born and brought up in Wallasey. I went to Liverpool University three years before the First World War broke out. At that time the Liverpool Repertory Company had close links with the University, and it was the Repertory Theatre that stirred my interest in plays and play-acting and playwriting. I remember being overwhelmed by young Miss Sybil Thorndike's performance in the Gilbert Murray translation of *Medea*. I thought on and off for some years about that revelation of Euripides. It was Miss Thorndike's Medea that gave me my first idea of a kindred character in Welsh legend; later on I wrote the first two acts of my own play *Blodeuwedd* in the hope that some day and some where there might be a Welsh-speaking Sybil Thorndike.

The war broke into my university course, and when I got back to Brownlow Hill after the war, Lascelles Abercrombie was on the staff of the English school. I used to meet him for lunch at the Central Station Restaurant sometimes on Mondays. He had a train to catch at five o'clock for Colwyn Bay, where he had a tutorial class. So from one to half-past four we lunched and sat on and talked.

He had been writing plays in verse for some years. They are neglected now, unwisely as I think. I have a memory of a one act play of his *The End of the World*, acted by the Liverpool Repertory. It was quick poetry and exciting drama ... Abercrombie was concerned to make his speech and speech-rhythms living, likely, dramatic talk - the poetry should be in the energy of the speech. His characters put more of themselves into every statement just because they speak in verse. That was a thing we discussed over the Central Station lunch table.

SAUNDERS LEWIS
in *Dock Leaves* (Vol.III., No. 8) 1952

A weekend in Liverpool, c. 1923
from *Emlyn Williams' Early Autobiography*

..."What's Miss Cooke written about now?" It was to suggest my going once a week to Liverpool for an hour's German at the Berlitz School, and enclosing pound-notes. I obeyed readily, taking a cheap day-ticket from Shotton to Seacombe, then my lesson from an impassive lady in a cubicle, 'das ist ein rote Bleistift', lunching off a meat-pie in a workman's café, then loitering outside cinemas scrutinizing the photographs like a detective; if I had enough pocket-money I went inside, continuous, for the degenerate thrill of sitting through a film twice.

One week-end, with a pound Miss Cook had sent me 'for extras', I went for my Deutsche Uebung on the Friday, and arranged to stay the night at Uncle Jab's so that I could queue up for Martin Harvey in *Oedipus Rex*. As I sat in the front row of the pit watching the theatre fill, an animated man came up to me from the stalls, said he had taken me for his nephew, and would I care for the free seat next to him: I was delighted and talked freely, it was ideal practice for Oxford. I explained that I had only seen plays in Paris, he said he had noticed that Continental accent, and I confessed that I was a local foreign boy.

The play was a revelation to me. When I thanked my benefactor he asked me was I doing anything for supper, I said yes my uncle and aunt were waiting for me in Bootle thank you very much, and we shook honest hands. Next morning I met Enid at the landing stage; on my way, I made a point of passing the back of the Royal Court, where they were moving Oedipus out and Sydney Carton in. In the sun, wings were threadbare and battered; but scenery was made for footlights, and it was right that it should all look like a busy railway station. I gave Enid a tea-shop lunch and treated her to *Dear Brutus* at the Repertory Playhouse; the impression on me of the two plays, my first in English, was to deepen with the months. Enid was amiable but unable to participate - "It tells a nice story doesn't it?" - and I would have preferred last night's companion, though looking back there had been something funny about him. I felt guilty being bored, but it was good to think that I had taken a girl out and spent money on her. Miss Cooke's.

EMLYN WILLIAMS
George (1961)

Canadian Tern Schooners in Albert Dock, c. 1920

The Landing Stage

The most exciting of our Sunday airings were undoubtedly those to the Landing Stage. Jumping off the tram, we proceeded along the Pier Head, hurrying ahead of our parents. The covered gangways were delightfully steep at low tide. If you ran down you couldn't stop until you reached the chains on the Landing Stage. Trying to run up was an Olympian task and called for a sharp agility to avoid the out-of-control, down-running flotilla of vociferous youth, with anxious parents vainly trying to catch up and shouting words of caution. The sounds of human cries and the staccato clatter of pounding shoes echoed and re-echoed in those cavernous gangways, making a cacophony of sound never to be forgotten.

Then the walk along the whole length of the Landing Stage, over half-a-mile long, and stated to be the longest in the world. Tied up at the Stage, rising up and down rhythmically with the swell of the water, were the busy ferry boats which all seemed to leave at the same time in close order, then separated to make for their four destinations 'across the water'. There would be the tug boats, Pilot boats, coasters, and then the Isle of Man and North Wales steamers, and the giant transatlantic liners towering over their embarkation bridges.

And if we were lucky, there would be the exhilaration of a short voyage - a ferry trip across the Mersey.

JOHN P. REID

New Brighton Ferry

You were eight years old, on the New Brighton boat.
You had watched the quayside sailors, blind to their own miracle,
unspinning eight-coil hawsers from bollards, to hurl them
idly as snake charmers to the teak palms
of the sailors on board...who, in hangy jerseys and gulping boots,
stowed them, went striding off.
You were astern now, waiting for screws suddenly to thrash, lather.
Then turning with the ship, the dinosaur cranes grazing the docks' skyline.
The gold bell shone from the bridge. You could see the Captain.
Below, like piano hammers, engine rods glistened, fell.
The ship was faster than its bows, fast
as the sparks tearing back from the funnel.
You went gunwale to gunwale, wild as a squirrel,
you couldn't miss anything – from the bucketed dredger
to the tramps, tankers, coming hugely in.
You were five, spelling out letters on sterns,
seeing who'd shout the answer first,
seven, picking out ocean flags
to check with your fag-card album at home:
a changeling, on fabulous water, one
with the globe-strutting lion, the white star.

Any moment now the ship would be a tug
with a liner slid solemnly at heel,
the place Lisbon, Acapulco. Off New Brighton pier
the one-legged diver was stumping his iron ladder,
climbing the sky, as he always would,
to fall deathless as a rainbow.
You were eight years old. Never, never coming back.

GEOFFREY HOLLOWAY

from *Shining Morning - Honora Collins' Wallasey Childhood*
I came to the beach when the morning was shining.
A barque on the waters sailed gloriously on....
THOMAS MOORE

Across Virginia Rd, down the slipway between Victoria Gardens and the Palace Fairground, and there is the promenade, the Lighthouse with the rock pools surrounding it, Perch Rock Battery, the bright sand, and the sun glittering on the water of the River Mersey...

I spent my childhood years 'within a walk of the sea', at New Brighton. I was born there in 1912, the second eldest of five children. Every day we saw the ships sailing up the river from foreign parts bringing their cargoes to the busy docks, and the ships departing, out beyond the Bar to the Irish Sea, some heading for the Atlantic. As a family (the Callanans) we were closely involved with both sides of the Mersey. My three brothers crossed on the ferry each day to St Francis Xavier's College (where they joined our Liverpool cousin, John Reid); later, my sister Pauline and I attended Mount Pleasant Training College; four of us were to teach at one time or another at Liverpool schools. The sea was in my youngest brother's blood - like his paternal grandfather who sailed in the Blue Funnel line, Francis, after completing his academic studies, joined the Merchant Navy and became a Master Mariner. My father and my eldest brother Philip were in shipping, in Liverpool, again crossing by ferry every day. We felt that we belonged to both sides of the river.

Our childhood world, however, was bounded by the stretch of promenade from the New Brighton Pier and Ferry to the 'Boards' by Marine Park. This was the liveliest part of the seaside town. The 'Boards' were high wooden boarding which extended from the wall of Marine Park (at the end of the prom), down to the tideline. They were built in such a way as to have an opening at a slant to give people access to the sandhills beyond. Immediately behind the 'Boards' was a single rail track which led to the tideline: its function was to carry trucks filled with sand down to the water's edge to be washed away by the tide. I can remember the prisoners of war being employed on this job. I was nearly seven at the time and I thought what a silly occupation this was for grown-up men, because often when the sand dried it would blow back and build up again.

Beyond the 'Boards' and above the sandhills were the large houses with gardens, many of these the dwellings which James Atherton had built, once owned by wealthy cotton merchants in the years when 'Cotton was King'. Most of them had high garden walls to protect them from the blowing sand. New Brighton was then called the Dormitory of Liverpool because so many people who worked in the city came home at the end of the day to the seaside resort and its environs. It had been Atherton's vision which had first brought this development, his idea that New Brighton could become a fashionable watering place for the 'Nobility and Gentry, and the rich proprietors of Liverpool's expanding industry.' In 1830 he bought plots of land to sell, and built houses in an elevated part, looking out to sea, nurturing the idea of creating a rival for Brighton

Honora and her brother Philip Callanan

in Sussex. Atherton did not live long enough to pursue completely the scheme he and his son-in-law William Rowson, had begun. Atherton St. and Rowson St. honour the memory of these speculative builders. I doubt, however, that many of my childhood acquaintances and myself were aware of the significance of these names as we tobogganed down the slopes of Atherton St. on snowy winter days.

Opposite the Pier was the tram terminus at the bottom of Victoria Road - a very busy road with every facility. How many little seaside towns of that time had, in one road, two banks, two cinemas, and the crowning distinction of an Empress Ballroom? There were more than fifty shops in the five hundred yards of Victoria Road, many of them duplicated. Down towards the promenade were the restaurants and tea-shops, such as 'The Golden Teapot Café', and even an oyster bar. I must single out for special mention Mumfords, our photographer; Palfrymans, Jeweller and Clockmaker (we hurried past on our way to school, and if it was open we knew we were late); and Theckston the Chemist. Mr Theckston was nearly as good as a doctor, a distinguished figure as he stood in his white coat,with his bald forehead shining antiseptically, his spectacles on the end of his nose. He would lean forward over his beautiful mahogany counter with its glass front, and ponder on the appropriate treatment. Behind him, on the shelves, were his labelled jars, and high up in his window were the coloured glass bottles which commanded total trust and respect.

The part of the beach most frequented by summer visitors and the locals was the area where the soft sand built up to the promenade walls between the Pier and the 'Boards' - this was closest to the amenities and the attractions. Supreme among these were the Tower Grounds. The Tower itself was demolished in 1920, but the Grounds were a place of delight, with winding paths, trees, and a lake with gondolas. The top of the hill was dominated by the Tower Building, its Theatre and Ballroom decorated in white and gold, and with a parquet floor laid on 2000 carriage springs. I learned ballroom dancing there, at a Saturday morning children's class, for about a shilling for two hours.

The Tower and Grounds. The Tower was 621 ft. above sea level, the tallest structure in England. The Tower was demolished in 1920 due to neglect during the war.

We were proud of the beautifully-kept Victoria Gardens, extending from Virginia Road at its rear to the promenade in front. Entertainment here was provided from the Bandstand, the open-air stage, a glass-covered hall for rainy days (and later, the Floral Pavilion), with Pierrot Troupes and Theatrical Companies such as Frank Terry's.

While Victoria Gardens was our favourite place, the stretch of promenade and beach facing the Palace Fairground was our stamping ground. Here were Uncle Joe, the banjo player, a man who sold *Tit-Bits*, comics and other periodicals, Clark's Donkey Rides and the photographer whose pictures were developed more or less on the spot on a kind of tin surface. During the summer holidays we would go down to the shore as early in the morning as possible and stay there all day. In our particular spot the sand had blown up to cover the steps up to the promenade, so that we virtually walked straight on to the shore from the prom.

Speaking of these steps reminds me of some specially interesting characters who came to New Brighton in those early days - the Orange Ladies - who had their regular sites at the bottom of the steps. They were market ladies who came over on the Ferry with their oranges in large circular baskets on their heads. It was quite unique the way they carried them, having a circular support of thick lengths of cloth, twisted into a circle, on the top of their heads, rather like a Bedouin headress. They walked along the promenade in their long black dresses, with a black shawl over their shoulders, their baskets perfectly balanced as they went along with a swaying motion of great dignity. Our own Orange Lady sat at our set of steps with her basket beside her; she made herself comfortable on the soft sand, looking out to sea. She always greeted us with "Hello love", and minded our shoes when we went in to paddle. I can still recall the feel on bare feet of wet ridges of sand left by the continual wash of the outgoing tide.

As the summer visitors departed to their boarding houses for their evening meal, the deck chair boys would collect the chairs and stack them securely under canvas. Gradually the shore began to be deserted, the lights would go on at the Pier and in the Tower Grounds and the Palace; the sound of the Carousel from the fairground would accompany our walk home. My thoughts return once more to Thomas Moore's song, which my mother used to sing to us:

I came to the beach in the evening's declining,
The barque was still there but the waters had gone.

HONORA COLLINS
from an unpublished essay, 'Shining Morning'

The pier, New Brighton; with the Tower Building and Tivoli Theatre.

Victoria Gardens, New Brighton; the beach, pier and ferry.

159

Jung's dream of Liverpool, 1927

I found myself in a dirty, sooty city. It was night, and winter, and dark, and raining. I was in Liverpool. With a number of Swiss—say, half a dozen—I walked through the dark streets. I had the feeling that there we were coming from the harbour, and that the real city was actually up above, on the cliffs. We climbed up there. It reminded me of Basel, where the market is down below and then you go up through the Totengässchen ("Alley of the Dead"), which leads to a plateau above and so to the Petersplatz and the Peterskirche. When we reached the plateau, we found a broad square dimly illuminated by street lights, into which many streets converged. The various quarters of the city were arranged radially around the square. In the centre was a round pool, and in the middle of it a small island. While everything round about was obscured by rain, fog, smoke, and dimly lit darkness, the little island blazed with sunlight. On it stood a single tree, a magnolia, in a shower of reddish blossoms. It was as though the tree stood in the sunlight and was at the same time the source of light. My companions commented on the abominable weather, and obviously did not see the tree. They spoke of another Swiss who was living in Liverpool, and expressed surprise that he should have settled here. I was carried away by the beauty of the flowering tree and the sunlit island, and thought, "I know very well why he has settled here." Then I awoke.

On one detail of the dream I must add a supplementary comment: the individual quarters of the city were themselves arranged radially around a central point. This point formed a small open square illuminated by a large street lamp, and constituted a small replica of the island. I knew that the "other Swiss" lived in the vicinity of one of these secondary centres.

This dream represented my situation at the time. I can still see the greyish-yellow raincoats, glistening with the wetness of the rain. Everything was extremely unpleasant, black and opaque - just as I felt then. But I had had a vision of unearthly beauty, and that was why I was able to live at all. Liverpool is the "pool of life." The "liver," according to an old view, is the seat of life - which "makes to live."

This dream brought with it a sense of finality. I saw that here the goal had been revealed. One could not go beyond the centre. The centre is the goal, and everything is directed towards that centre. Through this dream I understood that the self is the principle and archetype of orientation and meaning. Therein lies its healing function. For me, this insight signified an approach to the centre and therefore to the goal. Out of it emerged a first inkling of my personal myth.

After this dream I gave up drawing or painting mandalas. The dream depicted the climax of the whole process of development of consciousness. It satisfied me completely ... The clarification brought about by the dream made it possible for me to take an objective view of the things that filled my being.

Without such a vision I might perhaps have lost my orientation and been compelled to abandon my undertaking. But the meaning had been made clear. When I parted from Freud, I knew that I was plunging into the unknown. Beyond Freud, after all, I knew nothing; but I had taken the step into darkness. When that happens, and then such a dream comes, one feels it as an act of grace.

CARL G. JUNG

Memories, Dreams, Reflections, trans, Richard and Clara Winston (1963)

The Angel Skipper

Fifty or sixty years ago,
    Away down the Mersey swinging,
We sailed away in the misty morn,
With a skipper never of woman born,
And a light on his hair like April corn,
    And the bells of Liverpool ringing.

Fifty or sixty years ago,
    Away down the Mersey swinging,
When the scimitar moon hung low in the night,
There came a sea-bird wraith and white,
Hovering low on his hair so bright,
    And the bells of Liverpool ringing.

Fifty or sixty years ago,
    Away down the Mersey swinging,
The sea rose up like a green glass wall,
Wall of a sea palace, gate and all,
And the skipper went through ere the wave could fall,
    And the bells of Liverpool ringing.

Fifty or sixty years ago,
    Away down the Mersey swinging,
They say he is dead, and they saw him die,
They say he was man, as you, as I,
They say he is drowned dead, but they lie,
    And the bells of Liverpool ringing.

Fifty or sixty years ago,
    Away down the Mersey swinging,
I feared the light on his hair so pale —
The one man living to tell the tale —
By this dim bright fire, and this deep bright ale,
    And the bells of Liverpool ringing.

DOROTHY STAPLETON (1931)

Liverpool is recommended

..."You say you are going round looking at the cathedrals - that's the plan isn't it? Well, have you seen Liverpool?"

No, she had not seen Liverpool.

"Go to Liverpool at once," he commanded, and was so impressive that she felt she ought to hurry away that very moment. He was as bad as Mr. Chillingford. And what a pair they would make!

"Now you can't say I'm not interested in these medieval creations," he continued earnestly. "You can't say I don't appreciate them. This morning you probably thought I was a little too interested and appreciative, the way I dragged you round and talked your head off. But at Liverpool there's a brand-new cathedral, finished the other day - so to speak. Not a town-hall or a railway station or a block of offices, but a cathedral, the very thing you're talking about."

He paused to take breath, and Miss Trant, who was reminded a little of her father, regarded him with friendly amusement.

"Now what's it like, this cathedral? Is it a little shuffling jerry-built hotch-potch thing? It is not. It's large, it's solid, it's enduring. It's beautiful, it's sublime. And who made it? The men of today. Don't be misled by this medieval nonsense. We're better men than they were, and we live in a better world. Building was their chief trick; it's not ours; but when we want to build, we can outbuild 'em. You never give a thought to most of our building," he lectured away for ever taking up his fork and then putting it down again. "Take the big liners - there's building for you. Look at one of 'em." He said this as if there were several just outside his window. "There's adaptation to ends, there's beauty of design, there's solid craftsmanship and workmanship, everything there in a big liner. You go to Liverpool, look at the cathedral, then take a peep or two at some of the liners in dock, and you'll soon change your mind about our building. You were going there anyhow, I suppose?"

Miss Trant found herself compelled to say, untruthfully, that she was. It would have been terrible to have told him that she had never even thought about Liverpool; he would never have eaten any lunch.

"Then go there at once, my dear young lady," he replied, eager as a boy.

J. B. PRIESTLEY
The Good Companions (1929)

R. M. S. Mauretania,
holder of the Blue Riband
1909-29

Cunarders

I'd hear them in the night, baying like stags
over the sleeping forest of small boys
that was Liverpool, down past the Crosby lightship
where the sea-drunk bellbuoys wagged their star-struck heads.

I'd draw them in my rough books, with coloured funnels,
make impossible models of them in chunky wood
that capsized in the bath but always came up streaming,
exultant as dogs with sticks in their teeth.

Mauretania, Berengeria, Aquitania - these were never
keel-blocked skeletons Meccano pieced together,
straitjacketed with cunning rivets, plates -
but avalaunched epiphanies out of some triton's head.

Their soundscapes built my youth, were my long gods -
always in the offing, never wharf trussed;
those twelve ton anchors, those burly sirens
commanding even the spouts and flukes of white whales.

They were everybody's, yet peculiarly mine -
mine and the Liver Bird's that green tip-toed to see them,
their smoke, their hulls, the Mersey that breathed to hold them,
coming in from everywhere, across the world.

GEOFFREY HOLLOWAY

Graham Greene in Liverpool

The huge Liverpool hotel had been designed without aesthetic taste but with the right ideas about comfort and a genuine idea of magnificence. It could probably house as many passengers as an Atlantic liner; passengers, because no one goes to Liverpool for pleasure, to the little cramped square and the low sky-signs which can almost be touched with the hand, where all the bars and the cinemas close at ten. But there was a character hidden in this hotel; it wasn't chic, it wasn't bright, it wasn't international; there remained somewhere hidden, among its long muffled corridors, beneath the huge cliff-like fall of its walls, the idea of an English inn; one didn't mind asking for muffins or a pint of bitter while the boats hooted in the Mersey and the luggage littered the hall; there was quite probably a boots. Anyway enough remained for me to understand the surprise of Henry James when he landed in England, "that England should be as English as, for my entertainment, she took the trouble to be".

The natural native seediness had not been lost in the glitter of chromium plate; the muffin had been overwhelmingly, perhaps rather nauseatingly, enlarged. If the hotel was silly, it was only because magnificence is almost always a little silly. The magnificent gesture seldom quite comes off... But in the huge lounge at Liverpool, like the lounge of a country inn fifty times magnified, one was at home on the vast expanse of deep dark carpet, only one business man asleep with his mouth open ...

Next morning in the public-house near the Prince's Stage, four middle-aged women sat drinking with an old dirty man of eighty-four. Three had the dustbin look; they carried about them the air of tenements, of lean cats and shared wash-houses; the fourth had risen a little way in the world; she was the old man's daughter over from America for Christmas. "Have another drink, Father?" He was seeing her off. Their relationship was intimate and merry; the whole party had an air of slightly disreputable revelry. To one the party didn't really matter; she had caught the American accent. To the other women, who must return to the dustbin, it was perilous, precarious, breath-taking; they were happy and aghast when the old man drew out a pound note and stood a round himself. "Well, why shouldn't he?" the daughter asked them, asked Jackie boy, the bar-tender, the beer advertisements, the smutty air, the man who came in selling safety-razor blades, half a dozen for threepence, "it's better than spending it on a crowd of strange dames".

The Liverpool waterside at least had not changed since James's day: "The black steamers knocking about in the yellow Mersey, under a sky so low that they seemed to touch it with their funnels, and in the thickest, windiest light"; - even the colour was the same, "the grey mildness, shading away into black at every pretext".

The cargo ship lay right outside the Mersey in the Irish Sea; a cold January wind blew across the tender; people sat crammed together below deck saying good-bye, bored, embarrassed and bonhomous, like parents at a railway station the first day of a term, while England slipped away from the porthole, a stone stage, a tarred side, a slap of grey water against the glass.

GRAHAM GREENE
Journey without Maps (1936)

from *The King of the Castle*

Liverpool Jack that's born in a jersey
Round the world for Liverpool sighs
Give me a mist, the mist of the Mersey
You can have all your African Skies.

A. P. HERBERT and WILLIAM STRONG
(written for and performed at Liverpool Repertory Theatre 1924).
Rhyme to the tune of 'Lillibullero'.

Ode for the Liverpool Repertory Theatre

"Coming of Age", 1932

Here, in this port of ships, we built a stage,
Where the crusaders of the sea should find,
Their travels done, another pilgrimage
Calling them as crusaders of the mind;
We built a stage, that thereon should be told
All arguments that ever went to school —
We sheltered beauty crying in the cold —
We built another port of Liverpool.

We are of age to-day. We thank you, friends,
Who kept with us the hard, the happy time;
We have dreamt dreams, found vision, heard the ends
Of wisdom manifested in a rhyme;
Together we have learned that all things may
Be fathomed in the splendour of a Play.

JOHN DRINKWATER

A Liverpool Playhouse Romance, 1930s

... I had written a note to William Armstrong at the Liverpool Playhouse, saying that I would be coming up to see the Saturday matinée, and would he please give me an interview. Before catching the train to Liverpool I called at Chapel Street to collect some photographs. There was no one at home, but I found two letters for me, and one of them was from the Old Vic, offering me a contract for the next season for three pounds a week.

Armstrong was polite, but seemed rather abstracted, more or less pushing my photos aside.

'I know your mother, of course, a delightful actress, but, you see, my company is nearly filled. I have some very good young men - oh, and an excellent new young assistant director - you have some experience of directing, didn't you say ? - but I'll let you know.'

'When could you let me know, Mr Armstrong?' - and here I made as if to reach into my breast pocket. 'When could you let me know? Because, you see, I have a contract for the Old Vic.' I paused.

Willie looked at me with something like alarm. 'A contract for the Vic?' he said. 'How much for?'

'Three pounds a week,' I said.

'I'll give you four,' said Willie. And four it was. For an instant I regretted my honesty, as I told Willie later, having the impression that if I'd said seven, he would have capped it with eight.

The Liverpool Playhouse theatre had just been redecorated. It was, and is, one of the most attractive old theatres in England. I saw the matinée, of a play by John Van Druten, and enjoyed it. The company seemed to play to a high standard. But my mind kept wandering to the photographs in front of the theatre. How, I wondered, would mine look amongst them ?

MICHAEL REDGRAVE
In My Mind's Eye: an Autobiography (1983)

*   *   *

Michael

At Liverpool I was a paying guest with a Mrs Winter in Gambier Terrace, which faced the cathedral. Mrs Winter was a friend of some people we knew in Dartmouth. They had suggested I should stay with her on account of my health.

I arrived late in the evening after a seven-hour journey and took a taxi up the hill to Mrs Winter's. A rather scruffy-looking little girl who was the housemaid opened the door, but standing behind her was Mrs Winter with her yellow-white hair and her eyes smiling behind her gold-rimmed spectacles. We took to each at once. No one could have felt insecure in her company. She took me up to my bedroom where a huge coal fire was giving a tremendous heat into the large, dark room. which looked rather dramatic with its enormously high ceiling, royal blue velvet curtains and a huge screen between the door and the bed to keep out draughts. Having unpacked, I went down to dinner, which was at a long table in the dining-room. There were a number of other paying guests, mostly elderly, a man and three women of Dickensian personalities. I sat next to Mrs Winter, who immediately showed she was going to cosset me delightfully.

From Gambier Terrace you could see beyond the bulky, red cathedral then half built, down to the Mersey River. The birds on the Liver Building near the quay gleamed white in the sun. As it was such a lovely morning I decided to walk down the hill to the Playhouse instead of taking a tram, so I set off along the terrace, turning left into the main street which went straight into the city. It had rained during the night, and so the air was clear and the streets looked washed. There were streets and streets of shabby-looking Georgian houses. Their windows were beautifully proportioned and many doors had fine fanlights, but the buildings were all covered with the black smoke and grime given off by the factory chimneys in all northern towns. Even in the most prosperous streets the houses looked grim and forbidding. However, as I walked down the hill in the sun I felt far from depressed. I was full of that nervous excitement that precedes any new venture in the theatre .

Once in the town, which was noisy with trams, bursting with passengers going to work, I thought everything looked very lively, and quite soon I found my way past the Bon Marché to Williamson Square and the Playhouse. I found the stage-door and as I was forty minutes early I walked round to the front again to look at the entrance. Outside hung two uniform frames containing the photographs of the company, all taken by the same photographer, which was a very good idea and looked much tidier than the usual hotch-potch of frames outside the ordinary commercial theatre, where they have every shape and size of glamorous pictures of those who play within. The name of each actor and actress was printed underneath the photograph.

My eyes were held by the one of Michael Redgrave. He looked as if he might have been a naval officer in civvies, or indeed in any profession except the theatre.

Shortly I returned to the stage door, went in and asked for William Armstrong. I was shown into a little office off a passage and opposite the entrance to the stage. In a few minutes William came in, followed by the tall, extremely goodlooking young man I had seen in the photograph.

'Rachel, this is Michael, your leading man,' he said.

Michael and I shook hands and he said, 'Oh good, you're tall. I thought you were going to be tiny.'

William took us on to the stage and I was introduced to the rest of the company, Lloyd Pearson, Deirdre Doyle, Louise Frodsham, Valerie Tudor, Geoffrey Webb and others. From the stage I saw the perfect little auditorium. It was horseshoe-shaped with two circles, with lots of scroll decoration on the plaster-work, which was painted white, picked out in gilt. The walls were dark green, and there were footlights, which I have always loved and which have now largely gone out of fashion.

Chairs were placed in a circle on the stage and I sat next to Michael. We read *Flowers of the Forest* during the morning. Although I was nervous at first I soon forgot and became absorbed in reading the long part of Naomi, who starts the play aged 40 and in Act II goes back to about 20. William seemed pleased and said that as I looked very young we would have to take especial care over my dresses for the middle-aged part. 'But don't worry, it'll all be all right,' he said in his delightful optimistic way.

Michael asked me to have lunch with him and took me to the restaurant of the Bon Marché. The lunch was slightly overshadowed by my shameful indigestion powder, which I had to take at the end of meals.

Finally I said, 'It's rather a nuisance, but I have to have some medicine.'

Michael's face lit up. He called a waitress and asked for a spoon and water, and the whole thing became rather amusing. He told me later how this had pleased him because, he said, 'I am an awful hypochondriac and keep taking things, and it's wonderful to find someone else who does too.' We left the restaurant singing Polly and Macheath duets from *The Beggar's Opera*. We felt happy; he started singing and I joined in.

Rehearsals were mostly enjoyable. William was a most loving and amusing director, always over-praising: 'So moving, so moving ... oh! I have such a clever company,' etc etc.

My life was changed now and I entirely forgot my wretched stomach, which suddenly behaved perfectly. ...

At Mrs Winter's I was spoiled. In the theatre I loved the work and the daily lunches with Michael. One day Michael asked me to tea at his room at 23 Faulkner Street to go through our scenes together. I was already falling in love. We had two scenes which were flashbacks to the First World War, when Naomi was in love with Richard, a young officer in the army (Michael). The first scene in Act II is when Richard tells Naomi how he loves her and the second scene is when Richard comes back from the front, bitter and disillusioned, and Naomi is pregnant and they know they must marry although he'll go back to the front and probably never return, as is the case.

We had tea, and then in the dusk light in his sitting-room we went over our words. They were so real to me that I dared not look at Michael but gazed out of the window, so that he shouldn't see the truth in my eyes.

RACHEL KEMPSON
A Family and its Fortunes (1986)

Visiting Liverpool, 1933

I have never been near Liverpool in spring, summer and early autumn. My visits have all been wintry. I find it impossible to imagine what the city looks like in clear bright sunshine. I think of it existing in a shortened year, only running from November to February, with all its citizens for ever wearing thick overcoats. Just before you reach Lime Street Station your train runs into a deep cutting and daylight promptly vanishes, never returning, I feel, until your other homeward train has left Lime Street and Liverpool well behind. It has, in my memory, more fog about than other cities, not excepting London. The centre is imposing, dignified and darkish, like a city in a rather gloomy Victorian novel. Does spring ever arrive in St. John's Gardens? Do the birds ever twitter and flutter before the solemn façade of St. George's Hall? Is there a Mersey, so much green flowing water, not simply a misty nothingness hooting dismally? I must go there in June, some time, to find out ...

We arrived at the edge of the Mersey, and below us was a long mudbank. The water was a grey mystery, a mere vague thickening of space. Something hooted, to break a silence that immediately closed up afterwards to muffle the whole spectral scene. We walked slowly along the water-front, from nothing, it seemed, into nothing; and darkness rose rather than fell; and with it came a twinkle of lights from Birkenhead that reached us not across the river but over a gulf that could not be measured. I have rarely seen anything more spectral and melancholy. It was hard to believe that by taking ship here you might eventually reach a place of sharp outlines, a place where colour burned and vibrated in the sunlight, that here was the gateway to the bronze ramparts of Arabia, to the temples and elephants of Ceylon, to flying fish and humming birds and hibiscus.

J. B. PRIESTLEY
English Journey (1934)

A Liverpool Morning

Our kid,
cheek as smooth as a White Heart Cherry,
all of a tangle in a Liverpool morning,
takes ship to Valparaiso,
                    sees
an old man standing on the landing-stage limbo
pinning memories up like poppies
                         hearing
the long gone dray horses,
the overhead railway,
the Jack-in-the-Box of rattle and sound,
swift as an abbatoir blade.

Our kid,
cheek as smooth as a White Heart Cherry,
all of a tangle in a Liverpool morning,
proud of his first ship,
                    shouts
"God Bless you Grand-dad."

The Mersey,
a wanton bland with summer,
yet loving her sons and daughters,
carries the valediction away in her arms,
wears it on her breast,
a white carnation,
all of a tangle in a Liverpool morning.

MARGARET BROWNE

from *Ultramarine*

... But there was a queer elation in the eyes of the Liverpool men as they shuffled into the forecastle. Something had happened, at any rate, a tender voice from home had whispered for a moment to those in exile, a mystery had shown its face among the solitudes. Hilliot stood apart from the others, leaning over the rail. After all . . .

What was the good of understanding? The pigeon might be the very messenger of love itself, but nothing would alter the fact that he had failed. He would hide his face from Janet forever, and walk in darkness for the rest of his days. Yet if he could only see her at this moment, she would give him another chance, she would be so gentle and companionable and tender. Her hands would be like sun gently brushing away the pain. His whole being was drowning in memories, the smells of Birkenhead and of Liverpool were again heavily about him, there was a coarse glitter in the cinema fronts, children stared at him strangely from the porches of public-houses. Janet would be waiting for him at the Crosville bus stop, with her red mackintosh and her umbrella, while silver straws

169

of rain gently pattered on the green roof ... "Where shall we go? The Hippodrome or the Argyle? ... I've heard there's a good show on at the Scala—"

Oh, his love for her was not surely the fool of time like the ship: it was the star to the wandering ship herself: even labour, the noble accomplishment of many years, could be turned into an hourglass, but his love was eternal.

Had he not sought her in the town and meadow and in the sky? Had he not prayed to Jesus to give him rest, and found none until the hour he met her? ... Again they seemed to be sitting together on the sand dunes, staring at the sky; great wings had whirred above them, stooping, dreaming, comforting, while the sand, imprinted like snow, had been whistled up about them by the wind. Beyond, a freighter carried their dreams with it, over the horizon. And there had been nothing that mattered, save only themselves and the blue day as they scampered like two children past the Hall Line shed to the harbour wall just in time to see the Norwegian tramp steamer *Oxenstjerna* pass through the gate of the inner dock, while a scratch four paused on their oars watching her entrance steadfastly, their striped singlets dancing in the afternoon sunlight.

* * *

... yourself, Dana Hilliot, the syphilitic, as he strolls aimfully down Great Homer Street. Look! How everyone he touches is smitten with the dire disease. It is just that one little word, the word that kills. Now everything is wasted. *Dies Irae.* They have fallen from ash and are grey. This is he, the human husk, the leaf of ash, ashes to ashes and dust to dust. As he passes down Church Street the wind rushes round him with a cold, monstrous, final insistency. He walks without thinking where he is going. Tramlines run in front of the offices; mothers with warm-smelling furs are fussing with their school-capped sons into the Bon Marché; further away secret tunnels bore through the gloomy buildings, and the overhead railway and a number of sloping bridges leading to the landing stage spread round in bleak and bare confusion. Tram bells clang. Brutal buildings stride into the air above Dana Hilliot .... But the wind has enveloped and overarched all these masses of iron and concrete, all this little humanity, and is sweeping these sparkling buildings with rushing, tremendous shadows. *"Yacko,"* shout the newsboys, wearing, like aprons, the announcement: "Norwegian liner aground in Mersey!" "Last *Echo Exprey!*" He retreats up Church Street, Castle Street, down old Ropery again. The wind blows up from the road an old copy of the *Liverpool Express,* rumples and whisks it down the Goree Piazzas. It clings finally to a lamppost, like some ugly, cringing wraith. The lamppost was an erect viper, poised in climax of anger, to bite.... Crowds drift to and from the ferries, battling with the wind, their coats whipping round their knees, or blowing over their heads. A drove of black cattle clatter past, herded by a hooligan with a twisted stick. A dockside train with its diminutive engine is rumbling along cautiously beneath the Overhead Railway bridges in the direction of Mann Island and the Canning Dock, the sinister bell of warning singing out its desolate nostalgic phrase, *y'lang y'lang y'lang y'lang.* The voice of the chiming bell buoy, chiming and wallowing and rolling. The voice of the leper tolling, enforcing his sad solitude. 'Ware Shoal! A woman passes. *Y'lang y'lang.* Norwegian liner aground in Mersey!

It is the *Oxenstjerna* they are talking about, the *Oxenstjerna* that has gone aground. It is the *Oxenstjerna* which now turns over and sinks into the sand, while the oil spreads a mucous film over the Mersey; and now the white sea gulls, which knew once the dark, smoking rocks, the white sea gulls known by name to the dockers, are dying by the score - ...

MALCOLM LOWRY
Ultramarine (1933)

Paddy's Market, 1933

There is a very large Irish quarter in Liverpool. Two cheerful young journalists took me across the city to see it. Paddy's Market was about to finish business for the day. A few Lascars, like men cut out of brown paper, lurked in the entrance. All the seamen know this covered market, where they frequently come to replenish their wardrobes. Even those natives who have never seen England before and speak no English can ask for "Paddee Markee," as if the place were our pride and joy, the diadem of the Empire. It is surrounded by slum streets, dirty little pubs, and the Irish ... The two journalists and two trams brought me back to the centre of the city, whose essential darkness made a good background for quite a metropolitan display of Neon lighting and flashing signs. Cinemas, theatres (though Liverpool could do with several more), dance-halls, grillrooms, boxing matches, cocktail bars, all in full glittering swing. The Adelphi Hotel had dressed for the evening, was playing waltzes, and for the time being did not care a fig about the lost Atlantic traffic ...

J. B. PRIESTLEY
English Journey (1934)

Queuing in misty rain, Mann Island (D. J. Kewley)

Proving Catherine's Age
North End, Liverpool, 1936

"I was born in County Clare, sir.
No word of a lie, I'm sixty-five
this very year of Our Lord."
No cause to doubt those clear
blue eyes. Jet hair, soft speech
establish her geography, but State Laws
State servants should obey:
"A birth certificate," I insist.
She sighs. "I have none. Lost, I think.
And isn't it bad luck the place
was burnt to a cinder in The Troubles, so."
A baptismal paper from the parish priest?
She clicks her tongue, that she should have
to set a busy man this pointless task,
but God's good, a pension's a pension.
Yes, she'll ask.

It comes. Wrong name, wrong date.
Catherine suddenly Bridget, sixty-eight.
She's nonplussed that I find snags
in something quintessentially simple.
If some priest she's never seen says
she is Bridget, Bridget she must be.
And, as for age, she rocks with laughter,
What's in a year or two or three?
I feel my face go stiff, English, prim:
"That bit of paper, it could refer
to some other child with your family name."
Now, she's shocked. "Ah, no, impossible, sir!"
Why would a priest do a thing like that?"

Deadlock, while she rocks in her chair,
regards me with maternal care.
A clock ticks, I stare at papers,
coals fall in the grate.
Oh, what the hell! A rose by any other name,
she *looks* the age, has raised
five kids, paid life its full whack.
I'll make some story up,
sign in the right places.
It's not my money, anyway.

JOHN WARD

The Overhead Railway and Dock Road traffic (E. Chambré Hardman)

from *Man With A Plan*

(The play, Man With A Plan, was co-authored by George Garrett with other members of Merseyside Unity Theatre. It is set in Liverpool, from the Thirties' depression through the Second World War years to the first twelve months of uneasy peace).

LABOUR EXCHANGE QUEUE, 1932

B. Cheer up, mate. We'll all be working soon. Baldwin says prosperity's just round the corner.

A. Which corner?

B. He doesn't say which corner. He only says it's round the corner.

A. It'll be a hell of a time reaching this corner. This is dead-end corner.

B. I bet you're off the stones before I am. I haven't an earthly. Too old at forty!

A. Too old at forty! You're lucky, mate. I was too old at sixteen. Funny that, isn't it?

B. No, I...

A. Well, I didn't think it funny, see? Selling Echoes every night after school till I left. Then a butcher's boy. OK that was. Ten bob a week and a bit of meat on Saturdays. But at sixteen they have to stamp your cards. You wouldn't know that, Pop.

B. Look here, who are you?...

A. So at sixteen I was out of a job and I've been out ever since except for a day or two here and there.

B. Stop moaning, mate. We're all in the same boat.

A. Yes, a boat that's been on the rocks for years.

GEORGE GARRETT

173

George Orwell's impressions of Liverpool, 1936
from *"The Road to Wigan Pier Diary"*

27 February

On Wednesday (25th) went over to Liverpool to see the Deiners and Garrett. I was to have come back the same night, but almost as soon as I got to Liverpool I felt unwell and was ignominiously sick, so the Deiners insisted on putting me to bed and then on my staying the night. I came back yesterday evening.

I was very greatly impressed by Garrett. Had I known before that it is he who writes under the pseudonym of Matt Low in the *Adelphi* and one or two other places, I would have taken steps to meet him earlier. He is a biggish hefty chap of about 36, Liverpool-Irish, brought up a Catholic but now a Communist. He says he has had about 9 months' work in (I think) about the last 6 years. He went to sea as a lad and was at sea about 10 years, then worked as a docker. During the war he was torpedoed on a ship that sank in 7 minutes, but they had expected to be torpedoed and had got their boats ready, and were all saved except the wireless operator, who refused to leave his post until he had got an answer. He also worked in an illicit brewery in Chicago during Prohibition, saw various hold-ups, saw Battling Siki immediately after he had been shot in a street brawl, etc etc. All this however interests him much less than Communist politics. I urged him to write his autobiography, but as usual, living in about 2 rooms on the dole with a wife (who I gather objects to his writing) and a number of kids, he finds it impossible to settle to any long work and can only do short stories. Apart from the enormous unemployment in Liverpool it is almost impossible for him to get work because he is blacklisted everywhere as a Communist.

He took me down to the docks to see dockers being taken on for an unloading job. When we got there we found about 200 men waiting in a ring and police holding them back. It appeared that there was a fruit ship which needed unloading and, on the news that there were jobs going, there had been a fight between the dockers which the police had to intervene to stop. After a while the agent of the company (known as the stevedore, I think) emerged from a shed and began calling out the names or rather numbers of gangs whom he had engaged earlier in the day. Then he needed about 10 men more, and walked round the ring picking out a man here and there. He would pause, select a man, take him by the shoulder and haul him forward, exactly as at a sale of cattle. Presently he announced that that was all. A sort of groan went up from the remaining dockers, and they trailed off, about 50 men having been engaged out of 200. It appears that unemployed dockers have to sign on twice a day, otherwise they are presumed to have been working (as their work is mainly casual labour, by the day) and their dole docked for that day.

I was impressed by the fact that Liverpool is doing much more in the way of slum-clearance than most towns. The slums are still very bad but there are great quantities of Corporation houses and flats at low rents. Just outside Liverpool there are quite considerable towns consisting entirely of Corporation houses, which are really quite livable and decent to look at, but having as usual the objection that they take people a long way from their work. In the centre of the town there are huge blocks of workers' flats imitated from those in Vienna. They are built in the form of an immense ring, five

Liverpool dockers unloading fish

storeys high, round a central courtyard about 60 yards across, which forms a playground for children. Round the inner side run balconies, and there are wide windows on each side so that everyone gets some sunlight. I was not able to get inside any of these flats, but I gather each has either 2 or 3 rooms, kitchenette and bathroom with hot water. The rents vary from about 7/- at the top to 10/- at the bottom. (No lifts, of course.) It is noteworthy that the people in Liverpool have got used to the idea of flats (or tenements, as they call them) whereas in a place like Wigan the people, though realising that flats solve the problem of letting people live near their work, all say they would rather have a house of their own, however bad it was.

There are one or two interesting points here. The re-housing is almost entirely the work of the Corporation, which is said to be entirely ruthless towards private ownership and to be even too ready to condemn slum houses without compensation. Here therefore you have what is in effect Socialist legislation, though it is done by a local authority. But the Corporation of Liverpool is almost entirely Conservative. Moreover, though the re-housing from the public funds is, as I say, in effect a Socialist measure, the actual work is done by private contractors, and one may assume that here as elsewhere the contractors tend to be the friends, brothers, nephews etc of those on the Corporation. Beyond a certain point therefore Socialism and Capitalism are not easy to distinguish, the State and the capitalist tending to merge into one. On the other side of the river, the Birkenhead side (we went through the Mersey tunnel) you have Port Sunlight, a city within a city, all built and owned by the Leverhulme soap works. Here again are excellent houses at fairly low rents, but, as with publicly-owned property, burdened by restrictions. Looking at the Corporation buildings on the one side, and Lord Leverhulme's buildings on the other, you would find it hard to say which was which.

GEORGE ORWELL
in *The Collected Essays, Journalism and Letters of George Orwell
Vol. I, 1920-40*, ed. Sonia Orwell & Ian Angus (1968)

175

Liverpool Overhead Railway in the 'Thirties

Seventeen stations to Seaforth Sands,
their names a sort of History Quiz,
a mark for every one you knew:
Nelson, Clarence, Huskisson, Gladstone.
Journey's end, the *Caradoc* bar
and a congress of whores from Regent Road.
The Overhead drip-fed gutter-hungry
sailors, urgent to let the salt sea
out of their system for a night,
from ship to bar, from bar to bed,
and if their luck was in to ship again.
(If not, the lock-up, or a split head
and empty wallet down some dark ginnel.)

Six miles it stuttered and clattered over
bowstring bridges in which the gale sang.
To port, the river and half a hundred docks,
With piers, jetties, cranes, gantries,
and the lonely wail of sirens in sulphurous fog.
To starboard, empty warehouses,
as big as Pyramids; halftime mills;
mansions built from profit in slaves,
let out in rooms to lascar greasers,
firemen from Lagos and Accra:
bed, chair, no oilcloth on the floor,
two bob a week. The fleas came free.

Meccano-construct of some mad engineer,
less magic carpet, more aerial tram,
it served as butt for adenoidal jokes
by those Murphys and Quinns who scuffed its boards
in hobnailed boots, settled ample backsides
on varnished slats, spat on its floor,
were hidden in acrid smokescreens
laid down by their gnarled and spittled clays,
and at the drop of a hat wore the Green
to burnish stories of old hungers, rapes,
massacres and half-forgotten wrongs.

Had its uses by darkness, too.
Under its watertight umbrella,
lost souls slept in sacks, dreamt of jobs,
of food, and fire, and fields of lavender.

JOHN WARD

176

Early Days of a Scouse Mouse
from *George Melly's autobiography*

Surrounded by large late nineteenth-century houses, ringed by a sandy ride where middle-class little girls cantered self-consciously past on horses hired from a local riding school, Sefton Park forms a valley bisected by a string of lakes, the largest of which, 'The Big Lake', had boats for hire in summer and, when frozen in the winter, became black with skaters. On the other side of the lakes, dominating the landscape, is the Palm House, a large, circular, domed building of steel and glass in imitation of the Crystal Palace. When it was cold it offered a steamy refuge to expressionless men in bright blue suits and red ties, many of them missing an arm or leg. They were the institutionalized wounded of the 1914-18 war, and would sit all day smoking Woodbines on the fern-patterned Victorian benches. Behind them grew a contained circular jungle, its tropical trees and plants neatly labelled, and here and there, a small marble statue of a coy nymph or simpering maiden with a quotation from a poet carved on her plinth. In summer the men sat outside on similar benches.

Statues ringed the exterior also, life-size and representing historic figures in the arts and sciences. Before I could read, my father invented false identities for those frozen worthies. A Swiss botanist, he assured me, represented the Prince of Wales, while Galileo, holding a globe of the world, he maintained to be Dixie Dean, the celebrated footballer. Beyond the Palm House the park levelled out to form a great plain big enough to accommodate the annual fair; below it a steep hill swept down to one of the little lakes.

At the bottom of this hill were two stone posts aimed to discourage cyclists as there was then only a few yards across a road before the iron railings which ringed the water. I had at one time a small yellow motor car with push pedals and on one of our visits to look at Dixie Dean and the Prince of Wales my father made the following proposition. He would squat behind on the yellow pedal car, in itself a rather precarious operation, and we would then free-wheel down the hill between the posts whereupon I would have to turn the wheel abruptly to the right in order to avoid the railings. At five or six, for I can't have been any older, this seemed a perfectly reasonable if exciting thing to do, for I trusted Tom entirely and the danger didn't occur to me. We did it, gathering considerable speed, and shot between the posts missing the railings by a few inches. The mystery is that I cannot imagine what got into my father. It was most unlike him, and either or both of us could have been killed or badly injured. He told me not to tell my mother who 'wouldn't understand', and I never did. Perhaps though, like Maud's driving, it is a false memory.

The Park, like much of Liverpool, paid its reluctant homage to London. The sandy perimeter ride was called 'Rotten Row'. At the end of the 'little lakes' was a cast of Kensington Gardens' Peter Pan. During my childhood, a full-sized replica of Piccadilly's Eros was installed opposite the café at the bottom of the hill which led down from the Lark Lane gates. The café was rebuilt at the same time. The wooden 'Elizabethan' shack was replaced by a more solid art-deco structure. Peter Pan and Eros belong for me in Sefton Park. When later I saw the originals *in situ* I

177

thought of them as 'displaced'.

There was a Happy Valley and a Fairy Glen, a solemn statue of William Rathbone, after whom Uncle Willy was named, in a marble frock-coat, his hand on a marble book staring in side-whiskered indifference over the Big Lake.

If the park formed the 'landscape' of my childhood, the tram was its most potent presence.....

Rattling along Park Road for example - a street of smart shops, innumerable solid pubs and great soot-blackened Catholic churches - the cobbled, hilly streets of two-up two-down houses which led down to the river did so always at the same angle, and the horizon of the Mersey with its shipyard cranes on the other shore and the Welsh mountains beyond them remained fixed, imprinted on the memory with extreme precision. Trams were noisy. I could hear them whining and clanking from my bed in Ivanhoe Road, and occasionally a blue or green flash from some faulty electric contact would illuminate the night sky. The names of their destinations were printed on cloth and rolled into place behind a glass-fronted panel on both the back and front of the vehicle: Garston, the Dingle, Fazakerley, St Domingo's Pit, the Pier Head. ...

Liverpool people never called a tram a tram. It was either a tram-car or, more commonly, the car. 'I went into town like on the car.' The tram conductors had a certain bravura. They seemed to enjoy pulling on the leather strap, strung down the centre of the lower deck, which went 'ting-ting' in the driver's cabin. They cracked their ticket punches with enthusiasm, and shouted 'I theng yow!' when offered the fare (or 'fur' as most of their customers pronounced it). The late Arthur Askey adopted that 'I theng yow' as his slogan but few outside Liverpool knew where it came from. Tram conductors' fingers were black from handling the change in their big leather satchels. The tickets were very beautiful, rectangular, printed on slightly furry paper in faded colours, pink, pale green, beige, mauve, a washed-out blue. Painter Schwitters would have loved them. Children knew how to fold them in such a way as to construct concertinas. ...

In the late thirties the old red and cream trams were replaced by green

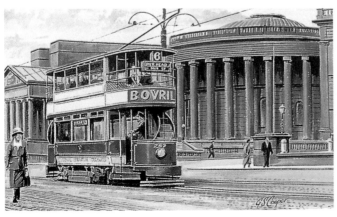

streamlined models with seat upholstery, springing and more silent machinery. They were called 'the Green Goddesses' and were considered an enormous improvement. They continued to run for some time after the war and were then scrapped in favour of buses. I never took to them. It's the old red bone-shakers which sway and clang through the Liverpool streets of my memory.

GEORGE MELLY
Scouse Mouse (1984)

Tram car passing the Picton Library and Museum en route to the Pier Head (G. S. Cooper)

Cautionary 'Traffic Nursery Rhymes', 1930s

Little Jack Horner
At Whitechapel Corner,
Crossed with the red light high:
He fell in the scrum,
And was lucky, by gum
To escape with a nasty black eye.

Mary, Mary, quite contrary,
That's not the way to go.
Just mind your step
As you pass the Rep.
Or a taxi will tread on your toe.

Came Jack and Jill
Down Brownlow Hill,
Much faster than they oughter:
And ere they could stop
At Lewis's shop,
Ran down the Adelphi porter.

in *My Liverpool*
by FRANK SHAW (1971)

At Formby

From that wide empty shore,
No foot had ever trod before
(Or since the sea drew back the tide),
I climbed the dune's soft slide
To where no higher than my hand
Wind-bitten pines grew in the clogging sand.

But farther from the beach
The trees rose up beyond my reach,
And as I walked, they grew still taller
And I myself smaller and smaller,
Till gazing up at a high wood
I felt that I had found my lost childhood.

ANDREW YOUNG
Collected Poems (1936)

The Conway *Bell*

Do you remember the *Conway,*
How sweetly she rose to the swell?
And the *Conway* Boys like clockwork toys
And the sound of the *Conway* bell?

To and fro on the ferry,
Caught in a magic spell
Of mast and spar and rigging we sailed
To the urgent calling bell.

The never ending pacing
To the engine's rhythmic pound,
Would pause as we passed the *Conway,*
And wait to catch the sound.

They towed her away from the Mersey;
They took her out of our care.
How could we bear to cross to school
And our own ship not there?

Beyond the Lightship Bar she sailed,
Beyond the Rip Rap buoy,
In Menai Strait to an alien shore
They moored our pride and joy.

She never returned to the river,
They let her drift away,
She broke her back, we broke our hearts,
And there she lies today.

Oh I remember the *Conway,*
Remember the tears that fell,
For part of childhood' s magic fled
With the *Conway* bell.

DORA KENNEDY

Evacuees with gas masks, boarding a train to leave Liverpool, 1939

The Blitz
from *Helen Forrester's Autobiography*

... Everyone in Liverpool needed as much strength as they could muster. That autumn, we endured over fifty consecutive nights of air raids. Brian, Tony, Avril and little Edward looked washed out and old, because of fear and lack of sleep. They never complained, however, and the three younger ones went to school daily, no matter how late they had had to sit up. Fiona was rarely at home during these raids; she continued her social life as if the bombings never occurred. She would return home after the raid was over, with stories of playing cards in hotel shelters or eating in a restaurant while the lights dipped from time to time, as the building rocked.

We worried when Brian was on duty during a raid. The more intense the attack, the more likely that telephone wires would be brought down, and the more messages he would have to carry through the pandemonium of the streets. A cyclist has not even the protection of a vehicle roof over his head; and, for once, Mother and I were united in our worries. He would turn up, however, soon after the all clear had sounded, covered with dust, eyes bloodshot, triumphant and cheerful, after having helped the police and wardens dig out victims.

After one particularly heavy raid, he breezed in rather later than usual, saying casually to our horrified mother, "Sorry I'm late. We had to find the heads."

Without the production of the head of a victim, a person could not immediately be pronounced dead — arms, legs, even torsos, did not count, and this caused boundless difficulties to many families. So, quite phlegmatically, seventeen-year-old Brian had been hunting heads at the site of a bad incident.

I wondered if the highly strung, imaginative little boy had really grown into an iron-nerved man, or whether he had just learned, of a necessity, to live with his fears. In any case, his experience as a police messenger must have helped to prepare him for the greater horrors he saw later in the Royal Navy ....

HELEN FORRESTER
Lime Street at Two (1985)

from *The Cruel Sea*

The corvett Compass Rose *comes into Liverpool, after a fortnight in the Atlantic, to find Merseyside shattered but unbowed at the end of the eight-day blitz in 1941*

Even far down river, at the Crosby Light Vessel, they knew that something was wrong, and as they made their way upstream at the tail of the convoy many of the crew clustered on the upper deck, shading their eyes against the strong May sunlight and looking towards the city they had come to know as home .

Morell, who was standing on the fo'c'sle with the men getting out the mooring-wires, trained his glasses up the river towards the Liver Buildings: there seemed to be a lot of smoke about, and here and there a jagged edge to the sky-line which he had never noticed before. ... At his side he suddenly heard Leading-Seaman Phillips exclaim: "Christ! It's copped a packet!" and then he smelt – they all smelt – the acrid tang of the smoke blowing down river, and his eyes, focusing suddenly on a big warehouse just above Gladstone Dock, discovered that it was split from top to bottom, that one half of it was a gigantic heap of rubble, that the rest was blackened and smouldering.

His binoculars, traversing steadily across the city and over to the Birkenhead side, showed him many such buildings, and scores of small houses lying ruined in the centre of a great scorched circle: there were fires still burning, there was a heavy pall of smoke lying over the northern part of the city, there were gaps, whole streets missing, rows of houses mis-shapen and torn.

He dropped his glasses, shocked by the scale of the destruction, the naked ruin of a city which they had left prosperous and unharmed; and then he caught the eye of one of his fo'c'sle party, a young seaman whose wife, he knew, had recently come to live in Liverpool.

"What's - what's it like, sir?" asked the man hesitantly.

"Not too good, I'm afraid." answered Morell. " It looks as if they've been raided several times."

The smoke and the dirty air, the smell of destruction, blew thick and strong across the river towards them: and such was their home-coming.

As they came alongside the southern quay of the dock-basin, a berthing-party of half-a-dozen men from the nearest destroyer ran along to meet them and to take their mooring wires.

One of the berthing-party, a tough, three-badge able-sea-man, looked up and grimaced.

"You've missed something, mate! " he shouted back.

"Eight nights on end - that's all we've had; bombers coming over every night as thick as bloody sparrows. They've made a right mess of this town, I can tell you."

"Go on," said Phillips. "What's got it worst?"

The A.B. gestured vaguely.

"All over, I reckon — Bootle, Birkenhead, Wallasey. And down in the town too; there isn't any Lord Street left — they got the lot, both sides. Worst bombing of the war, the papers said. I don't want any worse myself ... There was an ammunition ship just along-side here, blazing all over, but they towed her out into the middle of the river before she went up." He gestured again, more vividly. "Best dose of salts I've ever had . . . Give us your head-rope."

Presently, they were secure.

There were a lot of candidates for the telephone: a small procession of men, anxious to establish contact, queueing up outside the single dockside call-box, waiting patiently, not talking to each other. Ericson got through and spoke for a moment to his wife: she sounded subdued, but at least she was there. ... Ferraby, whose small house was on the outskirts of the city, had the same comforting luck: but Tallow, when it came to his turn. could not get his number at all, simply the high continuous note which meant " line out of order." When he was back on board and making a hurried toilet in the petty officers' mess before going ashore again, Watts said tentatively:

"I'd like to come with you, Bob."

Tallow, who was shaving, nodded his head. " Yes, Jim. You come along."

"They might just have damaged the telephone wires," said Watts after a pause.

Tallow nodded again. "It might be that."

But the nearer they got to the house, after crossing the river by ferry-boat, the more they knew that it was not that. From the landing stage they walked uphill towards the Dock Road, slowly because of the blocked roads and the rubble and glass and smashed woodwork which was strewn over the streets; the trail of wrecked houses and the smell of newly-extinguished fires was a terrible accompaniment to their journey. They did not talk to each other, because the cruel destruction was saying it all for them.

There wasn't a great deal left of Dock Road.

It must have been a stick of bombs, as neatly placed as the button-holes in a dress .... Tallow looked at the farthest point of destruction sick and hurt; he said, somewhere between surprise and fatalistic calm: " That's the one, Jim, I know it is," and started foolishly to run. Watts, possessed by the same urgency, kept pace with him, and they went at a steady jog-trot down the street; past the first lot of wrecked houses, past the second, past the crater in the roadway, and up to the last shattered corner. Number 27 was half ruined by blast; so was number 31. Number 29 had taken the full force of a direct hit.

No. 29 Dock Road ... Under the bright afternoon sunshine the wreck of the little houses seemed mean and tawdry; there was flayed wallpaper flapping in the wind, and half a staircase set at a drunken angle, and a kitchen sink rising like some crude domestic altar from a heap of brickwork. The house had collapsed upon itself, and then overflowed into the garden and the roadway; the broken glass and the rubble slurred under their feet as they came to a halt before it. It was not a house any more, this place where, between voyages, Tallow had been so comfortable and content, and Watts had stumbled out a halting proposal of marriage, and Gladys had made a warm cheerful haven for them all; it was simply a shapeless mass slopping over from its own foundation, a heap of dirt and rubbish over which drifted, like a final curse, the smell of burnt-out fire.

Some men — a rescue squad in dusty blue overalls — were picking over the ruins Iike scavengers who did not know what they were seeking.

After a moment of hesitation, Tallow accosted the nearest of them, a big man in a white steel helmet.

"How did it happen?" he asked.

Scarcely looking at him, the rescue man said: " Don't ask bloody silly questions, I'm busy."

"It's my house," said Tallow, without expression.

"Oh, ... " The rescue man straightened up. " Sorry, mate ... We get more bloody fools hanging round these jobs than I ever saw in my life."

He looked at Tallow with rough compassion. " Direct hit, this one. Middle of the raids — about five days ago. You been away?"

"Yes. Just got back."

By his side, Watts said: "We didn't know about this."

There was silence, while the dust stirred and settled. With an effort Tallow put his question.

"How about the people inside then?"

The rescue man looked away from him and across the street.

"You'd better ask at the warden's post, down there." He pointed. "They see to all that."

"But what about them?" said Tallow roughly. "Do you know, or don't you?"

This time the man looked directly at him, searching for words as he stared.

"You can't expect much, mate, not after this. We got them out. Two women. Don't know their names. Ask over there at the warden's post. They'll tell you all about it."

"Were they dead?" asked Tallow.

A moment of hesitation, then: "Yes, they were dead."

NICHOLAS MONSARRAT
The Cruel Sea (1951)

Barricade the Stars, *May Blitz, 1941*

Barricade the stars
for there must be no intercourse
between them and the light.
When the drone comes
crouch in the womb of the stairs,
and wait until the great bees
hold their breath.
Then if you close your eyes
you'll see death spurt
upon such waiting prey,
penetrating from a great height,
in a stinging climax of flame,
tearing open the seedbed
while gougeing out a rough grave,
there, where the bleeding broke.

BRENDA WALKER

Homecoming

Due on the tide, my father's rusted hulk,
weary from landings at Sicily, sailed
into blitzed Liverpool under the waving swords
of searchlights, into the flash and batter of
the ack-ack guns. Under a sky in panic,
into the erupting port, up-river he came
urging home his helpless and unspeaking love.

Next morning, docked, he slung his canvas bag
about his shoulders like a drunken mate, himself
unsteady in the smoking, settling air, and walked
into our street, turning the corner by
the foundry. The street was flattened - brick and wood
in scorched disorder. 'I thought that you were goners,'
he afterwards said, finding us safe up-town
at my grandma's house.

And I remember the last few days,
the quivering run-up hours to that street's death:
a five year-old and his mother hunched
under the stairs, with the fat chrome springs
of an obsolete pram jigging over my head
and plaster puffing white dust in our hair,
the sky droning and tingling blasts
as a neighbouring street went down.

'We moved that day,' my mother used to say,
'and that same night your dad came home.'
She prized the weird coincidence. It was
as if someone had given her flowers.

MATT SIMPSON

Wartime Merseyside
from *Helen Forrester's Autobiography*

In the dim electric light of Central Underground Station, we picked our way
carefully through families sitting or lying on the dusty platform - people were
easily incensed at passengers who brushed them when passing, or who trod on the
blankets they had spread to mark their space. The reek of urine, of babies who
needed their nappies changing, of old sweat, and musty clothing, was mixed with
the peculiar, clammy odour of underground railways, and the sound of a myriad

conversations rose and fell around us like the sea washing up on a shore. I thought with misgiving of the disease and vermin which could run through such a tightly packed crowd sleeping together, with inadequate lavatories and no water supply. It was only a very few years since we had ourselves finally got rid of body vermin, and I remembered how body lice could carry typhus, and how quickly influenza and typhoid could plague such a gathering.

Two feet from the edge of the platform had been kept clear by the station staff, for the use of passengers, and we waited there.

On the tram bringing us to the station, Mother had maintained a forbidding silence, and she continued frigidly silent, as we sat in the unlighted train, surrounded by an Air Force contingent. For servicemen, they were unusually quiet. They clutched bumpy-sided kit-bags and seemed to be festooned with other canvas bags hanging from their shoulders. I did not know then that close to Moreton was a Royal Air Force transit camp where men were collected prior to being sent overseas, and that the thought of being overseas was not always greeted with excited anticipation.

Looking down at my hands tightly clasped in my lap, I began to worry about how I was to get to work each day. There would be train fares from Moreton to Liverpool, I fretted, and then tram fares out to the Installation. I remembered the unbearable effort I had made to reach my work in Bootle. Would I have the same difficulties all over again?

There had been a time when I had looked out over the Mersey river and prayed to God to send me twopence, so that I could take the ferryboat across it and escape to grandmother's house. Now, it seemed a cruel joke that I should be passing underneath the river and was worried about getting back into Liverpool.

With eyes cast shyly down I sat tightly wedged between two tall servicemen carrying on a desultory conversation over my head. I began to tremble, and one of them looked down at me and asked if I was all right. Mother scowled at him from the opposite seat, and, after a sheepish grin at me, he resumed his conversation with the other airman.

The little train rattled out of the tunnel into fading day-light. Birkenhead Park and Birkenhead North. Memories of childhood journeys to Grandma's house overwhelmed me for a moment. Then Bidston, a country station, and Leasowe, a clean waste of fields. Moreton was the next red brick station, eight miles from the Birkenhead ferry. The airmen began to stir and haul their kitbags closer.

I had never been to Moreton. I had merely passed through it on the train. I knew that much of it was twenty feet below sea level and was, in those days, protected by a sea wall which was much admired by Dutch experts when they visited the village. As a child, and I had viewed with disgust the shanty town built between the railway and the sea wall after the First World War, by people who could find no other cheap place to live. I had been told that there was only one source of water there, to serve several hundred people, and I had seen that when there was heavy rain or a very high tide these miserable shelters were flooded.

Immediately adjacent to the station a neat village of council housing had been built, but some people still lived in the old shanties. The original village of Moreton was clustered round Moreton Cross about a quarter of mile away.

As we trudged silently towards the Cross that mild May evening, a familiar odour was borne on the clean breeze. I could smell the sea!

How wonderful it would be to run along the shore, dance in and out of the oncoming waves, and look for sea-shells again. Despite my worries, I took a big breath to savour the familiar odour, and my spirits rose.

We turned into a road lined with fairly new houses. Each had a front garden. In some there were more weeds than others - those would be the houses where the menfolk had gone to war—but in others, spring flowers were in full bloom. I could not remember when I had last seen tulips growing in a front garden.

We turned into a garden where the weeds were beginning to choke out the smaller plants. We crowded on to the porch.

Before Mother could get the key out of her handbag, the door was opened by a stout, white-haired lady. I stared at her, utterly confused.

In a soft Irish accent, she welcomed me effusively 'Come in, come in.' Then she realised my surprise, as I stepped over the doorstep, and said, with a note of puzzlement in her voice, 'Your Mam must have told you? I'm going to share the house with you. I was bombed out.' She ushered me into the modern little hallway.

'I didn't know,' I replied, as I shook her hand, and Mother, wearing her best society smile followed me in.

'Well, I'm Mrs Callaghan,' she told me. 'I met your Mam in the butcher's queue the other day, and we got talkin'.'

HELEN FORRESTER
Lime Street at Two (1985)

May Blitz, 1941 (Keith Medley). Bomb devastation in the city centre; the domeless Custom House is in the background.

187

This Game of War

"Come on, Ducks, play under the table,
and get your dolls in with you,
then when Gerry planes come over,
you'll be safe and sound, love.

See what Mum's got for your birthday
and your name on it and all.
Put it safe around your wrist now
and then they'll know who you are.

Sling gas mask over your shoulder.
Now Bren girl, don't take it off.
You may need it even in classroom
if Gerry drops the lot.

Wake up girl, the siren's going,
best take to the shelters tonight
I can hear Gerry over the city
and the sky's like bonfire night.

We can't go back to Gran's now
there was a fire next to the Pub,
bloody Germans dropped an
                incendiary
but thank God she's fine, love."

One day a German plane landed
in a field by the side of the road,
and when the pilot got out
I could see he was just like Dad.

I was too young to understand
                what I saw,
too young to say what I thought,
I just knew they'd got it wrong
this game of war.

BRENDA WALKER

In the Merseyside Blitz 1940-41, approximately 4,000 people were killed, 7,000 seriously injured, 184,840 houses damaged, 10,840 houses destroyed. On 14th May 1941, 1,000 dead were given a mass burial in a common grave at Anfield Cemetery. In Bootle, 16,000 of its 17,000 houses were damaged or destroyed.

Search for survivors in Virgil Street, Liverpool, after the raid of 9th & 10th January 1941.

188

from *The Dressmaker*

It was late August when Valerie Mander asked Rita to the party.

'Well, it's more of a sing-song, really,' she amended. 'But you'll enjoy yourself. Tell your Uncle Jack you're a big girl now.' And off she went up the street, swinging her hand-bag and tilting her head slightly to catch the warmth of the sun.

Rita had first seen her on the tram coming home from work, but she hadn't let on. She had been travelling since the Pier Head, wedged hard against the window near the platform. When the tram stopped opposite the bomb site that had been Blackler's store, she hadn't noticed the people boarding, only moved her feet to avoid being trampled, gazing out at the rumpled meadow on the corner of the city street; thinking of Nellie working there at the beginning of the war, on the material counter facing millinery, shearing with her sharp steel scissors through the yards of silk and satin and velveteen, taking such pride in the great bales of cloth, smoothing them with her hands, plucking with disapproval at the minute frayed ends. To no avail. When the roof split open, the prams and bedding spilled from the top floor to the next, mingling with Auntie Nellie's rolls of dress material, snaking out wantonly into the burning night, flying outwards higgledy piggledy, with the smart hats hurled from their stands, the frail gauze veils spotted with sequins shrivelling like cobwebs, tumbling down through the air to be buried under the bricks and the iron girders — covered now by the grass and the great clumps of weed that sprouted flowers, rusty red and purple, their heads swinging like fox-gloves as the tram lurched round the corner and began the steep ascent to Everton Brow. Only then did she glance up and see Valerie standing with one white-gloved hand raised to clutch the leather strap for support, her head swathed in a cream turban and a diamante button clipped to the hidden lobe of her ear.

*   *   *

Jack came to take them for a run in the car.

'One of these days,' warned Nellie darkly and left the room to fetch her coat.

'Don't you want a run out?' he asked when she returned, but she drew in her narrow lips and kept silent.

'I'm allowed a certain amount of petrol,' he said mildly.

'It's not right, Jack, and you know it, buying black-market stuff.'

'Good God, woman!' he exploded. 'Anyone would think I was the Gauleiter of Anfield, plundering the poor.' He felt quite nettled and put out.

'Take no notice,' said Margo, and told Rita to get her things on.

Nellie sat on the front seat beside him and he wound a rug about her knees. It was raining and the streets were gloomy; he didn't know where to go.

'Do you fancy anywhere special?' he asked Nellie, driving down Breck Road towards the cemetery and turning into Prescot Avenue. He would have suggested a cup of tea at Winifred's Cottage on the East Lancs Road, but it was a fair run and he didn't want another scene over his petrol ration.

'I want to go to the Cathedral,' said Rita, tapping his shoulder....

They were driving up Princes Road toward the Park, over-taking a solitary tram. The tall trees in the centre of the boulevard were heavy with rain. They swayed and dripped, turning the interior of the van into a green box full of shadows.

Marge was laughing in the back of the car. Jack looked in the mirror and saw her wiping her eyes with her handkerchief.

'What's up with you, Marge?'

'I just thought of that chappie from the Wirral with the short pants.'

'The what?'

'With the bike.'

'It was a tandem,' said Nellie, and her lips curved upward at the corner and she let out a little abrupt snigger.

'By heck,' said Jack delightedly, 'I'd forgotten him. With red hair - '

'And his mam rubbed his legs with goose fat to keep them ready for his bike - '

They were all laughing now....

They went down hill towards the river. Passing the old black houses built by the shipping owners, four-storeys high with pillars at the front door and steps of granite - occupied now by riff-raff: washing hung sodden on the wrought-iron balconies, a pram with three wheels in the gutter, a running herd of children without shoes. Some of the railings had been taken away to be melted down for the war-effort and there was wire meshing to stop people breaking their necks in the blackout. There was the new Cathedral rising like an ocean liner out of the sunken graveyard, tethered to its dry dock by giant cranes, coloured all over a soft and rusty pink. Rita wouldn't let him take her round to the front entrance. They parked on Hope Street and watched her push her way through a portion of broken fencing to the cemetery

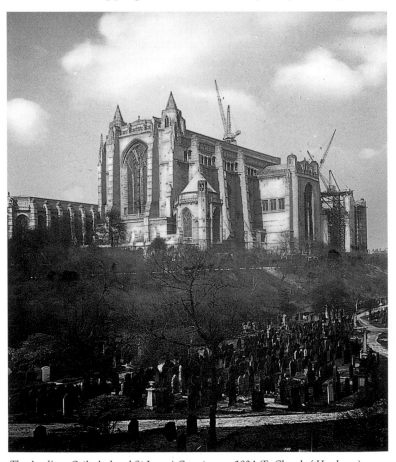

The Anglican Cathedral and St James' Cemetery, c. 1934 (E. Chambré Hardman)

BERYL BAINBRIDGE
The Dressmaker (1973)

Liverpool becomes the nerve-centre of the Battle of the Atlantic

Early in 1941, Winston Churchill gave orders for the Headquarters of Western Approaches Command to be transferred from Plymouth to Liverpool. At Derby House (Exchange Flags) the underground restaurant was converted into a huge operations room.

Winston Churchill described the Battle of the Atlantic as a war of groping and drowning, of ambuscade and strategy, of science and seamanship. Later he admitted that what most frightened him about World War Two was the U-boat menace. On this war at sea hinged Britain's fortunes. Allied shipping brought vital supplies, and if German Grand Admiral Doenitz's fleet cut the lifeline, Britain would almost certainly sink.

Merseyside was the core of that lifeline. The Western Approaches Command, whose job was to ensure safe passage of Allied shipping, had other sea-going bases, but none more important than Gladstone Dock. The heavy bombing which Merseyside had endured and the harrowing losses at sea only strengthened resolve to beat Doenitz....Captain Johnny Walker, ace U-boat killer, from Devon, who came to regard Bootle as a second home, reflected that determination as he set sail in sloops based at the Gladstone system, to the sound of his signature tune, 'A Hunting We Will Go'.... The plan's architect was Admiral Sir Max Horton, Commander-In-Chief, Western Approaches. He arrived on Merseyside in November 1942, already a naval legend....He was based at Derby House, the main plot and operations room of the Battle of the Atlantic. This headquarters below ground was protected by steel doors and 12 feet of concrete. Facing the great map boards, where every shipping movement was plotted, were the 'choir stalls', from which duty officers watched. Above them in the 'upper stalls', Horton analysed the battle day and night.

Derby House, or The Citadel, as it was called, had its own radio for communication with ships and aircraft. It was connected by cable with the U.S.A. and other countries. During the war, staff handled more than 30 million coded messages. Horton took over command at a crucial time. He planned to surprise the enemy in mid-Atlantic with co-ordinated counter-attacks by several highly-trained frigates working in groups with carrier-borne and long-range aircraft....

The Battle of the Atlantic went first one way, then the other. There was near despair at the toll wrought by the U-boats, but then jubilation as escort and support ships coming home reported more and more success ... in May, 1943 no fewer than 40 U-boats were sunk, and Doenitz sent out a signal recalling home his sea wolves. On May 23, 1943, the tide turned - a date in British naval history to rank equal to that of Trafalgar.

The lifeline of Britain was kept intact. During 68 months of war Allied shipping brought 19 million tons of food, one million tons of shells, bombs and ammunition, 66,000 tons of tanks and war vehicles, as well as petrol, cotton, iron and steel into Liverpool Docks - a remarkable achievement. 3.5 million British and 1.2 million American fighting men and women were transported from Liverpool.

JOE RILEY
from 'The Battle of Derby House' in *Front Line: When Merseyside Went to War*
(with the *Liverpool Echo*), September 1979

A Wren recalls her years of service at the Citadel
- Edith Pargeter's memories recorded by Harold Brough

Petty Officer Pargeter worked the first night watch at Derby House in 1941 through to the eve of the very last day of the war. The teleprinter room was a place of "noise, heat and frenzy" and she loved it....it was a time when there was nothing worth doing that was not aimed at winning the war. She resisted transfers and promotions to stay at the Citadel: "I wouldn't have missed it. All of it, not just the ending. It has left an honorable record. Girls fresh from school and 40 year-olds straight from bringing up a family learned in a few weeks to do jobs normally a couple of years in training, and did them amazingly well."

Her memories include the hunting of the *Bismarck,* "how every watch rushed on demanding 'Where are they now? What's happening?' until the great German battleship was caught and sunk."

She grew to love Liverpool for its force of character, superb musical and theatrical life. Even in the darkest days when British ships were sunk with depressing regularity, there was no atmosphere of depression. Even then there was a faith in ultimate victory....

While the city celebrated, work continued at the Citadel. But the frantic pace had slowed. Edith Pargeter says " we were able, in turn, to escape to the Pier Head to see and hear the ships blaring and blazing their victory."

HAROLD BROUGH, interview with EDITH PARGETER (Ellis Peters)
from 'In the Underground Citadel', in *Darkest Hour*
(with the *Daily Post*) February 1991

Say not the struggle nought availeth,
The labour and the wounds are vain,
The enemy faints not, nor faileth,
And as things have been they remain.

And not by Eastern windows only,
When daylight comes, comes in the light.
In front, the sun climbs slow, how slowly.
But westward, look, the land is bright.

ARTHUR HUGH CLOUGH

These lines from Clough's poem were
quoted by Winston Churchill in a wartime
speech.

V.E. Day, 8 May 1945.
Celebrations on Lime Street.

High Windows

No mines but always coal;
the smell of coal
and the smack in the mouth
of gas across black hills.
And, further on, squat dockside
cranes, their lines spun out
into the grey Mersey.

Bootle this, backstreet upon backstreet
upon backstreet and gaps
like missing teeth.
A hard-case place, proud
of its bomb scars,
of its fires in blitztime.

And here, from high windows,
above the sudden squares of grass,
the speckle of fog-lights poking
through the shapes of streets, I am
drawn to absences,
to spaces in the air
where buildings pressed and steam
blew from slithering trains,
where songs from pubs and parlours
rose and burst, and slow men
tugged horses, ringing,
over grinding lanes.

BRIAN WAKE

from *The City of Departures*

...When she came in sight of the Castle Street corner, she saw Tom standing, resting his hand and his left hip on a strong, unpolished walking-stick with a rubber tip. He was standing close to the windows of Austin Reed's. He never wore a hat, and now his hair glinted a very bright gold where the unimpeded sunshine fell on it. In his green tweed coat and his rumpled flannel trousers he looked, to a casual glance, what indeed he was: a student at a provincial university. He was tall, thin, and he held himself loosely in his still pose. Not many would have guessed that he had been a soldier and had emerged from his campaigns maimed in body and nerves. He did not see her approaching. He was staring southwards, to where, under the high vertical walls and towers of office buildings, James Street sloped away from the bomb damage down to the river, a narrow chasm of shadow thrust into the afternoon sunlight. She noticed he was stiff-faced and blank-eyed: that might be merely because he was tired of waiting, and tired of scanning the crowds for the sight of her. If she had had any common sense or consideration, if she had not been moidered by luxurious food and drink and the sympathetic generosity of Charles Thorneycroft, she would have boarded a tramcar outside the hotel and arrived punctually. She felt penitent and apologetic before she spoke.

When he saw her, Tom moved forward, shifting his weight rather clumsily on to his artificial leg. He smiled, and it was a boy's smile, sudden and radiant. But Nora had learned to watch his face closely and she noticed that the creases on his forehead and round his mouth did not fade completely away, and his eyes retained their sharp watchfulness.

She apologised for being late, and he waved his right hand, level with his waist, in a rapid gesture, sweeping her explanations aside as unnecessary. " Where shall we go ? " he asked. She ought to have thought about that before now....

At Castle Street, they were within a few hundred yards of the river. "Let's go over the water. It'll be crowded. But if you don't mind that... "

He started to walk towards the Pier Head. Nora suggested the Mersey Railway, half expecting that he would guess that she wanted to spare him the exertion of walking on hard pavements and jostling through the crowds on the ferry. Usually he resented anything which could be interpreted as pity or consideration for his lameness. But this time he agreed, saying they would be the sooner alone.

The under-river railway was draughty and cool, the air tinged with sulphurous odours: someone had once told her it smelled like the Metro in Paris. It carried them quickly to Birkenhead, and there they caught a bus, and in half an hour they were sitting on the heather on the crest of a small hill looking down on the broad turn of the Wirral Peninsula, with its sandy flats and undulating grassy dunes, as it thrust out seaward between the Dee and the Mersey estuaries. Below and around them were arable fields and pasture, farm buildings, heathland and villages, and on the shores the bleached whites and pinks and yellows of bathing huts and cottages. There were people about, but none near. They had the minimum of solitude they required. Far away on the long sea horizon two thin trails of smoke were visible; the ships, moving north, were already out of sight.

" Well," Tom asked, " what did they have to say ? "
She knew then what she had suspected for several days, that he was jealous of Charles Thorneycroft and Paul Beldon, jealous because they were older than he, and successful, well-to-do, established in the world.

* * *

... The hospital to which Tom Venables had to report was at Fazakerley, on the outskirts of the city, not far from the Aintree racecourse, a train journey of twenty minutes. After the examination, while the specialists conferred apart, he was glad to rest; the journey, short as it was, had tired him. What little he learned from the doctors was not reassuring. It was in an angry and despondent mood that he set out to catch the next train back to Liverpool.

When he came out from under the glass roof of the Exchange Station he saw Charles Thorneycroft, on the pavement outside, talking to an officer wearing the olive drab tunic and pinkish-fawn trousers of the American Army. He nodded and walked on as fast as his artificial leg and the pain in his back would allow. But almost at once he heard his name called. He stopped, and Thorneycroft came hurrying up.

" What did they say ? "

" Who ? "

" The doctors."

The tall youngster, leaning heavily on his stick, his big head uncovered, scowled as if he were about to demand, And what business is it of yours ?

JOHN BROPHY
The City of Departures (1946)

The new Empress of Canada, about to make her maiden voyage from Liverpool to Montreal, April 1961 (Keith Medley)

Chinese Liverpudlians

Da Bei Feng kitemaker

Liverpool's Chinese community is reputed to be the oldest in Europe and at one point was said to have been the largest in Britain. Located within walking distance of the city's South docks and initially contained almost exclusively within Cleveland Square and Pitt Street, the city's 'Chinatown', unlike those established in America, has never been wholly separate. The cosmopolitan character of the area in which it developed, coupled with the fact that, in the absence of Chinese women early Chinese settlers tended to marry women from within the locality, prevented its total isolation. In contrast with other dockland areas, the streets surrounding Cleveland Square and Pitt Street were home to people of a variety of nationalities. Scandinavian and African seafarers lived cheek by jowl with European Jews and Irish immigrants who fled persecution and famine respectively. Economic migrants from various countries on the Continent as well as those from Scotland and Wales, alongside temporary residents such as the Lascar seamen, also contributed to this multicultural jigsaw.

Although the exact date of the earliest settlement of Chinese immigrants in Liverpool is unknown, Chinese sailors first began to arrive around the middle of the nineteenth century. But why should the community develop in Liverpool first? The answer to this question has been thought to have related to the founding (in 1865) of the Ocean Steam Ship Company, more specifically, the Blue Funnel Line, the company behind the first direct steamship link between Britain and China. However, whilst the company was to become the largest single employer of Chinese labour, we must beware of equating its beginnings with that of the community... Chinese immigrants have been contributing to the port's economy, as well as its social and cultural life, since at least the last quarter of the nineteenth century....the community in its early years, did not consist solely of seamen....

The development of Liverpool's Chinese sector began with the opening of a few shops and services aimed specifically at the then embryonic community....a fairly wide variety of services were provided by enterprising Chinese people, some of whom settled here for very short periods. For example, in the early decades of this century there could be found a lodging house run by Chow Ghee; Ko Foo Kee, a chandler; Chow Too Kee, a huckster; Emily Ah Foo, a Chinese agent; Chong On a tailor; and Kwok Fong, a private detective.

Among the first services to be provided were the boarding houses which accommodated the thousands of seamen who began to pass through the port....

During the 1940s Liverpool, as the wartime headquarters of the Western Approaches, was the home of the Chinese Merchant Seamen's Pool which led to a massive expansion in the number of seamen based here. There are said to have been between eight and twenty thousand men registered and the majority of these appear to have come from Shanghai and other areas of the Chinese mainland....

As in other dockland communities, gambling was often seen by Chinatown's participants as a way to increase income ... The game of Pak a Pew ... The game of fan tan...for example, Edie's husband would sell his wares at The Nook and other establishments in Chinatown and then visit the gambling house afterwards...

Food featured highly in many aspects of Chinese culture. Belief in life after death had led to the development of elaborate funerary rites which are meant to prepare the deceased for the journey ...The funerals of the more prosperous Chinese people in Liverpool apparently followed national custom until around the 1940s:

> *There was a pig, a full pig, with all the food and rice, bags of rice and everything in the procession...and they buried them for the journey on. I was only young but I can remember they used to have open broughams and hundreds of wreaths....When F.S.'s first husband died, well they actually stuffed money down his throat ...ready for when he came back.* (interview)

The annual festival of Ch'ing Ming is yet another aspect of Chinese culture which maintained its currency for many years:

> *...they used to buy flowers, wholesale, the Chinamen, and they used to take all the kids up and all the Chinamen used to go up in taxis to Anfield Cemetery. We used to be thrilled to bits because we went in a taxi - with your dad and all your uncles, your suckies - and we'd have these boxes and we'd all run, throw a couple of flowers on each grave while the men would light the joss-sticks.* (interview)

MARIA LIN WONG
Chinese Liverpudlians - A History of the Chinese Community in Liverpool (1989)

Nelson Street, centre of the Chinese Community, today. The Nook is on the left.

197

The Mersey on a stormy day, with a high tide, September 1957. The Royal Iris approaches the Landing Stage and 'Green Goddess' trams are at the terminus. (Keith Medley)

The Empress of Canada passes New Brighton's Marine Lake (Keith Medley)

Arriving at Liverpool

How strange the landing at Liverpool, the Liver Building seen once more through the misty rain, that murk smelling already of nosebags and Caegwyrle Ale — the familiar deep-draughted cargo steamers, harmoniously masted, still sternly sailing outward bound with the tide, worlds of iron hiding their crews from the weeping black-shawled women on the piers: Liverpool, whence sailed so often during the war under sealed orders those mysterious submarine catchers Q-boats, fake freighters turning into turreted men-of-war at a moment's notice, obsolete peril of submarines, the snouted voyagers of the sea's unconscious . . .

MALCOLM LOWRY
Under the Volcano (1947)

Leaving

I loved it that morning
At seventeen knots
With its Cammell Laird beaches
And ferry-boat yachts.

I loved all the sunlight on the Pier Head glass
And the sound of the bell for the eight-o-clock mass
And the cranes like steel scarecrows clambering the side
And the dome in New Brighton as we passed on the tide.

I loved it that morning
When I left her for good
With salt-tears in my mouth
And gulls on the mud.

JOHN REYNOLDS

The Leaving of Liverpool

Fare thee well the Prince's landing stage
River Mersey fare thee well
For I'm off to Californ-i-a
It's a place that I know right well

Chorus
So fare thee well, my own true love
When I return united we will be
It's not the leaving of Liverpool that grieves me
But my darling when I think of thee

Extract from traditional song

199

The Manor House, Hale, near Liverpool

In early twilight I can hear
    A faintly-ticking clock,
While near and far and far and near
    Is Liverpool baroque.

And when the movement meets the hour
    To tell it, stroke by stroke,
"Rococo," says the pendulum,
    "Baroque, baroque, baroak."

Encrusted vases crowd the hall,
    Dark paintings grace the stairs
And from the wild wind's harp withal
    Sound soft Lancastrian airs.

On a bend sable three garbs or —
    Th'achievements hold my gaze;
Though fierce without the tempests roar
    The banner scarcely sways.

O'er Mersey mud and Mersey flood,
    Rust-red above the holly
How trimly rides the brick façade,
    As flimsy as a folly.

The Manor House, the Green, the church —
    From Runcorn to West Kirby
You will not find howe'er you search
    So sweet a *rus in urbe.*

JOHN BETJEMAN
Collected Poems (1958)

First Days of the Beatles

Once John and Paul had met, the nucleus of what would finally be the Beatles was nearly complete. Only guitarist George Harrison was missing, and he wasn't so very far away. George lived near Paul and, like him, went to the Liverpool Institute. They travelled in to school together every morning on the same bus route and changed buses at the Penny Lane terminal, at the intersection of Penny Lane with Smithdown Road, the main route into the centre of the city. The terminal was only small, it had a Ladies and a Gents, and there was a shelter place where the bus drivers sat in their break and drank cups of tea...

George was a little 'un, in the year below Paul, and looked more like twelve than fourteen. But he was music mad and that was enough, even when a school year was almost a generation gap, to make them friends out of school as well. They began spending much of their spare time together practising guitar chords until, through Paul, George joined The Quarrymen.

Paul told me: 'George was always my little mate. But he could really play the guitar, particularly a piece called "Raunchy", which we all loved.

The Beatles statues in Cavern Walks (Richard Lloyd-Jones)

'If anyone could do something as good as that, it was generally good enough to get them in the group.

'I knew George long before John and any of the others. They were all from Woolton, the posh district, and we hailed from the Allerton set which was more working class. George and I had got to learn the guitar together and we were chums, despite his tender years as it seemed to me then. In fact, George was only nine months younger than I was'...

George's formal audition took place on the top deck of a green Liverpool bus one summer day in 1957. This, says Paul, is what happened: 'George slipped quietly into one of the seats on this almost empty bus we were on; took out his guitar and went right into "Raunchy".

'Some days later, I asked John:"Well, what do you think about George?"

'He gave it a second or two and then he replied, "Yeah man, he'd be great!" And that was that. George was in and we were on our way.'

After that, all they ever did was practise and practise. 'Where are we going lads?' John would suddenly cry out in the middle of one of these sessions. 'To the top!' they all yelled back.

'What is that then?' was John's next line.

'Why, to the toppermost of the poppermost!' was the final exchange, the baby Beatles' war cry.

JULIA BAIRD with GEOFFREY GUILIANO
John Lennon, My Brother (1988)

from **No Trams to Lime Street, a television play by Alun Owen, 1959**

Three sailors disembark at Liverpool; they are, Alun Owen says,
'searching for themselves'. Extract from Act One.

ACT ONE

CASS is standing on the deck, looking out at the lights of Liverpool.
He breathes a sigh of contentment.

CASS   Isn't it marvellous, eh ! She's like the wink from a fancy woman ! Liverpool... the Garden of Eden of the North ... *(looking at his watch)* Eh up ... mustn't keep you waiting love ... *(He blows a kiss out to the city.)*
(He skips off down the ship, down the stairs and along the corridor, kicking one door, slapping another. He thunders on Billy Mack's door.)

CASS   *(shouting).* Billy Mack! William Mack Esq.!! Go to the top of the class and fill up the inkwells! Billy Mack! Billy!

BILLY   *(almost dressed, opening the door).* Oh, for God's sake, Cass — you're like a big, soft kid !

CASS   *(entering the cabin).* First night home in Liverpool and you're not ready yet !

BILLY   *(continuing dressing).* Some people have to work, like, for their living, y'know !

CASS   Go on, you're only the Second Engineer on this rotten old tub — you're not on the *Queen Mary*, son !

BILLY   If a job's worth doing ...

CASS   I know, it's worth doing well. Oh, change the needle. *(looking around the cabin)* Eh ... where's Taff, then?

BILLY   Having a shower, he'll not be a minute.

CASS   He better hadn't be! Anyroad, forget your work, Billy, we're home ! Liverpool's waiting like a turkey dinner with stuffing. Grab your knife and fork and let's get stuck in !

BILLY   All right, all right, keep your hair on. I'm nearly done.

CASS   Well, what'll it be ? A 1, a 33 or a 45 ?

BILLY   What are you on about now?

CASS   Which way d'y'want to go, son? Down Mill Street, down Park Road, or along the boulevard? Which tramcar ?

BILLY   You've done nothing but talk about Liverpool trams for the past two months.

CASS   Go on! Y'know you can't wait to gerron a tram. Ooooh — them old bone rattlers ! Umpty-umpty-umptyump ! All the way down to Lime Street ! *(imitating)* ' Pass right down the car please ! All change for Penny Lane !' *(Laughs.)* Past the Lyceum ...

BILLY   The old picture house ...

CASS   That's it. Kids' matinées on a Saturday avo — a penny bun and an orange!

	Rin-Tin-Tin the lightning warrior !
BILLY	Do we go past the big field?
CASS	Aye y'mean by me sister's school, the Sacré Coeur Convent.

BILLY	That's right. Now didn't they always have ...
CASS	Y'mean, the donkey in the field ! *(Laughs.)* Of course they did ... Many a time I tore me breeches pinching a ride when I was a kid !
BILLY	*(smiling).* I bet you did !
CASS	And how about all the churches along the boulevard, eh? Our lot, your lot, 'Scotch Orange', Synagogues, Welsh Chapels ... even a Greek one ...
BILLY	Oh aye, they're very religious up here, y'know ! *(They both laugh.)*
CASS	Oh, and there are some lovely boozers up here and all ! Well me old skin, in about half an hour's time we'll be off that tram and up and down Lime Street. We can dump Taff off at that Merchant Navy place.
BILLY	Y'mean the Atlantic Club ?
CASS	Aye, that's right. Then you and I can go and have a few beers and then go back and collect Taff and take him somewhere for a bloomin' good meal.
BILLY	*(deliberately).* Look, Cass, before we start this 'few beers and a bloomin' good meal' caper, I want to tell you something. I've got some private business to attend to first.
CASS	Private business? It's the first I've heard about it.
BILLY	Well I have. It'll only take about half an hour, then I'll meet you in that big pub off Duke Street — what's it called ?
CASS	The Welsh Harp? Oh aye, that's a smashing pub. But where are you going to ?
BILLY	Mind your own business.
CASS	I didn't mean to be nosy ... *(Grins.)* I just wanted to know where you're going.

ALUN OWEN
No Trams to Lime Street

After transmission of No Trams to Lime Street (1959)
Alun Owen's reply to complaints about his use of the Liverpool accent

. . I have made recordings of my own family - who live in Liverpool - and they just won't believe they are hearing their own voices. I have fought for two years now to get plays performed in the Liverpool accent. I've had a battle to get a love scene played in the dialect. I was told the accent was ridiculous, comical, absurd and very ugly. But I believe it is a very lovely accent. People get married, live and die using the Liverpool accent, so I see no reason why they should not make love in the Liverpool accent. I could quite easily have set this play in some never-never land of the north with everybody talking like Gracie Fields. ...

ALUN OWEN
Liverpool Echo (1959)

William Brown Street (Keith Medley). Walker Art Gallery, Picton Library, Museum (right); the Steble Fountain, St. John's Gardens, Mersey Tunnel entrance (left).

Architects plant their imagination, weld their poems on rock,
clamp them to the skidding rim of the world and anchor them down to its core; ...

They see through stone, they cage and partition air, they crossrig space
with footholds, planks for a dance; yet their maze, their flying trapeze
is pinned to the centre. They write their euclidean music standing
with a hand on a cornice of cloud, themselves set fast, earth-square.

A. S. J. TESSIMOND
from 'Earthfast'

PART FOUR

*"Liverpool... is at the present moment the centre
of the consciousness of the human universe."*

ALLEN GINSBERG

*"Don't want to go to Kirkby,
Skelmersdale or Speke,
Don't want to go from all I know
in Back Buchanan Street."*

GORDON & HARRY DISON

*"If Liverpool can get into top gear again
there is no limit to the city's potential..."*

IAN NAIRN

Liverpool *after William Mc Gonagall*

O Liverpool on the Mersey River
Noble city, how I shiver
With pride at the thought of your history
And your great men who are gone
Like Huskisson, and Mr Gladstone.
After each you have named a dock
From Bootle to the Liver clock
And some miles further on,
Even to Dingle and gay Garston.

You are the second greatest port
                          in all the land,
And your population runs to eight hundred
                          thousand.

Twenty miles of busy docking
Thanks to all the good men working
On them. The brave stevedores
And men in crane-driving
Have helped to make this great port thriving.

Your flour mills and other famous industries,
Biscuit, pea, soap and sugar factories,
All play a very important part;
And of all industrial south-west Lancashire,
Liverpool is the very heart.
Noble city astride the River Mersey,
I am sure we all salute thee.

ROGER MCGOUGH

Of Scouse and Scousers

Scouse - or to give it its full title, Lobscouse, is of course a food rather than a dialect; it is the native dish of the Liverpudlian, or Scouser. Scouse is to Liverpool what Bouillabaisse is to Marseilles or the Schnitzel to Vienna, but unlike many other dishes identified with their place of origin Scouse is derived not from a gourmandising love of food, but from sheer grinding poverty. It is a simple stew...

The etymology of Scouse or Lobscouse is, like so many Liverpudlians, of uncertain origin, though of greater antiquity than is generally supposed. It seems always to have been something of a joke: Ned Ward, the London gossip writer, in 1706 writes in his *Wooden World Dissected,* "He has sent the fellow to the Devil that first invented Lobscouse"...The Oxford English Dictionary defines Lobscouse as "a sailor's dish of meat stewed with vegetables and ship's biscuit or the like" and a Lobscouser as "a sailor, a tar".

But somehow the word did not look like an English one. I discovered a clue, if not an answer, in a large, nearly a century old, German cookery book that had belonged to my mother: **Labskaus** (Sailor's dish, original recipe)...Brockhaus, the German Encyclopaedia Britannica... declares Labskaus to be "a Norwegian sailors' dish of salt beef or fish, with mashed potatoes". ...We may, therefore, safely conclude that the origin of Lobscouse is to be found in some ship's galley on the high seas; it matters little of which nationality, for sailors had a habit of giving international status to their songs, their yarns and certainly their diseases.

There is, however, nothing insipid or soft about the Scouse that is spoken rather than eaten. ...Scouse is unique, highly evocative and often deliciously witty, but no one can say that it is beautiful.

Cartoon by Lindsay Coles

*

A Scouser is a Merseysider who conducts his ordinary, everyday conversations in Scouse, complete with the correct cold-in-the-head intonation and to the accompaniment of all the appropriate nods, winks and elbow-digs. A Scouser is not necessarily a Liverpudlian though the odds are in favour of it....It should not be (but is) necessary to say that not all Merseysiders speak Scouse. Some come from places like Llanbrynmair or Llanfaircaereinion or Penrhyndeuddraeth and are able to pronounce a mysterious foreign word like *twlldene*. Some speak Glasgow or Edinburgh Scotch or plain, ordinary *och awa'* Scotch...

Above all there is the pride and joy of official and socially conscious Merseyside, namely many enclaves of people who *talk proper* or think they *talk proper* or are believed to *talk proper*.

FRITZ SPIEGL
Lern Yerself Scouse, Vols One and Two (1990 reprints)

Scouser's Birthday Card

Toodaze yor sumpink berfdee, Ma,
I want yer terrav a gud time,
So t' cheer yer up on yer berfdee, Mam,
I've rittf yer diss pome.

MATT SIMPSON

The Beatles on the Mersey Ferry

In My Life

There are places I'll remember all my life,
Though some have changed,
Some forever, not for better,
Some have gone and some remain.

All these places had their moments,
With lovers and friends I still can recall,
Some are dead and some are living,
In my life I've loved them all.

JOHN LENNON AND PAUL McCARTNEY

The Mersey (Keith Medley)

An architect's response to Liverpool

June 1964

...the city seems to have wakened out of a drugged sleep. Everyone knows about the Mersey Beat, but this could not have been so successful if it had not been a symptom, drawing its vitality from some common resurgence... if Liverpool can get into top gear again there is no limit to the city's potential. The scale and resilience of the buildings and people is amazing - it is a world city, far more so than London or Manchester. It doesn't feel like anywhere else in Lancashire: comparisons always end up overseas - Dublin, or Boston, or Hamburg.

The city's structure is tremendous, and so, right up to the First World War, were the abilities of the architects who built over it - the less said about the last forty years the better.... The centre is humane and convenient to walk around in, but never loses its scale.

And, in spite of the bombing and carelessness, it is still full of superb buildings. Fifty years ago it must have outdone anything in England.

...joy and duty met in the Gothic building which is somehow the true heir of Liverpool's classic tradition. The Anglican cathedral was won in competition by the young Giles Gilbert Scott and begun in 1903. His inspiration was Spanish, his own descent was impeccably academic. Yet he not only caught the spirit of Gothic, but the spirit of Liverpool too. The first part to be finished, the Lady Chapel, is a *tour de force* of recollection that might belong anywhere. But the rest of the cathedral, which is still being built two years after the designer's death, is part of Liverpool in its immense warmth and open-heartedness.

Half a mile to the north, Frederick Gibberd's 'crusader's tent' is going up on the vast crypt of Lutyen's design for the Roman Catholic cathedral....

I have kept off the Beatles because I don't want to add more than I can help to the nonsense that has been written about them. But I do know that the exuberance and defiant grandeur of a song like "Twist and Shout" brings this great place like a gust of sharp air into the comfortable, leafy, slightly soggy London square where I am writing this. The Mersey glints sullenly in the haze, cargo boats hoot, seagulls scream, and scouse pies are on sale in The Vines. Ee-ay-addy-oh, this city's got me hooked.

IAN NAIRN
Britain's Changing Towns (1967)

Mrs Albion you've got a lovely daughter
(for Allen Ginsberg)

Albion's most lovely daughter sat on the banks of the Mersey
    dangling her landing stage in the water

The daughters of Albion
    arriving by underground at Central Station
    eating hot ecclescakes at the Pierhead
    writing 'Billy Blake is fab' on a wall in Mathew Street

    taking off their navy-blue schooldrawers and
    putting on nylon panties ready for the night

The daughters of Albion
    see the moonlight beating down on them in Bebington
    throw away their chewing gum ready for the goodnight kiss

sleep in the dinnertime sunlight with old men
    looking up their skirts in St John's Gardens

    comb their darkblonde hair in suburban bedrooms
    powder their delicate little nipples
    wondering if tonight will be the night

    their bodies pressed into dresses or sweaters
    lavender at The Cavern or pink at The Sink

The daughters of Albion
    wondering how to explain why they didn't go home

The daughters of Albion
    taking the dawn ferry to tomorrow
    worrying about what happened
    worrying about what hasn't happened
    lacing up blue sneakers over brown ankles
    fastening up brown stockings to blue suspender-belts

    Beautiful boys with bright red guitars
    in the spaces between the stars

    Reelin' an' a-rockin'
    Wishin' an' a-hopin'
    Kissin' an' a-prayin'
    Lovin' an' a-layin'

Mrs Albion you've got a lovely daughter

ADRIAN HENRI

Limestreetscene '64

Turned left into Lime Street
felt small
like a pelota ball
St George's Hall
black pantheonic
like a coalman's wedding cake
glows in the neonic
presence of Schweppervescence
and 'Guinness is good for you'

Proud buses turn up Skelhorn Street
and vomit and dribble up the hill
once more to fill
their 'no smoking' 'spitting forbidden' bellies.
Ahoy Doris, docker's delight
with cheeky breasts and indelible lips
tempting by
smart as paint
from your evilheels
to your brothelblackhair
laying a perfumed trail of gin
Irish linen and men

Outside the Chinese cafés
like buddhas bouncers stand
lest a band
of teds or sailors
or drunken Viking whalers
should seek to violate the chow mein
and trample on the waterchestnuts

Turned left into Brownlow Hill
felt big
as a pig

ROGER MCGOUGH

211

Seascape

gulls kiss the sun
and you walk on the beach
afraid of the tide

from the sea's warm belly
a lobster crawls to
see if we've gone

but mouths still talk
and finding out my lips
I say to you:

'lie silently
and stretch out your arms
like seaweed strangled by the wind'

out of a seashell
a sandcrab pokes his head
and sniffs the salt wind

now afraid we sit in silence
and watching the sun go down
I ask you your name

BRIAN PATTEN

New Brighton beach, ferry and pier, 1960 (Keith Medley)

The Liverpool Scene

The 'Liverpool scene' seems to have been born in the very early sixties....Any discussion of Liverpool poetry has to turn soon enough to the city itself....very much present in most of the poems - not only its various monuments, the street names and so forth, but in the very turns of speech and the attitudes to life which they express....Liverpool knows its own standards and imposes them firmly. Its inhabitants are gifted with a famous sarcasm.

...the success of the Beatles had a seismic effect on provincial culture as a whole. For the first time London had been left out in the cold till the very last minute. The upsurge of the groups went on for a long time after the Beatles had established themselves as international idols. The journalists and investigators came, and entertainers in Liverpool were suddenly provided with an acceptable identity.

Some of this glory was reflected on to the poets. If poetry was a branch of show business, it became, in Liverpudlian terms, respectable....poetry in Liverpool is more uninhibitedly colourful, more deliberately 'public', than at any other place in the British Isles.

ED. EDWARD LUCIE-SMITH
The Liverpool Scene (1967)

Roger McGough:

At the readings we did every Monday night at Samson & Barlow's the kids didn't look on it as Poetry with a capital 'P'; they looked on it as modern entertainment, part of the pop movement. They may go away crying, or they may go away very sad, but it was a certain experience to them, all part of experience.

ROGER MCGOUGH talking to EDWARD LUCIE-SMITH
The Liverpool Scene (1967)

from **In My Liverpool Home**

I was born in Liverpool down by the docks
My religion was Catholic, occupation hard knocks.
At stealing from lorries I was adept
And under old overcoats each night we slept.

Chorus
In my Liverpool home, in my Liverpool home
We speak with an accent exceedingly rare
Meet under a statue exceedingly bare
And if you want a cathedral we've got one to spare
In my Liverpool home.

PETER MCGOVERN

from *Prize Giving*

PLACE OF BIRTH .... Liverpool
FATHER'S OCCUPATION .... Carter
MOTHER'S SIGNATURE .... An X
ADDRESS ... Clancy's Boarding House, Hunter Street.

She was English by an accident. They skitted her about it back in Mayo - because she was so pale.

''Twas the English air,' her mother always said.

The date on her birth certificate seemed to grow larger, more entrenched with age.

'Surely that can't be right,' she had thought, genuinely shocked, the last time she had looked at it before stowing it away, back out of sight but not mind, into the darkness of the cold box. That was where they both belonged, somewhere out of sight where they would not be an embarrassment to their daughter.

They sat in at night; Siobhan doing homework, always reading always studying. In the corner the television showed them pictures of ideal families selling toothpaste and cornflakes, laughing with perfect teeth. They became comfortable in their seclusion.

They used to go out. When they were courting they went dancing. Saturday nights were spent at the Grafton Ballroom covered in moving flecks of light from the crystal ball and the feel of the smooth waxed floor underfoot. She remembered the smell of brillantine on the neatly combed hair of her partners as she stepped out with them to take the floor. She had been a fine careful dancer in those days, but he had the two left feet of a ploughboy and only danced on sufferance. She enrolled him for a course of lessons at Billy Martin's school of dancing but he said he felt embarrassed walking round a room counting 'one two three turn, one two three turn,' and everyone going in different directions. When she married him the dancing stopped. They had few excursions out together. He was not a drinker and although she would not have liked him to go off on his own and come in late smelling of beer and urine like her own father used to, she would nonetheless have enjoyed an occasional trip to the pub. But the more they hid themselves the more difficult it was to break their habits.

When they arrived at the hall there were already groups of people standing around outside in loose gatherings, talking comfortably together, recognising old acquaintances. Glossy, poised and perfect toothed. He felt her hold his hand as the courage drained out of him. Were they the only couple who did not know anybody? The doors of the foyer were wide open to the street on such a fine summer's evening.

His vision swam in the yellow light travelling from the sleeping docks out across the waterfront. It spread over the city bathing everything from the warehouses to the neat new council flats, mushrooming around the industrial estate, in a golden gleam of prosperity. At the Pier Head night-workers waited for the factory buses to take them out for their shifts, while in the distance, but never too far away, the dark slump was baying as it steadily advanced.

At the top of Brownlow Hill the cranes stood out against the skyline. The foundations for the new cathedral had been laid and the first stage of building was over. The crypt was finished, white walled and modern.

Two Cathedrals and the University tower.

'We talk with an accent exceedingly rare,
Meet under a statue exceedingly bare,
And if you want a cathedral
We've got TWO to spare,
In my Liverpool home.'

The audacity of the people, changing the words of the song before it was even finished! He wondered if he would see it in his day. The Anglican cathedral was still not complete after all that time. Cathedrals would not be rushed. At least the Anglicans had built theirs to look like a church, somewhere to go and pray in. The plans for theirs made it look like a space rocket. It would be like going to mass at a launching site. The Orange Lodge were going to have a bloody field day, he thought.

'Well, serves us right.'

He ached trying to move with the times, but how could he when it all got so fast like an uphill rush? His ecumenism was the sort that would live and let live as long as he was not expected to change. He did not mind the idea of Siobhan playing mixed games with a C of E school as long as she was safely back on the school bus to her own Catholic classroom at the end of it.

He felt he had lived all his life by divisions. His own country was divided. The boundary around the North may have just been a red line drawn on maps, but it made it into a different world. The people like goldfish that swelled or shrank according to their habitat, had become diverse. There was something about the set of the eyes of the Ulster Irish, a world-weary thing. His mother used to tell the old story of how Fintan from the seat of Tara had allocated all things to the separate provinces when Ireland was divided up. To the North was bequeathed conflicts and assault, so that Ulster should be ever battle-scarred and torn. He knew it was just a matter of time before it would all flare up again like the rising in the South. Now he lived in a divided city, torn by religion, its peoples needing two football teams for their different loyalties. It annoyed him when he saw the message on the wall changed to read 'God bless our Popeye'. It hurt him to see how little respect there was between them. The white walled monument rising from the rubble where the workhouse had once stood was important to him.

'This is the first time,' he told Siobhan, 'that two Cathedrals will face each other, recognising the other's existence and bowing with dignity.' Deep down he feared that theirs would not look half as dignified.

MOY McCRORY
from *'Prize-Giving'* in *The Water's Edge and other stories* (1985)

215

The Metropolitan Cathedral of Christ the King, at the northern end of Hope Street.
"A Cathedral in Our Time" - Archbishop Richard Downey

A Street Named Hope

High on a sandstone ridge, at one end of a street named Hope, Liverpool men have been toiling for over sixty years to build the biggest Anglican Cathedral in Britain and one of the six largest cathedrals in the world. Half a mile away at the other end of the same street, a second cathedral - the Roman Catholic Cathedral of Christ the King - was consecrated on Whit Sunday 1967. Thus, Liverpool, hard-as-nails Liverpool, bold-as-brass Liverpool, demonstrated to the world that beneath its tough exterior there beats a God-respecting heart. Liverpool will in the future be known throughout the world as the City of Two Cathedrals.

Alan Brack
Liverpool '67

216

Poem for the opening of Christ The King Cathedral, Liverpool

O Lord on thy new Liverpool address
let no bombs fall
Gather not relics in the attic
nor dust in the hall
But daily may a thousand friends
who want to chat just call

Let it not be a showroom
for wouldbe good Catholics
or worse:
a museum
a shrine
a concrete hearse
But let it be a place
Where lovers meet after work
for kind words and kisses
Where dockers go of a Saturday night
to get away from the missus
Tramps let kip there through till morning
kids let rip there every evening

Let us pray there
heads held high
arms to the sky
not afraid and kneeling
let Koppites
teach us how to sing
God's 'Top of the Pops' with feeling

After visiting you
may trafficwardens let noisy parkers off
and policemen dance on the beat
Barrowmen knock a shilling off
exatheists sing in the street

And let the cathedral laugh
Even show its teeth
And if it must wear the cassock of dignity
then let's glimpse the jeans beneath

O Lord on thy new Liverpool address
let no bombs fall
Keep always a light in the window
a welcome mat in the hall
That it may be a home sweet
home from home for all.

ROGER McGOUGH

After the baths

Time for the crier to clear the pool
And for the water to be still
And for the cubicles to dry out for morning.

Time for the boy and girl to walk down to the shore
And smoke quietly in the dusk
And not worry when the last bus is leaving.

Time to watch a tug move slowly past the lighthouse
And headlights flash on the promenade
And Liverpool to stand like a lighted train along the opposite shore.

Time to smell the tide on the sea-weed sand
And damp hair
And to cling together unbalanced by the stars.

Time for fish-pale bodies at the water's edge to be still
And for the night to run cool
And to rejoin the raucous town behind the baths.

JOHN REYNOLDS

The Estuary

A Nobby (Gladys Mary Coles)

Widening waters
whose sheltering lands
mist-wrapped on dew-sprung days
drop to the sea
while gulls and clouds
people the air.

So shall it be.
The tide will come
at each appointed time
to wash away the debris
cover up the slime
bear the little boats
far out to sea.
And fishermen
will glimpse their sails no more
but know they are not lost
if no longer
on this shore.

PEGGY POOLE

from **Meridians**

I am far enough from the river to be insulated from the atmosphere of fading maritime grandeur but it is impossible to be totally unaware of it; most of the big houses and their spacious rooms that make for the best parties, were originally built with money from the sea. Cotton money. Slave money.

Mirror, mirror on the wall. Whose party is this? The rooms are large, very large but although they are filled with people, the film has stopped running. In the huge, crowded kitchen the heads are still, the mouths silent, the fingers frozen to the glasses. In the large oval mirror I can see a brown dog asleep on a bed. At the corner of this still life my eye catches an impudent movement and a small black boy comes, pushing his way between petrified legs, playing on a penny whistle.

In the second room, larger than the first, the figures sit or stand in silent groups, locked into their stations by the two nightmare wooden puppets strung on the wall. Barbaric chessmen collect dust beneath the bowls of hyacinths. The mirror shows the back of a young man seated at a soundless piano and the black boy comes walking among the shadowy tableaux beating a drum.

The third room is as dark as a slave ship's hold, the couples stand motionless, oblivious to the heavy rhythmic beat of the amplifier's bass and in their midst the small black child dances and dances.

JIM MANGNALL
Meridians (1985)

The Last Resort

The slow meat grinder sea corresponds to soap suds, frothing
himalayas of a vulturous eye, a fumy resurrection
devoutly to be wished, the nauseous opiates
of a prickling humility, stinking to high heaven
with planetary grief, while close at hand
a barbarous viridian communes
with mushy peas on nightly promenades.

Behind diaphonous drapes along laburnum drives
gothic enormities perpetuate themselves -
while you wait antique glass guillotines
pronounce our names as death
stands mourning in us as we trudge the shore.

HENRY GRAHAM

from the comedy *The Liver Birds*

ACT ONE. Time - The present.

The action takes place in the living room of a ground floor flat in Liverpool. The general atmosphere of the decor is cheap and cheerful.

As the curtain rises it is obvious that it is the morning after a party. Plates, bottles, glasses, mugs and odd paper streamers are strewn about the set. The curtains are partly drawn, so the full morning light is somewhat obscured. After a moment **Sandra Hutchinson** *enters from the bedroom in her nightdress and a flimsy dressing gown. She is a very attractive girl of about twenty. She walks over towards the window.*

SANDRA:	*(calls to bedroom)* Beryl, did we have a party last night? *(There is no reply, so she opens the curtains and light streams into the room. She shields her eyes then looks around the room.)*
SANDRA:	*(contd.)* We had a party last night. *(There is a ring at the door.* **Sandra** *goes to open the door.)*
PAUL:	Hi, Sandra. (**Paul** *enters. He is a good looking young man of about 25.)*
PAUL:	I've come down to help you tidy up.
SANDRA:	You're early, it's only ten o'clock.
PAUL:	Well I thought the earlier I got here the more I'd be able to do.
SANDRA:	But I haven't had time to dress yet.
PAUL:	*(puts an arm round her).* I thought of that too. As a matter of fact living in the flat above it's difficult to think of anything else.
SANDRA:	Half of me is still asleep.
PAUL:	Don't worry. I'll concentrate on the other half.
SANDRA:	Look have you come to tidy up or what?
PAUL:	Well if there's a choice I'll have "what".
SANDRA:	Paul love I'm not very good in the morning.
PAUL:	Ah well that's where we differ. I'm at my peak in the morning. It's a well known fact that in the early hours a man is a bundle of enthusiasm.
SANDRA:	Good, well get enthusiastic about this lot *(indicating room).*
PAUL:	Right, well before I start there's a small service charge.
SANDRA:	What is it?
PAUL:	Just a little cuddle.
SANDRA:	Oh go on then. *(He cuddles her.)*
PAUL:	Plus V.A.T.

He kisses her as **Beryl Hennessey** *enters from the bedroom. She is in her early twenties, small, blonde and cheeky. What she lacks intellectually is made up for by her typical North Country drive and wit. She is wearing pyjamas and her hair is in rollers, with some green paper streamers caught up in them. She yawns, stretches and then sees* **Sandra** *and* **Paul** *kissing.*

BERYL:	Oh crikey, haven't you gone yet?
SANDRA:	He's just dropped in to help us tidy up.

220

BERYL:	He's always dropping in. I wonder you don't fix a fire-man's pole through that ceiling.
PAUL:	I'm working on it. Smashing party Beryl, you ought to have birthdays more often.
BERYL:	I'm glad you enjoyed it, 'cos it's the last one I'm going to admit to.
SANDRA:	It was lovely Beryl, you got all those presents and birthday cards.
BERYL:	*(going to the mirror).* The way I look, next year they'll be sending me get-well cards.
SANDRA:	Well take your rollers out, it's so undignified.
BERYL	*(looks at herself):* I don't remember putting them in. *(Suddenly)* Hey, me highlights have gone green.
PAUL:	Yes, well someone kept chucking streamers about. *(He starts to clear up).*
BERYL:	*(trying to remember):* Oh yeah, that's right. Idiot. Then they tried to do a clog dance on the sideboard.
SANDRA:	Yes.
BERYL:	And sang "Jesus Christ Superstar".
SANDRA:	That's right.
BERYL:	And to crown it all they tried to balance a jelly on their head. Nearly ruined my party they did.
SANDRA:	Well we did try to stop you Beryl.
BERYL:	Was it me?
PAUL:	'Fraid so.
BERYL:	Oh what a shame, I missed it.
SANDRA:	I think you had more to drink than normal.
BERYL:	I must've had a whole glass of wine.
SANDRA:	Anyway it cheered you up didn't it?
BERYL:	What?
PAUL:	You know, made you forget your troubles.
BERYL:	That's typical of you two isn't it. You think one little party can cure everything. But let me tell you something, if you think it only takes one glass of wine and a clog dance to make me forget my troubles then you don't know Beryl Hennessey. *(Then blankly).* What troubles?
SANDRA:	There, you see, you'd forgotten you were depressed about your age, that you'd lost your job, you're stoney broke and you haven't heard from Robert for two whole weeks.
BERYL:	Oh God, let's have another party.
PAUL:	Don't push your luck. Mr. Duval the caretaker's been complaining this morning.
BERYL:	Let him. Old fussy-drawers, he doesn't understand my problems.
PAUL:	You're just having a bad little patch.
BERYL:	I don't have bad little patches. I have great Sahara Deserts.

Paul exits with tray into the kitchen.

SANDRA:	You know Beryl, it's not as if you haven't got any boy-friends.
BERYL:	Name one.
SANDRA:	Brian.

BERYL: I don't like Brian.
SANDRA: What don't you like about him?
BERYL: His tandem.
SANDRA: They're coming back into fashion.
BERYL: Yeah, well you want to try sitting on one. Two hours of that and you
            stagger in with a bent back, bow legs and shredded knickers. *(The
            telephone rings)*. You get it.

  Beryl *starts to go to bedroom.*

SANDRA: *(going to the phone):* Hang on it might be for you.
BERYL: I'm out. *(She exits)*.
SANDRA: *(into phone):* Hello . . .

  N.B. **Robert's** *voice is heard over the loud-speaker.*

ROBERT: It's Robert.
SANDRA: It's Robert!
BERYL: *(running back into room):* I'm in! *(She hastily removes her rollers and then
            grabs the phone from* **Sandra***)*. Robert?

CARLA LANE & JOHN CHAPMAN
from *The Liver Birds* (1975)

The Pier Head Buildings and the Landing Stage from the river (Keith Medley)

222

from *The middle-aged couple at the back of the bus to Lark Lane*

Do we parody those teenagers
in the seat across or do they parody us
the middle-aged couple at the back of the bus?

This hot and hungry mouth-to-mouth
the travelling hands
the warm-sweet reek of drink and lust
must surely scandalise or does our heedless voyaging
vindicate their own
ticketing us all as tripping fools
or on some journey of the wise?

Of course this excursion cannot last
you're expected in a suburb called respectability
where sanity, security and duty wait:
husband, children, hi-fi set
and smooth-styled motor behind the wrought-iron gate.
I'm going to a street called consequence
where need, guilt, habit and gratitude reside
family, mortgage and uncancelled debts
and cells like terraced-houses side by side.

But now while our city lurches past the steamy windows,
churches and pubs and back-to-backs ...
crumbling brick-faces cosmeticked by grime
you don't seem to care where the route may take us
against my ear your mouth wet-murmurs,
"Darling aren't we having a wonderful time?"

DAVID EVANS

"Hullo ... That's knocked a few jokes on the 'ead!"   Cartoon by Bill Tidy

"Forget the cup defeats, let's hope it's played in the right spirit and Souness falls over again."

Cartoon by Bill Tidy

A Goalden Night

We went straight at them from the start,
Their whole defence was ripped apart.
Our pre-match plans went to the letter,
Has any Liverpool team played better?

Ray Clemence kicks a long high ball,
And Barcelona are about to fall.
For Kevin Keegan wins the race,
And flicks it on into a space.
By my right foot the ball is met,
And in a flash it's in the net!

A Goalden night and what a thrill,
It's Liverpool one, Barcelona nil.
One away goal will suit us fine,
And I'm so pleased that it was mine.

Now all we want to do is sing,
But let's remember just one thing,
Midst all the fuss let's not forget,
We haven't reached the final yet!

JOHN TOSHACK
from *Gosh it's Tosh* (1976)

224

Ellesmere Port - its origins and today's Boat Museum

By far the best way to approach Ellesmere Port is by parachute, dropping straight down into the town centre between the Civic Hall and the Central Library. Arriving more conventionally from any other direction could prove a disappointment. For Ellesmere Port is a modern boom town....A lot of it dates from only yesterday and, going back in time, only from the nineteen-fifties when the town expanded like an inflating balloon....Discounting the several villages and places like Willaston and Neston which go to make up the actual *Borough,* not much is left of any great age. Ellesmere Port itself is a name which had not crossed anyone's lips before 1796 and it was some years after that before it was in everyday use. Earlier it had been known as Whitby and the change was brought about by the cutting of a canal.

In 1793 an Act of Parliament authorised the construction of an eight-mile-long canal through the Wirral from Chester into the River Mersey to provide a deep-sea outlet for the Ellesmere Canal system in Shropshire, so enabling manufacturers in the Midlands and the Potteries to transport their wares directly to ships for export or conveyance round the coast.

The canal entered the Mersey through a series of locks in the tiny hamlet of Netherpool, but since the principal place at the time was nearby Whitby the area became known as Whitby Locks...often referred to as the 'Ellesmere Canal port' and that, in time, became shortened to 'Ellesmere Port'.

The canal was designed by the great Thomas Telford..(with) the construction of a tidal basin which connected the canal to the Mersey ... and (later) a comprehensive dock estate ...

The Boat Museum was set up in December 1970 by a small group of enthusiasts who had individually shown an active interest in preserving canal boats....The Museum opened to the public in 1976 and great strides have been made...the boats and the static exhibits give a good idea of what the canal-basin was like in its hey-day.

ALAN BRACK
The Wirral (1988)

(Richard Lloyd-Jones)

High-Rise Visit

The veranda was a hot tin-lined box.
It contained her whole summer.
High up she waved in the flapping wind
Like the Queen Mother but toy-doll sized.

Whirlwind whistled around this pebble-dashed
Monstrosity built like a towering cage.
There, mostly alone,
Unable to operate even the lift,
Too proud to be in "one of those wheelchairs! "

Some fragile flowers wavered in pots,
The fumes of braised meat escaped,
With twice stewed veg – lingering in the lifts.
I felt dizzy looking through hurricane cracks
At tiny objects in a miniature landscape
On visits which took the feel of my legs away;
Was this her paradise confined?

Sitting soaked in memories of Pears Soap
Working at Port Sunlight factory,
Her mind travelled the cracks across
The Mersey and back along the wet tram rails,
To the market, to Jack and the first meeting;
And looking over the veranda
She fitted it all into place.

No doubt the view was enough
For an active mind panning those years.
And there we left her looking out,
Tearful, faraway, waving;
A doll with two others, her sons,
Like the Russian one she showed me
When sitting at her lace-covered table.

We zoom off in a car, out of sight.
In my mind's eye I still see her waving,
In her wool-lined slippers and apron,
Shawl gathered against the wind,
Her mind a box of collected memories.

CERI COURTENAY

Coming to Liverpool

When we came to Liverpool in 1975/6, the dream of great new housing projects already lay in ruins. On the wall of a large block of flats on Everton Brow, now demolished, was a commemorative plaque which read, 'The Braddocks: opened by the Rt. Hon. Hugh Gaitskell, 1957.' The hope, which so many shared, was that such high-rise blocks would get rid of the long waiting lists for housing and of the mean, grey, terraced streets. With this went the belief that it would relieve the gross overcrowding of the past and that families would be given a flying start, if they could move from the over-populated inner city into spacious estates on green field sites. So rigorously was this policy pursued that a quarter of the whole population of Merseyside lives on those great estates around the perimeter of the city.

DAVID SHEPPARD: Our first year in Liverpool saw the production in the Everyman Theatre of the play Love and Kisses from Kirkby. *It was keen observation, often bitter, sometimes sensitive. There was Bessie Braddock, five feet square, dressed in red from head to toe, explaining the pressure of ten thousand on the housing list. There was the family buying new furniture and making everyone take off their shoes to enter the house. There was the councillor taking the blame when reality fell short of a dream. And then came the smashing of the dream - the broken glass, the endless delays for repairs, costly travel to see grandparents left behind, poor shopping facilities, the collapse of employment . . . Within fifteen years of being built, the great blocks of Netherley were deserted, then demolished.*

BISHOP DAVID SHEPPARD and ARCHBISHOP DEREK WORLOCK
Better Together (1988)

Netherley - 1985

They stood, strange, silent, gaping,
Gigantic black shells against a fading sky.
Erected to a new dream,
Now a nightmare.

Cold, dark, thankfully lifeless.
"They once were home," she said.
"We had no choice.
Our old homes rumbled to the ground,
While these new ones reached for space."

"We loved the view", she said,
"We had that.
We saw for miles and miles.
Trees, fields, and even rivers.

We heard the wind,
But not among the trees.
We heard the wind screech and scream
Down endless echoing passages.

We didn't hear the children play.
We heard, each side,
Our neighbours' muffled lives.
Closer to heaven,
We were closer to hell.

They solved housing problems,
We lived them.
Benevolent jackals said,
'Oops! Sorry, our mistake,
Wasted money, not to worry,
We'll sort it out - just a minute.'
Minutes grew to years,
Their paralysis scratched
On the blackboard of our lives.

Now, we're released.
We hear the children, we hear the breeze.
We hear the rustling leaves,
And demolition hammers."

Tomorrow though, they come tomorrow.
Tonight, scrap-metal scavengers, and rats,
Creep through ghostly rooms,
Salvaging what they can.

JENNY ROCHE

Jambo

The man in the grey overcoat who gets
the train into town at the same time
every morning has never met Jambo.

> He never wants to meet Jambo. He has
> these nightmares about Jambo - as big
> as the Incredible Hulk, as agile as
> Spider Man.

He must be. How else could he paint
his name across the top of every bridge
and half way up the brick embankment
all along the railway line?

> What he'll never know is that every night
> Jambo has nightmares too, where he's
> ordered from room to room along a maze
> of silent corridors by a mysterious man
> in a grey overcoat who looks just like
> the man on the train.

DAVE WARD

Calling Card

Dorothy Harris stepped off the pavement and into her hall. As she stooped groaning to pick up the envelopes the front door opened, opened, a yawn that wouldn't be suppressed. She wrestled it shut — she must ask Simon to see to it, though certainly not over Christmas — then she began to open the cards.

Here was Father Christmas, and here he was again, apparently after dieting. Here was a robin like a rosy apple with a beak, and here was an envelope whose handwriting staggered: Simon's and Margery's children, perhaps?

The card showed a church on a snowy hill. The hill was bare except for a smudge of ink. Though the card was unsigned, there was writing within. A Very Happy Christmas And A Prosperous New Year, the message should have said — but now it said A Very Harried Christmas And No New Year. She turned back to the picture, her hands shaking. It wasn't just a smudge of ink; someone had drawn a smeary cross on the hill: a grave.

Though the name on the envelope was a watery blur, the address was certainly hers. Suddenly the house — the kitchen and living room, the two bedrooms with her memories stacked neatly against the walls — seemed far too large and dim. Without moving from the front door she phoned Margery.

"Is it Grandma?" Margery had to hush the children while she said, "You come as soon as you like, Mummy."

Lark Lane was deserted. An unsold Christmas tree loitered in a shop doorway, a gargoyle craned out from the police station. Once Margery had moved away, the nearness of the police had been reassuring - not that Dorothy was nervous, like some of the old folk these days - but the police station was only a community centre now.

The bus already sounded like a pub. She sat outside on the ferry, though the bench looked and felt like black ice. Lights fished in the Mersey, gulls drifted down like snowflakes from the muddy sky. A whitish Object grabbed the rail, but of course it was only a gull. Nevertheless she was glad that Simon was waiting with the car at Woodside.

As soon as the children had been packed off to bed so that Father Christmas could get to work, she produced the card. It felt wet, almost slimy, though it hadn't before. Simon pointed out what she'd overlooked: the age of the stamp. "We weren't even living there then," Margery said. "You wouldn't think they would bother delivering it after sixty years."

"A touch of the Christmas spirit."

"I wish they hadn't bothered," Margery said. But her mother didn't mind now; the addressee must have died years ago. She turned the conversation to old times, to Margery's father. Later she gazed from her bedroom window, at the houses of Bebington sleeping in pairs. A man was creeping about the house, but it was only Simon, loaded with presents.

In the morning the house was full of cries of delight, gleaming new toys, balls of wrapping paper big as cabbages. In the afternoon the adults, bulging with turkey and pudding, lolled in chairs. When Simon drove her home that night, Dorothy noticed that the unsold Christmas tree was still there, a scrawny glistening shape at the back of the shop doorway. As soon as Simon left, she found herself thinking about the unpleasant card. She tore it up, then went determinedly to bed.

Boxing Day was her busiest time, what with cooking the second version of Christmas dinner, and making sure the house was impeccable, and hiding small presents for the children to find. She wished she could see them more often, but thcy and their parents had their own lives to lead.

An insect clung to a tinsel globe on the tree. When she reached out to squash the insect it wasn't there, neither on the globe nor on the floor. Could it have been the reflection of someone thin outside the window? Nobody was there now.

She liked the house best when it was full of laughter, and it would be again soon: "We'll get a sitter," Margery promised, "and first-foot you on New Year's Eve." She'd used to do that when she had lived at home — she'd waited outside at midnight of the Old Year so as to be the first to cross her mother's threshold. That reminded Dorothy to offer the children a holiday treat. Everything seemed fine, even when they went to the door to leave. ''Grandma, someone's left you a present," little Denise cried.

Then she cried out, and dropped the package. Perhaps the wind had snatched it from her hands. As the package, which looked wet and mouldy, struck the curb it broke open. Did its contents scuttle out and sidle away into the dark? Surely that was the play of the wind, which tumbled carton and wrapping away down the street.

Someone must have used her doorway for a wastebin, that was all. Dorothy lay in bed, listening to the wind which groped around the windowless side of the house, that faced onto the alley. She kept thinking she was on the ferry, backing away from the rail, forgetting that the rail was also behind her. Her nervousness annoyed her — she was acting like an old fogey — which was why, next afternoon, she walked to Otterspool promenade.

Gulls and planes sailed over the Mersey, which was deserted except for buoys. On the far bank, tiny towns and stalks of factory chimneys stood at the foot of an enormous frieze of clouds. Sunlight slipped through to Birkenhead and Wallasey, touching up the colours of microscopic streets; specks of windows glinted. She enjoyed none of this, for the slopping of water beneath the promenade seemed to be pacing her. Worse, she couldn't make herself go to the rail to prove that there was nothing.

Really, it was heartbreaking. One vicious card and she felt nervous in her own house. A blurred voice seemed to creep behind the carols on the radio, lowing out of tune. Next day she took her washing to Lark Lane, in search of distraction as much as anything.

The Westinghouse Laundromat was deserted. *0 0 0*, the washing machines said emptily. There was only herself, and her dervishes of clothes, and a black plastic bag almost as tall as she was. If someone had abandoned it, whatever its lumpy contents were, she could see why, for it was leaking; she smelled stagnant water. It must be a draught that made it twitch feebly. Nevertheless, if she had been able to turn off her machine she might have fled.

She mustn't grow neurotic. She still had friends to visit. The following day she

went to a friend whose flat overlooked Wavertree Park. It was all very convivial —
a rain storm outside made the mince pies more warming, the chat flowed as easily
as the whisky — but she kept glancing at the thin figure who stood in the park,
unmoved by the downpour. The trails of rain on the window must be lending him
their colour, for his skin looked like a snail's.

Eventually the 68 bus, meandering like a drunkard's monologue, took her
home to Aigburth. No, the man in the park hadn't really looked as though his
clothes and his body had merged into a single greyish mass. Tomorrow she was
taking the children for their treat, and that would clear her mind.

She took them to the aquarium. Piranhas sank stonily, their sides glittering like
Christmas cards. Toads were bubbling lumps of tar. Finny humbugs swam, and
darting fish wired with light. Had one of the tanks cracked? There seemed to be a
stagnant smell.

In the museum everything was under glass: shrunken heads like sewn leathery
handbags, a watchmaker's workshop, buses passing as though the windows were
silent films. Here was a slum street, walled in by photographs of despair, real
flagstones underfoot, overhung by streetlamps on brackets. She halted between a
grid and a drinking fountain; she was trapped in the dimness between blind
corners, and couldn't see either way. Why couldn't she get rid of the stagnant
smell? Grey forlorn faces, pressed like specimens, peered out of the walls. "Come
on, quickly," she said, pretending that only the children were nervous.

She was glad of the packed crowds in Church Street, even though the children
kept letting go of her hands. But the stagnant smell was trailing her, and once,
when she grabbed for little Denise's hand, she clutched someone else's, which felt
soft and wet. It must have been nervousness which made her fingers seem to sink
into the hand.

That night she returned to the aquarium and found she was locked in. Except
for the glow of the tanks, the narrow room was oppressively dark. In the nearest
tank a large dead fish floated toward her, out of weeds. Now she was in the tank,
her nails scrabbling at the glass, and she saw that it wasn't a fish but a snail-
coloured hand, which closed spongily on hers. When she woke, her scream made
the house sound very empty.

At least it was New Year's Eve. After tonight she could stop worrying. Why
had she thought that? It only made her more nervous. Even when Margery
phoned to confirm they would first-foot her, that reminded her how many hours
she would be on her own. As the night seeped into the house, the emptiness grew.

A knock at the front door made her start, but it was only the Harveys, inviting
her next door for sherry and sandwiches. While she dodged a sudden rainstorm,
Mr. Harvey dragged at her front door, one hand through the letter box, until the
latch clicked.

After several sherries Dorothy remembered something she'd once heard. "The
lady who lived next door before me — didn't she have trouble with her son?"

"He wasn't right in the head. He got so he'd go for anyone, even if he'd never
met them before. She got so scared of him she locked him out one New Year's Eve.
They say he threw himself in the river, though they never found the body."

Dorothy wished she hadn't asked. She thought of the body, rotting in the depths. She must go home, in case Simon and Margery arrived. The Harveys were next door if she needed them.

The sherries had made her sleepy. Only the ticking of her clock, clipping away the seconds, kept her awake. Twenty past eleven. The splashing from the gutters sounded like wet footsteps pacing outside the window. She had never noticed she could smell the river in her house. She wished she had stayed longer with the Harveys; she would have been able to hear Simon's car.

Twenty to twelve. Surely they wouldn't wait until midnight. She switched on the radio for company. A master of ceremonies was making people laugh; a man was laughing thickly, sounding waterlogged. Was he a drunk in the street? He wasn't on the radio. She mustn't brood; why, she hadn't put out the sherry glasses; that was something to do, to distract her from the intolerably measured counting of the clock, the silenced radio, the emptiness displaying her sounds —

Though the knock seemed enormously loud, she didn't start. They were here at last, though she hadn't heard the car. It was New Year's Day. She ran, and had reached the front door when the phone shrilled. That startled her so badly that she snatched the door open before lifting the receiver.

Nobody was outside — only a distant uproar of cheers and bells and horns — and Margery was on the phone. "We've been held up, Mummy. There was an accident in the tunnel. We'll be over as soon as we can."

Then who had knocked? It must have been a drunk; she heard him stumbling beside the house, thumping on her window. He'd better take himself off, or she would call Mr. Harvey to deal with him. But she was still inside the doorway when she saw the object on her step.

Good God, was it a rat? No, just a shoe, so ancient that it looked stuffed with mould. It wasn't mould, only a rotten old sock. There was something in the sock, something that smelled of stagnant water and worse. She stooped to peer at it, and then she was struggling to close the door, fighting to make the latch click, no breath to spare for a scream. She'd had her first foot, and now — hobbling doggedly alongside the house, its hands slithering over the wall — here came the rest of the body.

RAMSEY CAMPBELL
in *Dark Companions* (1982)

The Mersey from the Pier Head (Gladys Mary Coles)

Old Man

Like Nelson
on the quarter-deck of the Victory
he slowly paces the Pier Head parapets
above the river, his cradle.

He leans on the railings, blinks,
watery sunlight
warming thin memories:
the cast-iron roadway, carts,
cattle, Gladstone bags and collars,
his sticky lollipop falling,
grit on wet sweets,
black-shawled women
bartering for fish,
his father's calloused hand,
tarry wood and ropes,
fat bollards, creaking ferries,
smell of river ooze,
intermittent shrike of gulls
rending the air, the heart,
the memories.

He's part of it all
of generations of gulls of wingbeats
of the heavy clock tolling in the tall tower
of the Liver Birds, their copper cross of wings.
He came here with his Nelly,
evenings, in Sunday tie and boots.
Trams left for mysterious destinations
(Allerton, Fazakerley, Croxteth),
travelling inside twin hedgerows,
rattling and clicking to old sandstone villages
at the city's green fringes.

He watches light tacking on the Mersey,
the dark crocodiles of waves, urgent,
the river mouth beckoning
salt-hints from the sea-line
—in this his small freedom,
soon.

GLADYS MARY COLES

Intrada

This is one of the great buildings of the world.... The impression of vastness, strength and height no words can describe.... Suddenly, one sees that the greatest art of architecture, that lifts one up and turns one into a king, yet compels reverence, is the art of enclosing space.   SIR JOHN BETJEMAN

It is finished. After three quarters of a century of almost continuous building, Liverpool has given the world its fifth largest church, at a cost of £5 million.

If the explorer, George Mallory, born in Birkenhead across the River Mersey, could claim to have tackled Mount Everest 'because it was there', then it can be claimed with equal finality and simplicity that Liverpool Cathedral was completed because it was started. For although Mersey-siders have kept faith with the grandiose plans of their Victorian and Edwardian forebears, such a man-made, Everest will never be seriously considered again in this country: the cost, the ethics, and not least, the declining influence of the Church in society, would forbid it.

As it is, Liverpool now possesses the biggest church in Britain, capable of accommodating a congregation of more than 4,000 people...

The cathedral offers a monument to physical and artistic greatness. Here is a project that has been completed with no feckless compromise, one using age-old crafts which have themselves now passed into the looking-glass of history.

Viewed from the air or from out at sea, the cathedral tower, standing nearly 500 ft above the river, is the first major landmark to attract the visitor's attention. From the tops of the Clwydian Hills in Wales; across the Wirral peninsula; northwards beyond Southport; and east and south towards Cheshire and Greater Manchester, its bulk cuts the skyline like a symmetrical Hebridean sea stack. But however magnificent a cathedral may be, its aesthetic qualities are greatly aided by its site, and in this respect Liverpool is paralleled only by Durham for splendour. St James's Mount, with its ravine on the east side, and with the future hope of sensitive landscaping and planning to the west, was without doubt the best possible choice of position. The topography accentuates the cathedral's linear qualities with dramatic effect.

Yet the full glory of the building lies within and the interior is best approached from the great West porch. As one enters beneath the huge Benedicite Window, the complete majesty is revealed in a single uncluttered vision: the light grey marble of the floor and the pink sandstone of the fabric blend to lead the eye forwards and upwards. Beyond the first flight of steps is a 30 ft bridge-arch which frames the vastness of the building's central space, and in the distance up another set of steps, is the solid stone and gilded High Altar, backed by the stained glass of the Te Deum Window.

The relative simplicity of the architect Giles Gilbert Scott's design, with its breathtaking spaciousness, confirms his wish that the cathedral should be seen as 'a vast hall quarried out of a solid mass of stone, rather than a structure of separate units'. The horizontal stress is given by the lack of pillars, columns, and fixed furnishings; the vertical stress by the soaring arches, the lancet windows in the cliff-like walls of the undertower, and the pipework of the organ cases on either side of the Choir. This view is without doubt the greatest at-a-glance revelation in the history of British architecture. It demands a legion of superlatives, while at the same time a single phrase can achieve all that needs to be said. Sir John Betjeman, the Poet Laureate, has provided an unsurpassable description by defining this cathedral's unique quality as 'the art of enclosing space'.

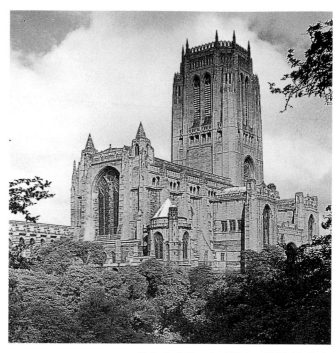

Cathedral Church of Christ, (Keith Medley).

The visitor is confronted with awe-inspiring statistics made visible reality: the highest Gothic arches ever built; the largest tower vault in the Gothic tradition; the noblest church organ in the world; and in the tower above, the world's highest and heaviest ringing peal of bells. All this has been brought to finality in a decade when the Church of England will make over 800 churches redundant, when organized religion is on the decline, and when many committed Christians (and non-Christians) would rather see money spent on direct social needs than on consecrated bricks and mortar, no matter how inspiring the result. ...

Liverpool is a city with two cathedrals. The Roman Catholic cathedral, which faces the Anglican one down the oft-quoted Hope Street (a great ploy for ecumenists) was consecrated at Whitsuntide, 1967. Coventry and Guildford also have cathedrals which belong wholly to the present century. But none has taken nearly so long to complete, nor been as costly or as controversial as Scott's building, spawned during the days of Empire, of intense inter-city rivalry, and of diocesan jealousies, when biggest was considered to be best. So, has Liverpool landed itself with an expensive religious dinosaur? Or, as a local folk-song asks, has the city of two cathedrals 'got one to spare'? Have our great-grandfathers left us an inheritance that owes more to pride and eccentricity than to common sense?

Building Liverpool Cathedral may have been less of a burden on the community *pro rata* than the construction of a medieval cathedral like that of Salisbury during the thirteenth century, but the position of the Church in society has also radically changed. Like the very arts which adorn Liverpool Cathedral, it has been graded as a minority interest. Now, after years of appealing to 'Finish the Cathedral', we are fully entering the era of 'Maintaining the Cathedral'. And without support and a real sense of meaning in the years ahead, even new Gothic cathedrals can start to fall down.

JOE RILEY
Today's Cathedral (1978)

Star performance at the Everyman

Les Hancock is quite simply the best-known (and probably the best-liked) doorman in Liverpool. He has been the fireman-cum-doorman at the Everyman Theatre in Hope Street since 1964, when he was offered the job in rather bizarre circumstances.

"I was walking past this building in Hope Street, and there was a man standing on the steps. I was curious, and I asked him what the building was going to be. He said: 'If I have my way it'll be a theatre, if I can get myself a fireman.' Well, I told him I was a fireman, and walked on. He caught up with me by the traffic lights and offered me a job there and then."

The man on the steps was Michael Freeman, the Everyman's first general manager, and when he took Les Hancock on as fireman and general factotum he probably had little idea of the type of man he was taking on. Les Hancock is a virtuoso doorman. To see him at his best, you have to go along to the theatre late at night at a weekend. The show has finished, and the ever-popular Bistro downstairs is full. There is a queue of hopefuls outside the door when Les appears.

"I'm sorry, ladies and gentlemen, it's full downstairs. Absolutely full. If you've got somewhere else to go to, then you'd better go there." Half the queue drifts away there and then in search of alternative entertainment. Les surveys the determined remainder, and a conspiratorial gleam comes into his eye. "Stick around, and I'll see what I can do," he says darkly. "I can't make any promises, mind you. It's absolutely full and Paddy (one of the Bistro's guiding lights) says I can't let anybody else in." He then drops a large wink.

Sooner or later a few diners come up the stairs and out into the night. One by one the queue is let in to replace those that leave, until the pavement is bare. For a few minutes it is deserted until the process begins all over again...

"The marvellous thing about this theatre is that the people love the place. Everybody here gets the same respect and welcome as the bosses, and it's great. The little children come out of the pantomime with a smile and they salute you as they go out. And then their mums and dads bring them over and tell them: 'It's Les. Say hello!' Marvellous!"

WILLIAM LEECE
Daily Post, 22 February 1978

The Everyman (Gladys Mary Coles)

The Playhouse (Gladys Mary Coles)

Seaforth Shore Revisited

A vague perversity has brought me here
to routine waves. Behind me now
the town that tried to push me out to sea,
into my family's element. And literate,
I've puzzled out new roads,
roundabouts, flyovers, to come to this
old tramping-ground of clinkered sand
and fifty visible miles of sea,

forgetting how much sky
included me.

A gawky know-all girl avowed
that Turner painted sunsets here
dipping his brush in the raging fires
that slither into Ireland. And Sassoon
tossed his medal in this sea's grey face
glaring across the estuary to where
Wilfred Owen chased the winds
on horseback on New Brighton sands
before that war which trampled them.
And here we rummaged in the sand
for skulls and shrapnel,
scavenging like gulls to prove
our war.

Behind, behind for good,
the town's indifference. The rubble of
my toppled street is long bulldozed away.
Only sea and sky renew the thought
of freedoms brighter than my father hoped
wishing me to take his turn
over that horizon there.

MATT SIMPSON

Don't have to be there tonight

December 8th, 1980

Don't have to be there tonight
to know it's raining

down the Scottie Road. Down Quarry
Bank, where kids scuffed with grit and grim
humour, before the cars got burnt out -
alongside mansions of fast-setting
concrete, the architects' cold
dream, that didn't need too much
money, but can't buy you love....

Don't have to be there tonight
to know it's raining

down Penny Lane. Down Strawberry
Fields, where the cottages of childrens'
Homes, nestle bleakly. And they - too
young to know another age
feel orphaned tonight....

Don't have to be there tonight
to know it's raining

down the Pier Head. Down the docks
where they stand united. Mostly
Dads now. With collars up and pockets
empty. Stubborn as their peaked
caps, and wishing it had been
a hard day's night, working....

They watch with the stoney-eyed
Liver Birds - waiting for ships to come in
and sail up the Mersey again -
it's nearly twenty years on,
and the flowers have almost gone, from
hair that's growing thin....

Don't have to be there tonight
to know it's raining
down Mathew Street, where
the Cavern stands out,
like a gap in a row of grey
gritted teeth....

Don't have to be there tonight
to know it's raining in Liverpool
don't have to be there
tonight, to know it's because

one of their kids made it
all the way to New York City ...

CELIA NOKES

The Merseyside Nomad

*(conceived on a Friday evening train
from Euston to Lime Street Station)*

He is one of the Merseyside Nomads,
  working Mon. through to Fri. in the Smoke.
Lonely nights in pad, down in Peckham,
  ever bored, ever bruised, ever broke.

There's a wife and three kids up in Kirkby,
  he goes back to whenever he can.
These days once a month's all he can manage.
  It was better when he had the van.

But then wheels is hard on the pocket,
  and the Halifax still want their whack.
Though the maisonette leaks and there's dry rot,
  no way will the Corpy buy back.

It's ten years since they chained gates of South Dock.
  At that time the lump sum seemed a lot.
And to own your own home was the message,
  though it left a great hole in the pot.

What you can't believe when you are working,
  is how stopping can screw you so low.
Come the writing, the ringing, the queuing,
  the echoing, "We'll let you know."

"See you don't have all that much to offer.
  No trade. Did you not serve your time?
There's no call for bale slinging these days,
  unless they bring back, 'What's My Line'".

She did afternoons packing biscuits.
  He O.D.'d on the Flower Pot Men.
Then Crawfords closed down so they'd nothing,
  And the Sharks started counting to ten.

So he hopped on his bike like the man said.
  Six days traipsing, then he made the grade.
But the week worked in hand meant Embankment,
  with the old Cardboard City Brigade.

Months of casual work on a Wimpey,
  stacking breeze block or heaving a hod.
Then days on the lump looking hopeful,
  and nights in the pad on his tod.

Letter to Brezhnev (1985)
An acclaimed film made on Merseyside, in
which two Kirkby girls meet two Russian
sailors in port. Written by Frank Clarke,
with Margi Clarke and Alexandra Pigg as
the girls.

Now a year of this is depressing,
  And three, he thinks more than he'll bear.
The kids treat him as they'd a stranger.
  Seems going home's not worth the fare.

But he finger-nails half an inch forward.
  Lots of ovies and he's back on track.
Maybe they could move down here and join him.
  Then rules change and knock him straight back.

The landlord in Peckham is preening.
  The new Rent Act's finally cleared.
If tenants move on, you can triple.
  Now his front door has just disappeared.

So it's hook slinging time for the Nomad.
  Still running hard just to stand still.
His head shouts that things must get better.
  His heart whispers, they never will.

JIM HITCHMOUGH

Closed Factory: Kirkby Industrial Estate

The building is disjointed
work-din gone
grass dislodges stone.
Barbed wire keeps the silence.

Once I heard them talk
undaunted, homely
in white overalls.
Their stories and words leapt
chutes of gravy, mountains
of peas, wavy puddings,
boxes that flapped open and shut
like kept birds.

KEEP OUT says the board. Yet some days
a white pigeon flies in from the city
to walk the gutter's shelf,
head tipped, listening.

No-one calls.
At nightfall a small ghost
flits across the roof.
Below lamp lights glisten: only
graffiti haunts the pitted wall.

SUSAN SKINNER

Patronise the Punch, Mister?

One of Liverpool's longest standing landmarks has gone. Did anyone notice? The old Punch and Judy which once stood on Lime Street, and later on St George's Plateau, and finally on Williamson Square, has disappeared. Perhaps forever.

And where is the Punch man who entertained generations of Liverpool children for a penny? Perhaps he is hidden in 'the wilds of a Liverpool cemetery' where, according to tradition, he found 'the necessary seclusion for undertaking operations of surgery and the stitching of costumes'.*

That little bit of folklore could have come straight from Dickens' *The Old Curiosity Shop:* the Punchman, Codlin, is discovered repairing his little wooden actors in a graveyard. In fact it is a little bit of family history. Not that of Codlin but of Codman, a whole family of Punchmen still alive and kicking - or should that be walloping?

No longer busking in the City Centre, Professor Ronald Codman, the fourth to bear the title in Liverpool, finds modern day audiences less willing to 'patronise the Punch 'n Judy, mister! ' He and his son, Robert, now rely on contracted work - that is, they are paid for each performance and they must travel many miles to maintain the family's tradition.....

In 1868, Richard Codman had established his winter pitch in Liverpool's Lime Street, after presenting his show in Llandudno from May 1864, with marvellously dramatic Punch & Judy figures which he carved from driftwood found on Llandudno beach, and an ornate booth topped with a lion (a symbol to other Romany travellers). In 1888 the oldest son of 'Professor' Codman, Richard II, took over the Liverpool site, establishing a tradition which the public so took to heart that in 1923 a new booth was commissioned from the Sandon Studios and presented amidst great ceremony, with a recital from the City Police Band, preceding its premiere appearance.

Richard II died in 1951 and his son - yes, another Richard - took over the family business, often crossing the Mersey to perform in the thriving resort of New Brighton. Richard III's son, *Ronald,* and his son Robert, continued the family tradition on a new site in Williamson Square, a pitch which proved impractical and unprofitable.

But the Punch & Judy man is still with us. Just like his great-grandfather, Ronald Codman travels the length and breadth of the country presenting one of Britain's oldest theatrical entertainments: *The Tragical Comedy or Comical Tragedy of Punch & Judy.*

* from '*Neath the Mask* by JOHN M. EAST (1967)

NICHOLAS GARRICK

Punch & Judy Show

Liverpool 8 (Lindsay Coles)

Adrian Henri's Talking Toxteth Blues

Well, I woke up this morning, there was buzzing overhead
Saw the helicopter as I got out of my bed,
Smelt the smell of burning, saw the buildings fall,
Bulldozers pulling down next door's wall.
Toxteth nightmare...
     ... yes ...
          ... city with a hangover.

Then I remembered what happened last night
The sirens and the shouting and the TV lights,
Banging on the riotshields, petrol bombs in flames,
Cars all ablazing, shattered window-frames.
     Felt sick to my stomach ...
          ... don't cry for me ...
               ... Upper Parly.

Saw a busy lying blood pouring from his head,
Saw one stop a paving stone, thought that he was dead.
Heard the sound of engines in the bright orange night,
Saw the headlights blazing, saw the crowd in flight.
     One of them ...
          ... didn't run fast enough ...
             ... Land Rovers ...
                 ... long way from the farm.

Well, I saw the Chief Constable up on TV
And the Superintendents, but they never saw me,
Saw the Home Secretary and the Minister for Riots,
And all them social workers who just never keep quiet.
     ... never met a one of them ...
          ... neither did the coppers.

Saw a woman walking in the firelight's glare,
"Hey, Aunty Maggy, what you doing there?"
Arms full of liquor and a portable TV,
Said, "All the rest are doing it, why not me?
　　　... do yourself a favour, son,
　　　　　... nice music centre ...
　　　　　　　... just over there."

Well, I thought a bit about it and I took her advice
Crowd was having fun and the goods looked nice,
Then a scuffer copped me and they threw me in a van,
Took me off to Risley and the Magistrate Man.
... exemplary sentence ...
　　　... act as a deterrent ...
　　　　　... law 'n' order ...
　　　　　　　... Toxteth nightmare ...
　　　　　　　　　... city ...
　　　　　　　　　　　... with a
　　　　　　　　　　　　　hangover.

　　　　　　　　　　　ADRIAN HENRI

from *Nuh blame Rasta (Dub poem)*

The riots inna Liverpool
Who is to blame?
Please don't call the RASTAMANS name
Peace and love is the RASTAMANS aim
Suh rioting is not the RASTAMANS game

Chorus:
The riots inna Liverpool nuh blame
RASTA
Oppression and injustice could never
prosper
All over England is a total disaster
The burning and the looting nuh
blame RASTA

　　　　　　　　　　　LEVI TAFARI

A Liverpool Dock, 1982

An empty sink.
No water, no ships.
A relief map of mud,
contours of ooze.
An opaque well.
Drop anything in here -
a ring, a boot, a body -
it will be stored without sign.

Memories too are sunk in there -
of cobbled quays with human throngs,
the clamour of cargoes, foreign tongues.
Above the mudline: 1849
the plaque's a reminder
everything falls
in the clogging hold
of time.

Pigeons and shadows inhabit warehouses,
weeds erupt through pavings,
bollards are fungus-furred.
And the river hurries by
preoccupied
with its own new silence.

GLADYS MARY COLES

Albert Dock silted up (Liverpool Echo)

Albert Dock: Regeneration, 1984

First, the Victorian grand design
named after the Prince
with an idealistic mind.
Jesse Hartley built a dock to survive -
and revive.
Functional solidity in form and line
yet Venetian style for each warehouse block:
where water doubled the thickets of rigging,
cranes swung cargoes through elegant arches
direct from vessels to vaulted rooms.
A century of storage,
dry, safe, and cold.

Then the death-phase:
crusted rust on cast-iron columns,
corrosion claiming the colonnades,
insinuation of silt and slime
into the basin abandoned by trade;
blind boarded-up eyes
of the riverside storeys -
frontage to phantoms and rats.

Next, the gradual reincarnation
after testing of timbers
for internal rot:
successive scourings and series of scrapings
restore the original rosy tones.

From mausoleum to Maritime Museum,
refilling the dock with river and people.

GLADYS MARY COLES

Regeneration in progress.
(Gladys Mary Coles)

Albert Dock redeveloped. Opened to the public, August 1984; official re-opening by HRH the Prince of Wales, 24th May 1988, on the same day as he opened the Tate Gallery, Liverpool. (Gladys Mary Coles)

Mersey Heritage at Stanley Dock; and the Tall Ships

On the banks of great rivers run the tides of dreams. Visions haunt the stardeep wharves of Liverpool. Rust-burnt capstans thrum in an Atlantic wind which brought the Liverpool Clippers home. 'The hardest thing a sailor ever did wasn't climbing the mast or stoking the filthy boilers. It was the leaving of Liverpool.'

Sometimes, working late in the dim stark yards of the old warehouse, we can feel long-dead dockers and sea-farers watching us, reluctant still to leave. Their grandsons pitch stones into the olive depths of the Stanley Dock and their sons amble across its yards, looking around at the great familiar walls, to tell their life testimony onto tape. They show us their discharge papers, their faded photographs, their medals. As they speak, in their old rough charming voices, they paint a picture. Of a seaport through which the tides of the world flowed. In a few generations, the grave hands of circumstance grasped Liverpool and wrung out of her mean little streets, her towering monuments and singular people, an era so magnificent, so terrible and profound that history cannot forget her. Through their eyes we see that her decline can only be a necessary respite before she takes the stage again. That is their dream. That is what they need to tell us.

At Mersey Heritage, we are building the stage. As the warehouses emptied of cargoes, they filled up with these people's dreams, of a future for Liverpool... If dreams are the ship to which hope entrusts its poignant, powerful cargo, on the Mersey, it must be well founded.

Even the gulls were spitting out damp the last time the river's dream awakened. The Mersey moved sourly, choppy and petty in a way only a great river could get away with. Beneath its surface, the silkgrey slide of its inexorable tide ebbed out to sea. It speaks a rough dialect, but persistently numbers itself amongst the great rivers of the world....Most of them motored to the start, fretting off New Brighton,

their clotted sterns speaking more of machines than canvas. At the mouth of the deep a million people watched the Tall Ships sail out of Liverpool. They watched not as people view an entertainment but as they witness a vision. This was their own heritage; their community's identity. They willed it not to take the tideway, but the mists still fell.

SUSAN PLACE
from '*Time to turn the Tide*',
in *Cheshire Life* (May 1987)

246

The International Garden Festival, 1984

This is a city surviving modern blitz and fire-bombs
and the battered image broadcast.

This is a cradle of nations still echoing
with sea-twinings of its once powerful Port.

This is a great garden of the nations
created on its rejuvenated shore.

Here are the hills scooped from silt,
salt-wind in the leaves and flowers.

Here are the fabled birds, anchored high,
with green growth in their beaks.

Here is the river shining intermittently
hinting the resilience of its city.

Here is the sound
of a new sea-page turning.

GLADYS MARY COLES

*The Yellow Submarine sited at the Garden Festival. Inset: plaque on submarine
and John Lennon statue which stood alongside. (Richard Lloyd-Jones)*

from *Shirley Valentine*
(Extract from Act One, Scene One)

The kitchen of a semi-detached house. It is a well-established kitchen, bearing signs of additions and alterations which have been made over the years. It is not a highly personalised palace of pitch pine and hanging baskets but nevertheless has signs of personality having overcome the bleakness of the chipboard and formica ... It is quite a comfortable and reassuring place.

Specifically the kitchen contains (apart from the obvious cooker, fridge, etc.) a door which leads out of the house, a wall with a window, a dining table and chairs.

In Act One, **Shirley** *is beginning preparations for cooking the evening meal - this includes opening a bottle of wine from which she pours a glass. Throughout the following scene she sets a table for two and she prepares, cooks and finally serves one of the truly great but unsung dishes of the world - chips and egg.*

... I wanted to be like Marjorie Majors. I used to pick on her somethin' rotten an' I really wanted to be like her. Can't y' be evil when you're a kid? I saw her a few weeks ago, Marjorie Majors. Didn't I wall? I hadn' even heard of her for years. I'm in town, loaded down with shoppin' an' what's the first thing that always happens when y' in town loaded down with shoppin'? Right. The heavens opened. An' it's funny the way all these things are linked but they are; once you're in town, loaded with shoppin' bags, caught in a deluge - it always follows that every bus ever made disappears off the face of the earth. Well I'm standin' there, like a drowned rat, me hair's in ruins an' I've got mascara lines runnin' from me face to me feet, so I thought I might as well trudge up to the Adelphi an' get a taxi. Course when I got there the taxis had gone into hidin' along with the buses. Well I'm just rootin' in me bag, lookin' for somethin' to slash me wrists with when this big white car pulls up to the hotel an' of course I'm standin' right by a puddle an' as the wheels go through it, half the puddle ends up over me an' the other half in me shoppin' bags. Well all I wanted to do by this time was scream. So I did. I just opened me mouth, standin' there in front of the hotel an' let out this scream. I could've been arrested but I didn't care. Well I was in midscream when I noticed this woman get out the white car an' start comin' towards me. An' she's dead elegant. Y' know she's walkin' through this torrential rain an' I guarantee not one drop of it was landin' on her. But the second she opened her mouth I knew who she was. I'd recognise those elocution lessons anywhere. 'Forgive me for asking,' she said, 'but didn't you used to be Shirley Valentine?' I just stood there, starin'. And drippin'. 'It is,' she said, 'it's Shirley,' an' the next thing, she's apologisin' for half drownin' me an' she's pullin' me into the hotel an' across the lobby an' into this lounge that's the size of two football pitches. Well, she's ordered tea an' I'm sittin' there, rain water drippin' down me neck an' plastic carrier bags round me feet an' I'm thinkin', 'Well Marjorie, you've waited a long time for your revenge but you've got me good style now, haven't y'? Well go on, spare me the torture, just put the knife in quick an' let's get it over with; come on tell me all about your bein' an air hostess on Concorde.' But she didn't say anythin'. She just sat there, lookin' at me, y' know really lookin' at me. I thought I'm not gonna let her milk it so I said, 'You're an' air hostess these days are y' Marjorie? Oh yes, I hear it's marvellous. You travel all over the world don't you?' But she still just kept lookin' at me. The waitress was just puttin' the tea an' cakes on the table in front of us. I said to her 'This is my friend Marjorie. We were at school together. Marjorie's an air hostess.' 'An air hostess?' Marjorie suddenly said, 'Darling whatever gave you that idea? I certainly travel widely but I'm not an air hostess. Shirley, I'm a hooker. A whore.' Marjorie Majors - a high class hooker! 'Oh really Marjorie,' I said, 'An' all that money your mother spent on elocution lessons.' By this time, the waitress was pourin' the tea into the cream buns! Well me an' Marjorie - God, we had a great afternoon together. She didn't come lordin' it over me at all. Y' know she told me about all the places she works Bahrain, New York, Munich. An' d' y' know what she told me? When we were at school . . . She wanted to be like me. The two of us, sittin' there at the Adelphi, one's like somethin' out of Dynasty, one's like somethin' out of the bagwash an' we're havin' a great time confessin' that all those years ago, we each wanted to be the other. I was sad when I thought about it. Like the two of us could have been great mates - y' know real close. We didn't half get on well together, that afternoon, in the Adelphi. We were rememberin' all kinds. I could've sat there forever - neither of us wanted to leave. But then the time caught up with us an' Marjorie had to get her plane. An' y' know somethin' - she didn't want to go. Paris she had to go to, Paris France, an' she didn't want to. An' an' on the way out ... d' y' know what she did? She leaned forward an' just kissed me - there on the cheek - an' there was real affection in that kiss. It was the sweetest kiss I'd known in years. An' then she, she held my shoulders an' looked at me and said, 'Goodbye Shirley. Goodbye, Shirley Valentine.' *(Pause.)* On the way home, on the bus, I was cryin'. I don't know why. I'm starin' out the window, tears trippin' down me cheeks. An' in me head there's this voice that keeps sayin', 'I used to be Shirley Valentine. I used to be Shirley Valentine . . . I used to be Shirley . . .' *(She is crying.)* What happened? Who turned me into this? I don't want this. Do you remember her wall? Remember Shirley Valentine? She got married to a boy called Joe an' one day she came to live here. An' an' even though her name was changed to Bradshaw she was still Shirley Valentine. For a while. She still . . . knew who she was. She used to . . . laugh. A lot. Didn't she?

WILLY RUSSELL
from *Shirley Valentine* (1988)
reprinted by permission of Methuen, London

Shirley Valentine was first performed at the Everyman Theatre, Liverpool, on 13 March 1986. The part of Shirley Valentine was played by Noreen Kershaw. The director was Glen Walford.

Shirley Valentine was subsequently produced in London at the Vaudeville Theatre, opening on 21 January 1988. The part of Shirley Valentine was played by Pauline Collins. The director was Simon Callow.

Shirley Valentine was made into a film in 1989, starring Pauline Collins.

Pauline Collins as Shirley

The Ballad of Hillsborough

The Liverpool supporters
Were given the smaller end;
Crammed behind the goalmouth
The fans were tightly penned —

Penned, penned in their thousands,
Penned in under the sky.
No one there had reckoned
That ninety-five would die.

The barriers all buckled,
They couldn't take the strain.
The cheers of jubilation
Turned into cries of pain.

And when at last they noticed,
The police unlocked a gate,
But the exit was too narrow,
And they'd opened it too late.

The nation watched in horror,
Stunned with disbelief,
As the shadows from the goalmouth
Stained a football pitch with grief.

An inquiry has been opened
To find out who's to blame,
But for those who lost their dear ones
Nothing will be the same.

For nothing brings the dead back,
Post mortems, flowers, or prayers,
It's like reaching the top of the stairwell
And finding there are no stairs.

That drop into the darkness
Goes down and down and down;
And grief's black waters well there,
Inviting you to drown.

Never to see your loved ones,
Or hear them on the phone —
It's hard to believe when it happens
That you'll never walk alone.

But down at the Kop at Anfield,
The goalmouth shows it's true:
The scarves around the crossbar
Are knotted red and blue.

Despite divided loyalties,
Liverpool loves its own,
And every tribute there proclaims:
You'll never walk alone—

Not by the banks of the Mersey,
Nor down the terraced streets;
Beneath the great cathedrals
A city's warm heart beats.

And now in the cold spring sunset,
The Liver Bird's aflame.
The Phoenix rose from the ashes;
A city can do the same.

SIMON RAE

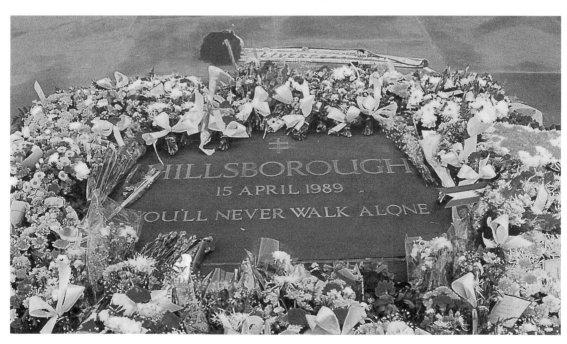

* The 96th victim, Tony Bland, died in Hospital in 1993, having never recovered consciousness.
Liverpool's FA Cup semi-final against Nottingham Forest on 18th April 1989
at the Hillsborough ground, Sheffield, turned into the worst sporting tragedy in British history.
*Pictured above is **The Hillsborough Memorial Stone** at the Anglican Cathedral. (Peter Kennerley)*

251

The Merseysiders
The First Local Radio Soap Opera

This twice weekly domestic drama series, broadcast by BBC Radio Merseyside, ran for 160 episodes between July 1988 and March 1990, attaining an audience of 500,000 (BBC audience research figures). It was the first local radio 'soap opera' and the inspiration of Keith Birch, the series creator and storyline writer.

The Merseysiders centred around a typical Liverpool family, the location inner-city working-class Liverpool, the story following a two-year period in the lives of Mary and Tommy Kelly and their three daughters: Margaret, Sarah and Kate.

The main characters

Thomas Peter Kelly, *aged 55. Ex-merchant seaman, docker and taxi-driver. Racist and sexist through ignorance, he is never short of an opinion on any subject but especially where the affairs of his daughters are concerned. He believes that a woman's place is in the home. Tommy has been unemployed for ten years and fears that he may never work again.*

Mary Kelly *is 53 years old. Married to Tommy for 35 years she is the outwardly calm rock around which the rest of the family ebbs and flows while she tries to hang on to her own identity. Apart from a weekly visit to the local bingo hall she has no social life. She spends most of her time knitting and massaging her husband's ego. She is a quiet woman who, up to now, has kept her own counsel. Mary Kelly is a secret writer of romantic verse but has never discussed her writing with anyone.*

Kate, *the youngest Kelly at 17, was conceived late in marriage and has been forced to look beyond the city of her birth for employment. Whilst working as a chambermaid in a south coast holiday camp she meets and falls in love with a Spanish cook. Kate loses her job and arrives home with a bun in the oven.*

Margaret, *the eldest daughter, is 33 and has been divorced for twelve months. There are two children from the mistake and Margi, unbeknown to the rest of the family, is heavily in debt to a loan shark, one Jed Malone. She is under physical and mental pressure from Malone to use prostitution as a way of paying him off.*

Sarah *is 27 and married to Sam Jackson. They have two children who both attend the local infant school. Marrying her childhood sweetheart, having his children and caring for his needs was all that Sarah ever wanted from life, until now. A chance meeting with an old friend makes her question the limitations she's accepted. Can she explore other possibilities within the framework of domestic bliss? We are about to find out.*

Sam Jackson, *aged 30. He has worked for the council as a painter since leaving school. Steady, dependable Sam. 'Everything in moderation' and 'Quality before quantity' are his watchwords. Sam can always be found at a certain time of day having a pint of bitter with his best mate, Dave Parker. They are in the* Rose & Crown *chatting to the landlord, Vinnie McIntosh. Sam has no warning that the storm, born of the Irish Sea and now gathering strength at the mouth of the River Mersey, will unleash a sequence of events that will leave an indelible mark on all those lives that mean so much to him.*

The two years that follow see dramatic changes in the lives of the Kellys and the Jacksons. Fate is to deal some cruel cards in their particular game of life, and flatters to deceive. We will be left with winners who become losers and losers who become winners, or so it would seem.

Dave Parker: *Friend and lover. A weak man with strong drink.*
Billy Stanley: *A lost soul with a lifebelt for Mary.*
Vinnie McIntosh: *A Godfather but never a father.*
Pat Askew: *A Lancashire lass who holds her own, and anyone else's!*

The Final Episode
SCENE 1: MARGARITA'S RESTAURANT INTERIOR.

DAVE: Hold the ladder still, Billy. I think I've found the problem.

BILLY: What is it?

DAVE: *(Whilst descending ladder)* You know the little plug that goes in the back of the speaker .... hold it, I nearly came off then.

BILLY: Sorry, I thought you were down. Is that it?

DAVE: Falling off the wagon's one thing, but ladders are something else. See that? The wire's not connected. Pass us that small screwdriver.

BILLY: Aren't you going to the A.A. meeting tonight?

DAVE: Yeah, tonight's the night. Kentucky John's picking me up at 7 o' clock .

BILLY: *(Sings)* 'And we went dancin' , we went dancin'.'

DAVE: Ar eh, don't start all that again. Sarah's in for a surprise today, isn't she?

BILLY: Valonia Park you mean? Yeah, I suppose so. I still can't get over that, y'know. Sam Jackson selling out to the bourgeoisie.

DAVE: There y'are, that should be alright now. You don't have to worry about Sam, he won't change, I've known him too long. He just wants a better lifestyle for his wife and kids, that's all. Everyone's entitled to that. Hold the ladder, comrade.

BILLY: Yeah, everyone should have the same standard of living, but we need solidarity to achieve it.

DAVE: You're an idealist, Billy, but we have to live in the real world. O.K., that's it, I'm coming down.
    (Cuts to)

VINNIE: Here's tonight's menus, Marg. They've made a good job of them, haven't they? What are Dave and Billy doing over there?

MARGARET: The sound system's not working. I thought it was all going too smoothly. I knew something would go wrong on our first night.

VINNIE:Stop worrying, love. The lads'll fix it. You've done a smashing job, Marg. The place looks a treat; fit for a prince to dine in.

MARGARET: The red tablecloths were a good idea, weren't they? The cutlery and glasses are sparkling. D'you think it's warm enough in here, Vinnie?

DAVE: I think we've sorted the problem. D'you want to switch it on and give it a try?

MARGARET: Thanks Dave. Well, go on then Vinnie. What are you waiting for? Music maestro, please!
    (Julio Iglesias singing 'Hey' followed by 'When They Begin the Beguine', can be heard in the background for the rest of scene.)

VINNIE: Thanks lads, that really gives the place atmosphere. D'you think it's cold in here?

BILLY: It is a bit nippy now that you mention it, yeah.

DAVE: You'll be alright when it's full of people. All the tables are booked up for tonight, aren't they Marg?

MARGARET: Yeah, but I don't want dew drops falling into me prawn cocktails. What can we do, Vinnie?

VINNIE: No problem, sweetheart. *(Gives her a kiss)* Never fear when Vinnie's here. Right lads, if you go out to the shed in the back yard, you'll find four of those mobile heaters. The gas bottles are inside and they're on castors so you won't have any trouble moving them. Put one in each corner of the room.

MARGARET: They won't stink the place out, will they, Vin?

VINNIE: Not at all! It's gas, not paraffin. Once they get going they'll have this place warmed up in no time. I haven't used them this winter 'cos it's been so mild, but they'll be O.K. We can turn them off just before you open for business.

DAVE: Can I ask a question Vinnie, before we bring the heaters in, like? It's just that, y'know, I thought the restaurant was supposed to have an Italian style to it. That's right, isn't it?

VINNIE: Yeah, so what?

DAVE: Then why are we listening to Julio thingy? He's Spanish, isn't he?

MARGARET: *(Laughing)* Oh that's for Juan. It's Vinnie's idea. To make him feel more at home, y'know.

BILLY: Where is Juan? I haven't seen him all morning.

MARGARET: He's in the kitchen showing Pat Askew his equipment.

DAVE: *(Distance)* Sooner him than me.
(Cuts to kitchen)

JUAN: So you see, Pat, these are my special pans for making the sauces, Si?

PAT: Ooh, that music's so romantic. It makes me want to lay down.

JUAN: And this is my special hubbly bubbly, how you say, my stock pot. The base for all my sauces. You like?

PAT: You can stock my pot anytime, darlin'. Come and sit down here with me while I tell you what I'm going to do to you tonight.

JUAN: Don't sit on that table! No, no, no! Sorry for the shouting. Sorry, sorry Pat. Look, sit here on the chair.

PAT: *(Puzzled)* What have I done?

JUAN: This is my preparation table for my foods. It have to be kept without the spot on it all the times. Very important. You understand? Good! This music you like, Si?

PAT: Julio Inglisis? Or whatever his name is. Oh yeah, it's lovely. Makes me go goosey all over.

JUAN: *(Laughing)* You can't say this, but in English it is 'church', Julio Churches.

PAT: Julio Churches? That's not very romantic, is it? Come here, Juan, I want to wrap meself round you and pretend we're somewhere else.

JUAN: Oh Pat, stop please. You are so .... s o ......

PAT: The word you're looking for begins with 'H' and ends with 'Y', and it isn't 'happy'. Come here, you!

TOMMY: Gang way! Right Juan, where do you want these? Eye, eye! Put her down will you, you don't know where she's been.

MARY: Pat Askew! Pull your clothes down, for God's sake. Have you got no shame?

JUAN: Senor Tommy, Mary. I just bring Pat here to show my equipment.

TOMMY: Yes, so I see. Listen, I know what you dago's are like. You can't control yourselves. Women aren't safe anywhere near you. Mary, fasten your coat up. Right, I'm not standing around here all day holding this lot. Here's your potatoes, you'll have to wash them yourself. *(Noise of sack falling)*

JUAN: *(Excited)* No, no! Not potatoes on my table. Please, senor Tommy, look what you do to my table. *(Sobs)*

MARY: Ah, what's the matter, Juan?

PAT: You wait, Cod's Gob, you've put them on his table.

TOMMY: This is a mad house. Mary! Bring them flowers and come out of it. They're definitely touched, them two. Where's our Margaret?
        (Cuts back to restaurant)

VINNIE: There you are, Marg, the last candle lit.

MARGARET: Vinnie, it looks brilliant. I feel like sitting down and ordering something.

VINNIE: The lads will have the heaters lit in a bit, so everything will ... Eh up, here's your Mam and Dad.

MARY: Hiya, Marg, here's your flowers. Why are the candles lit? Have the lights fused, or something?

TOMMY: Eh, Vinnie, you want to keep an eye on the Spanish fella y'know. He's gone soft. Him and the Wigan bike are up to all sorts out there.

MARGARET: We just turned the main lights off to see what it looked like in candlelight, Mam. What do you think?

MARY: Oh Margi, it's just like something from a film. And the Italian music an' all.

BILLY: It's Spanish, Mary. Vinnie, y'know these heaters?

TOMMY: Stay away from that kitchen, Billy. And you, Dave. He's crackin' up in there. I mean it y'know Vinnie, he's going berserk.

VINNIE: Hang on a minute, Tommy. What's the matter with the heaters?

DAVE: Well for a start, two of the gas bottles are empty, and they were in a bit of a mess, y'know.

BILLY: We had a bit of trouble lighting those two with gas in. They're going O.K. now, like, but when did you last have them serviced?

MARGARET: Oh Vinnie, are they safe?

VINNIE: Of course they're safe. They just haven't been used for a while, that's all. I told you.

TOMMY: There y'are then, Billy. Here's the keys to the van. You can go and get the gas refills from that place on the industrial estate. It'll only take you ten minutes.

DAVE: I'll go with you, Billy. They're heavy them things.

VINNIE: Come through and I'll get some cash for you.

MARGARET: Eh Dad, are you sure these flowers are fresh? Only they look a bit limp. You haven't been to the cemetery by any chance, have you?

MARY: Oh eh, Marg. Just as if. You haven't have you, Tommy?

TOMMY: Don't be soft. Me own daughter? Do me a favour. It's the heat that's all. Snip the ends off and put a cube of sugar in each vase. They'll last for days.

MARY: I wonder what's happened to our Sarah. I'm surprised she's not here giving you a hand, Marg. Maybe it's one of the kids, eh? I'll call round and see after.

SCENE 2: INTERIOR OF VAN WHICH IS MOBILE

SARAH: Sam, where are we going?

TRACY: I know! We're going to the fair, aren't we Dad?

CLARE: We're not going to the fair, Tracy. That's the other way. Are we going to the park, Dad? Mum, she's pulling tongues again.

SARAH: Who's *she?* The cat's mother? Sam, are you going to tell us where we're going? Our Margi would have expected me to be helping out there today y'know. Sam, are you listening to us?

TRACY: Are you listening, Sam? *(The girls giggle)*

SAM: Eh hard clock, I heard that. It's nice out here isn't it, Sarah? Wide streets with trees along the sides. Bags of space between the houses. I've been thinking about the last eighteen months; all the things that have happened y'know. In our lives, like.

SARAH: Did you see that? That woman pushed the pram out into the road first and *then* looked to see if anything was coming. Honest to God. How do you mean? What things?

SAM: Just think back. It started when we came home from our holidays the year before last and we'd been burgled.

SARAH: And you hadn't paid the insurance money.

SAM: Then you started college, and I got the sack from the corpy, remember?

SARAH: Our Kate and Neil died.

SAM: Yeah! You decided ... or we agreed, that you'd take up the 'Options' course and set your sights on a teaching degree. Then I went self-employed; Sam Jackson - Painter & Decorator. Best thing I ever did, although I wasn't too sure at the time.

SARAH: You never see 'and Daughter', do you?

SAM: I'm not with you. What do you mean?

SARAH: Well you see lots of 'and Son, or Sons'. But have you ever seen 'and Daughter'?

SAM: You mean on the side of the van? No, I've never seen that. It's an interesting thought, isn't it? 'Sam Jackson & Daughters - Painters & Decorators.'

TRACY: Mummy can I whisper to you?

CLARE: She wants to go to the toilet.

SARAH: I told you to go before we came out, didn't I? Sam, where *are* we going, and how long before we get there?

SAM: We're nearly there now Tracy, love. Eh Sarah, it was great when all that work was coming in, wasn't it?

SARAH: Yeah, and you met Annie Bradshaw and I met Jed Malone. You left home and our lives started to fall apart. This is Valonia Park, isn't it?

TRACY: That's when Clare ran away.

CLARE: I didn't run away. I went to see Daddy.

SARAH; *(Excited)* Sam, there's the house that I came to see with Pat Askew. The one with the porch and the yellow bush in the garden. Can you see it? It's brilliant, even better than I remember it. Sam, what are you doing? *(Sound of van stopping, engine turned off and doors opening and closing. Exterior house. Lawnmower in distance.)*

TRACY: Daddy, I need to go to the toilet now!

CLARE: I want to go as well, Dad.

SAM: *(Sound of doors opening as he speaks)* Right, here you go. Let me open this other door. That's it. See the stairs? The bathroom's the first door you come to at the top. Go on, hurry up, we're coming in now.

SARAH: Sam, are you going to tell me what's going on? What are we doing here? Whose is this house, and why have you got the keys?

SAM: This is the last secret I'll ever keep from you Sarah, I promise. But before I tell you what it is, I want you to do the same.

SARAH: *(Nervously)* O.K., I promise. No secrets between us from now on.

SAM: Welcome to Valonia Park Mrs. Jackson. *(Jangling keys)* Here's the keys to your new house.

SCENE ENDS

SCENE 3: INTERIOR OF VAN WHICH IS MOBILE

DAVE: Have you got the keys to the side door of the restaurant?

BILLY: No, I thought you had them.

DAVE: I must have left them on the bar when Vinnie was giving us the money for the gas bottles. I don't fancy humping these things through from the front, do you? They weigh a ton. *(Sound of police car overtaking them)*

BILLY: We'll have to give them a knock. He's in a hurry, isn't he?

DAVE: Probably late for his tea break. You know what they're like; do as I say, not as I do.

BILLY: It's getting more like a police state every day. Look what they got away with during the miners' strike and Wapping. There's two levels of law in this country; one for us and *(sound of fire engine)*. Hang on, I'll pull over and let this fella through. *(Fire engine passes)*

DAVE: A couple of months ago we couldn't get you to say anything, now it's hard to get a word in edgeways. I wonder where they're all going?

BILLY: I've got a lot to be thankful about. If it wasn't for Mary and Tommy taking me in and looking after me, I don't know where I would've ended up.

257

DAVE: Tommy? Looking after you? I thought he wanted you out?

BILLY: Oh no, I can see right through him. Under all that bluster he's a frightened man. Can you understand what it must be like for him? Long-term unemployed, no prospect of a proper job. He must feel as though he's been thrown on the scrap heap to rot. I don't support everything he does or says, but I admire him. He won't lay down and let them walk all over him, Dave. All that stuff with the tip and the rabbits, the car boot sales and now the fruit and veg; that's Tommy fighting back against the system.

DAVE: Yeah, I've made a lot of mistakes in my life Billy, and I'm grateful I'm still around to tell the tale. One of the biggest was losing Margaret. I had it all there in front of me and blew it away. Look how red the sky is above the school. The whole street must be on fire. *(another fire engine goes past)* Follow him in, Billy. You can see where they're heading, can't you?

BILLY: We'll soon find out when we get around this ... corner. Bloody 'ell, the pub's on fire.

DAVE: Stop the van, Billy . Stop the van. *(van screeches to a halt)*

BILLY: What's the matter? I can drive in closer .

DAVE: The gas bottles in the back of the van. They'll go off like bombs if they get too hot. *(Van door slams. Exterior with building on fire. Getting louder as they get nearer, shouts of fire crews, etc. Billy and Dave run towards the fire.)*

DAVE: Look at it! The whole place is on fire .

BILLY: The restaurant, Dave, it's like a big bonfire .

POLICEMAN: Keep back . Hey, where do you think you're going?

BILLY: The *Rose & Crown*. We've been working there. There's people inside. Mary ... Mrs. Kelly ...

POLICEMAN: Right, I'll need a statement from you. What's your name, sir?

DAVE: I know you, don't I? Remember me? Dave Parker. You found me, thought I was dead, hypothermia. What happened here? Did they all get out O.K.?

POLICEMAN: Well ... It seems there were two explosions reported. When the first appliance arrived the whole place was alight. Faces were seen at the second-floor windows, but that was a while ago. We haven't news of any survivors yet, I'm sorry.

         (The noise of the fire intensifies and far away with an echo we hear:)

MARY: You take no notice of him, Billy. You stay as long as you like.

PAT: You're a rum devil you are, Dave Parker.

JUAN: You like the *Cuba Libre,* Billy?

VINNIE: One more stunt like that, Dave Parker, and you're barred.

TOMMY: This is it, Billy, me ship's come sailing in.

MARGARET: I love you, Dave Parker. You soft sod.

Series ends

KEITH BIRCH
from *The Merseysiders* (1988-90)

City Tram

that year the draughty
crackling trams clanged
bowled like hoops
down Water Street
draughty and stiff
and full of noise
that night the tram lurched
and she fell
laughing and drunk into his arms
as chips fell hot
and scattered on her lap
'Let me' he said
'Let me' and kissed
her laughing lips
and turned her head
to face the swinging stars

now buses frighten her
the doors that hiss and snap
and angry drivers
chauffeuring their hate
the nights are colder
and the stars moved far away

and only at her feet the tracks remain
silver and still
they mark the path
that brought her down the years
from Water Street

RICHARD HILL

Water Street, 1932 (E. Chambré Hardman)

Liverpool Cathedral, 1987

Arches seen through arches frame the words. Good
homilies from Proverbs and the Psalter
for my great grandpapa who helped to carve the wood
behind the Lady Chapel altar.

The Sony system choir sings without a break
at the christening of a motordrive Minolta.
Traceys in dark corners confer blessings on their Daves.
At the breaking of the cake
an American announces: "Hell, Uncle Walter,
this coffee bar ain't got no cherry Coke."
The solemnisation of souvenir rock,
cathedral cards, cassettes, cathedral after-shaves.
For the architect, for each and every builder,
electrically self-rotating graves.

COPLAND SMITH

Alice Thomas Ellis's Liverpool

I was born in Liverpool in 1932 and as I poke around in the sludge of memory it seems I might just as well have been born in Ancient Rome, for the city then bears no relation whatsoever to the city now. To put it another way, watching *Brookside* I feel rather as a Sioux warrior might feel if he had survived long enough to watch, say, *LA Law* - baffled, resentful and wild with regret for the Good Old Days. The cast thereof are no more typically Liverpudlian than are the cast of *Neighbours* and, with some adjustment of accent and temperament, they could be interchangeable (the Neighbours, on the whole, appear unnaturally sweet while the Brooksiders seem unusually ill-disposed towards each other) - as could their dwelling places. The matter of accent is another source of bewilderment: the Liverpool manner of speech was always said to derive in equal parts from Welsh, Irish and catarrh, but I don't remember the glottal stop being part of it. (All accents seem to have undergone a change in recent years: at the other end of the social scale no one now talks like Celia Johnson.)

Bread comes closer to my memories, for large, scatty families were very much part of Liverpool life, due, I imagine, to the Irish Catholic influence. There were annual scenes as rival religionists processed for their various purposes: one redoubtable old lady always marching with the handle of her sewing machine concealed beneath her shawl to protect her altar-serving grandchildren from assaults by Orangemen, but communal violence was the exception rather than the rule. Liverpool 8, where my family lived, was a *truly* neighbourly district where everyone knew everyone else. It is now known as Toxteth and the atmosphere is entirely changed. My grandfather owned a pub called The Nook in Nelson Street and judging by the few surviving letters from my aunts to my father, his offspring led an idyllic childhood with frequent camping and fishing trips into the Wirral and Wales. 'Aug. 5th 1920 . Dear Alfy, I hope you are enjoying yourself at camp. As you will perceive by the above address I am staying at the Unicorn.'

Another letter addressed to my father at The Saracen's Head, Beddgelert, contains an account of an entertainment the children had been to. 'There was an Irishman from Cork who sang and told a few jokes. There was one where this man got on a car (tram) and at the first stop two or three men jumped on, at the next some more got on and all the time Pat had to keep moving up the platform, so when the conductor came for the fares Pat said: "Begorrah, you shouldn't ask me to pay, I've been walking all the way." He said ladies spend shillings on stuff to colour their lips but grudge their husbands 3d to colour his nose.'

The letter concludes with the news that 'Last night they played Net-Ball on bicycles at the Empire, and next week we're going to the theatre - I think either Daddy Longlegs or Little Women.' Sounds like there was never a dull moment. At one point a returned seafarer presented them with a large consignment of bananas - 'Hip Hip Hoorah. The bananas are ripe and we've had banana cream and Fried Bananas and Banana Fritters (Mother used the batter to thicken the sauce with next morning) and a banana whenever we want one.'

The picture that emerges from these letters is of a happy, relaxed and prosperous way of life - with a lot of bananas. 'Dear old Bean. Sorry we have bambooslet all the bananas, and besides "Love to have some" is not right. "Like to have some bananas" is correct.'

In February 1926 my Papa was fined a shilling,'... for that you, during the period between one hour after sunset and one hour before sunrise, to wit, at the hour of 6.55 pm on the 18th day of February in a certain street called Prince Alfred Road in the City of Liverpool aforesaid, being a person riding a certain carriage called a Bicycle, did not carry attached to the said carriage a Lamp so constructed and placed as to exhibit a light in the direction in which you were proceeding, and so lighted and kept lighted as to afford adequate means of signalling the approach or position of the said carriage, Contrary to the Statute in such cases made and provided ...' Later that year: 'At a meeting of the Liverpool Shipwreck and Humane Society, held at the Underwriters Room, Exchange Buildings Liverpool on the 8th day of December 1926, It Was Resolved Unanimously that the thanks of the Committee be presented to Alfred Lindholm with the Society's Bronze Medal for bravely rescuing a man attempting suicide in the River Mersey near the Dingle on the 22nd December 1926.' I think these fragments of ephemera demonstrate something of the difference in priority and attitude between then and now.

By the time I was born my grandfather had killed himself - there is still debate in the family about whether it was deliberate or accidental - and the family's circumstances had already altered. It seems that there were darker undercurrents than the children were ever aware of. It is said that all the flower-sellers of the city followed the funeral cortege but none of us knows quite why, and there were vague rumours of sexual indiscretion - but then, there always are.

I was taken to live in Wales when I was five and did not return to Liverpool until I was 17 when I went to the Art School. It was then still a living city with businessmen whizzing to and fro on the Mersey ferry-boats which were crewed by chaps in navy-blue jumpers, thriving theatres and cinemas, the Philharmonic usually filled to capacity, and a crammed Kardomah. There were small businesses and shops everywhere and The Nook had become the centre of the Chinese community. My father's sister still lived in Canning Street with her large (and scatty) family, still surrounded by the old tapestries and family portraits which her father had brought from Finland when he left the sea in favour of innkeeping. I found it entirely delightful...

Beryl Bainbridge said, 'Somebody has murdered Liverpool and got away with it ', and she's right. People now think of it mainly as the home of the Beatles, God help us. I prefer to remember it as the home of people like my uncle Percy, who played second violin in the Philharmonic all his life and hated music. He would have sailed on the *Titanic* as a member of the orchestra only my aunt had a premonition and wouldn't let him - but that's another story.

ALICE THOMAS ELLIS

Maritime Liverpool

The gulls indulge
their crow's-nest fantasies,
stiff-legged mariners
outward-bound.

Plump and fishy
and full of velleity,
they perch on top
of the silliest pinnacles.

Here is a bird
on a king on a horse
on a plinth, who sees
no more than Nelson did.

Fog encircles
the Wallasey ferry:
a gull on the flagpole
has taken command.

A motor-launch,
with its jewellery of tyres,
bobs at the quay
like a harbour tart.

I love these gulls'
uncalled-for heroics,
their swooping down
at the sea and missing it.

CHRISTOPHER REID

King Edward VII statue at the Pier Head
(Gladys Mary Coles)

Shaggy Sailor's Story

It's a long time since I was in the Isle of Man, but being there reminds me of a story once current in my home town. It had to do with a Liverpool sailor who met a desperate South American girl on the Dock Road.

"l trying to get on a ship," she said. "I got no money, no job. I want go home to my mama, my papa in Buenos Aires."

"Listen," the sailor said. "I can help you. My ship is sailing tonight. She'll be picking up cargo at quite a few places en route, but in three weeks she'll be in Buenos Aires. I can hide you in a lifeboat."

To the poor homeless girl this seemed like a heaven-sent offer, and she allowed the sailor to smuggle her on board and conceal her under a tarpaulin in one of the lifeboats. A few hours later, the ship sailed.

Every night the sailor brought food and water to the stowaway, together with a report on their progress from port to port. After a week, their friendship ripened to romance, and thereafter the sailor spent his nights in the lifeboat. Then one morning, a seaman noticed the untied tarpaulin on the lifeboat and in the process of fastening it, discovered the frightened girl. He took her up to the bridge where she poured out her story to the captain.

"Disgraceful!" said the captain. "What a scoundrel! You must tell me the bounder's name."

"He no bounder," protested the girl. "He no scoundrel. He nice man, kind. He taking me home."

"Madam," the captain told her. "You are on the Isle of Man ferry."

FRED NOLAN
The Bookseller 21 & 28 December 1990

Queen Elizabeth 2 in the Mersey, July 1990, marking 100 years of transatlantic voyaging by the Cunard Line
(Gladys Mary Coles)

The Real Liverpool

Philharmonic, this city,
Studded with theatres and an array of art galleries.
Some of the most magnificent architecture
you're ever likely to see...
Overflowing with humour
and cultural diversity.

Built on the treasures collected from slavery,
rich in a heritage that some never see.
Steeped in tradition,
a working-class history.

Champions of sport, with a keen creativity.
Poets, players, humble rate-payers.
Yet seldom is this how the media portray us.
As a rule they never show how cool
the full scope of 'The Real Liverpool'.

MUHAMMED KHALIL
(Eugene Lange)

Blacks Like Me

Before I ever came to Britain, back in 1983, I heard my father talk about the docks in Liverpool. As a Black American serviceman stationed here during the Korean War, he must have been disoriented in Chester. Certainly he never mentioned the Cheshire countryside to me —but the docks and the workers here, the parties, the weekends, the pubs, the be-bop, the drinking, the friends —I've heard stories about Liverpool as long as I can remember.

When I first came to Cambridge, I forgot all my father's stories. I was caught up in the storybook life at Emmanuel. As long as I stayed in the college gardens, more protected by my tutors than any of the ponds or ducks or flowers, it was a languorously wonderful existence. But out on the town, the chill set in. But with my friends — all New Zealanders, Scots, boys from Durham and girls from Manchester, and a lovely piano player from Liverpool —I could forget the eyes that shut in my face.

I didn't forget the lesson, and came up North to Manchester in 1988. But Manchester and Liverpool might as well be on different planets, for all the communication between. My only connection for four years was a wild Scouser named Colin —brilliant at be-bop sax —couldn't understand a word he said —and

264

the occasional gig, late at night. I didn't see Liverpool by day until almost a year ago, when I took the job as Black Writing Liaison Officer for the WALL* project at Toxteth Library. And I soon realised why my daddy always talked about the place, because for the first time in this country I was surrounded by blacks like me: blacks from an old, established community, blacks whose blood had been intermingled with other nations over so many years no one bothers to count; blacks whose skin spans the spectrum from gold to amber to ebony, and back.

And while I had been singing in Britain for years, reading my poems in Britain for years, I never got such a buzz from an audience as here in Liverpool. No jealousy, no jockeying for position — not from the performers here (at least I haven't seen it yet, and hope I never do); no too-cool-to-clap at a concert here. I love it. Everyone knows performers live on what audiences give them, and I never found a purer response than here. I hope I can find others who will lose themselves in writing or singing or acting, and help them find what I've found. Because I love it.

*WALL - Writing Activities in Liverpool Libraries   CHERYL MARTIN

from *Watching*

In the novel WATCHING Brenda and Malcolm take turns to describe how they met and how their unlikely relationship managed to stagger from one disaster to the next. In this abridged extract we start with the voice of Malcolm.

If Mr Ambrose hadn't suddenly decided we ought to re-stock the tie racks, and if Terry had helped instead of saying he had to leave early because he'd promised his landlady he'd pick up a couple of plaice fillets from Marks, I would have got away on time. As it was, by the time I got to Victoria Street the tunnel traffic was backed up to North John Street. Well almost; it certainly reached that traffic island near the top, which is why I decided it might be quicker to nip down Mathew Street and then come out half way along Whitechapel, except that there was a van unloading near the top and I couldn't get through. So after negotiating a rather difficult U turn just outside Cavern Walks I headed South towards Aigburth.

As it happened this wasn't the master stroke I'd intended as a lorry had broken down at the end of Paradise Street, by the Moat Hotel, well the far side of it actually, so that there was single line traffic for at least half a mile, possibly three quarters, certainly five eighths. Eventually I decided to nip up towards Sefton Park and to cut across that way. Then would you believe it, a burst water main.

So what with the delay at the shop and my mini tour of central Liverpool and the water gushing down Ullet Road I realised I needed to stop somewhere for a 'you know what'. Amazingly, just as I reached this decision I turned a corner and there, lo and behold, right in front of me was a pub. Unfortunately that was a bit too soon after reaching the decision so I drove on a bit until I eventually came to one called the Grapes.

With my helmet held firmly under my arm I headed for the Gents and as I reached the door wasn't it just my luck to meet a stock scouse comic on his way out who pointed at my helmet and said, "No need to bring your own mate. They've got big ones in there."

The thing about Scousers is not so much that they are particularly funny but they are quick. Given any situation there's a smart remark spat out before normal human beings have time to focus. I can take them in small doses. Very small doses.

On return I went to the bar to order a half of bitter. I thought that by the time I'd drunk it the traffic might have eased and after all I had used their facilities. Trouble was I couldn't get near and nor could I attract the attention of the barmaid. Then after I'd given my third hopeful wave it happened. This young Scots girl must have been standing close behind, when blow me if I didn't knock her drink with my elbow. Embarrassment plus plus. But she didn't seem too upset, not like the drink, (that's a joke), once I offered to replace it. So next I was waving for a half of bitter and a vodka and lime but still to no effect. Not that is, until she borrows a penny, tosses it amongst the feet of the people in front of us and then says in a very posh voice:

"I say, is that a pound coin on the floor?"

Of course the whole crowd scrum down and I'm straight in with the order. I was impressed. The move was funny and effective and I wasn't at all surprised when she said she was from Glasgow. They're quick too.

She was nice. Easy to talk to, or rather to listen to; something of an aerobics expert and she was down here visiting her cousin, and helping with some new fitness programme he'd devised. She asked what I was doing Sunday and when I told her she laughed a lot. Lovely sense of humour, though she insisted on calling me Arnold. Before I knew it we had a date.

Tunnel entrance at ten.

*   *   *

For once in my life I was early. Didn't mean to be but sometimes everything just conspires to go right in spite of your best efforts. Of course the fact that Pamela was snoring away like a tug boat in the fog, having been busy with overtime activities extending way beyond the call of stenographing, had something to do with it. So I could have a bath and not get moaned at for taking all the hot water, borrow her makeup without being screamed at and try on three of her tops and a jumper without fear of decapitation. Mind I finished up wearing my own gear. I mean I know baggy was in that year but me in Pamela's togs is just tentsville. I'm beginning to wonder if she doesn't keep her Giant Haystacks physique just to avoid being democratic in the wardrobe department. She's just that tight.

So there I was in the car park by the tunnel entrance, and didn't my gorgeous biker cruise up on a machine so black, so powerful, so throaty that my toe nails cut through my shoes. He didn't see me right away so I tip-toed up behind him and gave an 'anybody home' tap on his helmet. A big helmet it was. One that could hide a face completely, and that's just what I needed when he took it off. I felt myself scarletting so hot my eyelash glue was melting. He grinned. I dried. And then putter puttering into the car park came the real Arnold.

If I hadn't been so embarrassed about knocking on this other fellow's helmet I'd have walked out there and then. But you don't do you. They talk about wanting the ground to open and swallow you - well it's true. And for me, the hole in the ground was the sidecar tacked on to Arnold's bike. Otherwise there's no way I'd ever have climbed into that thing in the first place. Crazy isn't it. I made a mistake and felt I must look a right wally in the eyes of some stranger, so I dive into the first escape tunnel that comes along and finish up looking a mega wally in the eyes of the whole world and Birkenhead. But it happened. Another of the big *ifs* you see. *If* Pamela hadn't had a late night she'd have been awake in time to moan at me and make me late, and I'd have arrived after Arnold, seen from a safe distance him and his antique sewing machine with the semi-detached goldfish bowl and done a runner.

So it's all her fault really.

The trip through the tunnel was bad. We got stuck behind a lorry that belched diesel fumes like dry ice at a pop concert and twice as smelly. The sidecar had been carefully constructed so as to produce a steady draught up through the floor so it slowly filled with fumes. I pulled the canvas top back to let them out but this just let more in, so I settled to writing my will on the steamed up windscreen. There was worse to come. At least the tunnel road surface was smooth. When we hit the original Druids' road through deepest Wirral I got bounced around so much three fillings shot out.

I suppose it must have been a punishment. My Mum was dead against our Sandra going to any Hells Angels' Rally and I'd sort of agreed with her. Then the same day didn't I chat up this biker in the Grapes and get him to take me with him for a fun day Sunday, knowing it would be next stop Rhyl with a ton or two of ton ups. He didn't actually say where he'd be going but they play it very close to their leathers these bikers.

So that was it. My punishment for being a hypocrite, but you can only take so much. After half an hour that seemed like half a week I put my hand through the lid and waved a hanky. Perhaps I could get time off for bad behaviour. The response was a lot later than immediate. First I got a grin and a wave that reminded me why I'd christened him Arnold in the first place. He looked like one. But finally he got the message and we stopped at a country caff in the middle of nowhere. You couldn't imagine the relief. It had been like riding in a liquidiser. I told him.

"A couple more miles of that and you'd have had a sidecar slopping with pureed Brenda."

He gave me a very strange look.

*   *   *

Leonard had rung on Thursday evening. He had seen a hen harrier out on Burton Marsh and told me the precise spot. I wasn't too hopeful. This had happened before. You see a lot depended on the tides, and the week before there had been a high spring at Parkgate. Trouble was I could never remember whether you got the time of high water by adding an hour every day or taking one off. As things turned out my calculations were quite academic. Having first agreed to pick up the Scots girl by the tunnel entrance (Liverpool end) early Sunday morning it then turned out that the soonest she could make it was ten a.m. It was unfortunate but understandable. The problem was that before she left the house she had to see to her invalid sister.

The first shock came when I pulled in at a café. We hadn't spoken when I'd picked her up at the tunnel entrance, as she seemed to be in a bit of a hurry for us to get away. I didn't even cut the engine. Then, as I helped her out of the sidecar, she let rip with a nasal winge of pure scouse that I found depressingly familiar. Having lived in the area for so long now I hardly notice it, but when you do meet someone from abroad, Glasgow in this case, you do look forward to a little badinage in a different register.

"Hold on a minute," I said. "Where do you come from?"

She gave me a funny look.

"Are you soft or somethin'? I just got out the bloody sidecar."

Which just about set the tone for the day. It had all been a big act. She wasn't helping with any training, she knew nothing of aerobics and she wasn't even the most distant relative of Kenny Dalglish.

You may find it hard to credit that I could have believed any part of her meanderings in the first place. I do myself. But you see she is expert, and in the ensuing months I witnessed her fool more cynical types than me. Terry Milton for one and it took a bewhiskered French Canadian with a wooden leg to settle that score.

But I did believe and that's my problem. Even after twenty years in this land of the fairy tale I still can't get out of the habit of believing people. Silly isn't it. Actually thinking that when someone strings together a sequence of words that there should be sense to the sentence, sincerity in the syntax, instead of fabrication, fantasy and falsehood. (I can be quite poetic when roused). Particularly when it's a perky lass with a pretty face and a smile that can light a room. Now that I've known her longer I can see that I must have been easy pickings - but I'm sure that accent would have fooled Billy Connolly himself. And the smile, devastating, but it's seldom in use. Most of the time she's on continuous moan with auto reverse.

*   *   *

As we left the caff I told him straight that there was no way I would travel one more lousy inch in that stupid goldfish bowl. There was a vacant length of saddle sticking out behind him which I was quite prepared to keep warm.

"I'll get on the back and hang on to you," I explained.

"But you can't," he pouted. "It's not allowed. Not without a helmet."

Would you believe it. All the bikers in the world and I had to plck one who'd got an I SPY badge for law. Well given all the clues I'd had up to that point I should have guessed there was something phoney about the whole gig. But I was tired. I'd had a bad week, and what with a cold and sitting through Krypton Factor, Master Mind, two rounds of University Challenge and three Blockbusters my brain was sore. So it was back in the sidecar, but not for so long this time. I only lost one filling, caught my earring on the back of the seat, laddered my tights and broke my right thigh with my chin when we stopped suddenly. A doddle really. So I was just wondering if I should write my address in blood on the canvas bag so that they'd have somewhere to send the bits, when the lid opened. I peeped out and round. We were in central nowhere.

"What 's up?" I asked.

"We're here," he jested.

"Here?" I puzzled. "Where the bloody hell's here?"

"Burton Marsh," he lied, for the bike was not slowly sinking.

This was the first sign he'd given of having a sense of humour, so I sat back and waited for the punch line. But there wasn't one. Or rather that was it. He was, would you believe, a birdwatcher.

What can you do? He offered to run me into Neston and put me on the next bus to civilisation, or Birkenhead. It was cold, there was rain in the air and we were surrounded by a billion acres of green nothing but I thought, what the hell, I'll stick around for a bit. When it comes to stupid, I've got badges.

Of course once I took my brain out of neutral it was all so obvious. Him a biker! Even his leathers looked like off cuts from a worn settee. No studs, no earrings, no wrist chains, nothing manly at all. And what I'd taken to be the edge of a tattoo peeping out from under his cuff turned out to be a biro'd phone number.

We left the bike rusting under a tree and set out on a hike across a field that was probably Cornwall. This gave me time to think and time to worry. The thing that bothered me was the possibility that our Pam might find out. If she ever discovered that my little chat up had got me no further than a Wirral Marsh with a poncy birdwatcher, after me saying I was heading for a Rhyl rave up, she'd laugh till her shoes were full. So I asked him just one favour:

"Promise you won't tell our Pamela."

"I wouldn't know your Pamela if I fell over her," he sniffed.

"Some fall," I pictured. "You'd break your neck. She's thirteen stone and twelve of them's her bum." (You don't get repartee like that in Manchester.) "She was sitting in the corner by the Space Invaders."

He stopped and if there'd been a glass plate in his head you'd have seen the cogs turning.

"I didn't notice her." Wait for it. "Or her friends!"

It was the first of what I've come to recognise as a 'Malcolm joke'. Not completely unfunny, interesting because of its rarity value and carefully heralded by a smile that lifted like a pair of stage curtains as he first thought of it himself, then delivered with the finesse of a lumber jack.

We now have an understanding. I've promised not to call him Arnold, and he's promised not to crack more than two jokes each month, except for December when he just cracks one — as a sort of Christmas bonus to the rest of us.

JIM HITCHMOUGH
from the Novel, *Watching* (1990)

Something Great and Strange

'...it is a deep pleasure to us to come here today to open for the use of men a thoroughfare so great and strange as this Mersey tunnel, now made ready by your labour.'

HIS MAJESTY KING GEORGE V, July 18, 1934

BIRKENHEAD   **TUNNEL**

No headlights   and wind up
your window.   Sounding
                          the horn prohibited.

Go down, flat along the river's belly until you see
the carriageway rise   False dawn
of lights that snake
you away to the left and
again with orange, then open
you out into wet Birkenhead, to
overhead gantries now, instead
of pale green confessionals, toll-
booths with uniform men issuing the
large tickets we used to collect.
Now manned only to give change, it's
automatic for everyone. Wind down
the window, steer with one hand, select
a bin, toss in the correct money.

automatic   manned   manned   automatic   automatic   automatic
change   change   no change

MICHAEL CUNNINGHAM

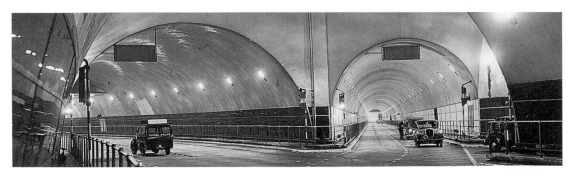

(Keith Medley)

from *Janet and John*

AUTHOR'S NOTE: The 'Janet and John' books were used to teach children basic reading skills in primary schools in the 50s and 60s through the adventures of a brother and sister. They were a white, middle class family. Mummy never lost her temper, Daddy never got drunk or hit Mummy. The sun always shone and the children never tried to assault or maim each other, play truant from school or experiment with cigarettes.

And so what happened to a generation of children who read the 'Janet and John' books?

This play is about one such Liverpool couple JANET AND JOHN.

Characters: JANET: aged nineteen; JOHN aged twenty.
The extract is from ACT ONE; the setting, 1980; Liverpool.

JANET: The church. I feel sick. Dad holds my hand. We sit and look at each other a moment, our last time together. Like lovers parting forever, his eyes glazed with tears. He hugs me tight, his baby girl, before she becomes a woman. I step out into the street to crowds of cheering neighbours, gasping with delight. A butterfly emerging from its chrysalis! I can hear the music. I feel... God, I don't know what I feel. I'm floating into the cold darkness, the cave of God. A glimmer of candle light, hushed silence, the smell of polished oak, the rustle of my dress, a waft of Chanel No. 5 and Aramis, flowers, candle wax. He's there at the front. He tries to turn to see me, he can't wait. I'm so lovely, so beautiful. A dream in white taffeta. I look down at my hands, my false nails still perfectly in place. I hold father's arm, every second counts. Drink it in, keep it forever. The stained glass lit by sunlight, colours falling into my path, my embroidered bodice flashing with a thousand different gems. I dazzle, I shine, alive with light!

JOHN: I didn't recognise her. She looks all sort of... squat and puffed out. Like the frilly doll me Mum keeps in the bog to cover the toilet roll. I can hear me Mum sobbing quietly into me Dad's hanky, you'd think it was her son's funeral. I've got a terrible urge to run but it's gone too far for that. Why's Janet's uncle smirking, it's alright for him. "We are gathered here". He beckons me to step forward, the condemned man's last act of will. Karen takes the bouquet from Janet then slips on her train and crashes uncontrollably into the pews. I hope she's broke her leg. Janet's veil slides softly to the floor leaving a little halo of flowers framing her nose. Me Mum's starting to laugh now, too many gin and oranges lashed down her throat. I think me Dad's stuffing his hanky into her mouth. "Do you take" as Janet's mother nails the veil back onto her head, making her dolly perfect for the sacrifice. The sacrifice, that's me.

JANET: It's gone like a dream. Two birds flying in the roof of the church, the soft flutter of their wings above us. My uncle's workless hands, soft as kid leather, bless our union. The joy in his eyes as he takes this man and this woman to the precipice of love. "Man and wife", he's mine.

JOHN: Bloody stupid birds flapping around, beating their wings against the windows, shitting desperately, like drunken B 52s, dropping great watery blobs of napalm on unsuspecting heads. It's like the dance of the zombies, everyone's eyes raised, blank with booze, swaying to avoid the inevitable. I'm calm. *My* suit's hired.

Janet and John start to dance a waltz

JANET: The Adelphi, only the best for me.

JOHN: And what was wrong with The Everton Supporters Club I'll never know.

JANET: I'm your wife now. And you're my husband. Mr. and Mrs., man and wife, mums and dads, a couple.

JOHN: I love you Janet.

JANET: You said it! Say it again, only ... call me Mrs. Connor.

JOHN: I love you Mrs. Connor. I feel like I'm talking to me Mum.

JANET: I love you, Mr. Connor. Shall we go and consume our marriage upstairs?

JOHN: Let's wait a bit. People will notice and I don't fancy your dad bursting in on us. You make a terrible racket.

JANET: I'll bite the pillow.

JOHN: If we stood up, the bed springs wouldn't squeak.

JANET: I'm not consuming my marriage standing up. I want a proper consumption.

JOHN: Wrong word. *(SEXILY)* It's fuck.

JANET: Don't talk dirty to me, I'm your wife ... Mrs. Connor. Did you see Clare's face? It was a picture, all smiling sweetly but seething with jealousy inside.

JOHN: I'm going for a pint. The lads'll want to say their goodbyes. I won't see them for two weeks.

JANET: But what about me?

JOHN: You can come as well. I'll get you a cider and black.

JANET: Say it. Go on, again.

JOHN: I love you.

JANET: Mrs. Connor.

JOHN: Our flight is at eleven, courtesy of her mum and dad. Two weeks in sunny Greece.

JANET: Speke airport, two weeks with my Adonis. ...

PAT ANDERSON
from *Janet and John*
Performed at the Liverpool Playhouse Studio, 1990.

The Argonauts

I saw a jet
Catching the fallen sun
Spewing a golden curve in the west.
The black spot,
Giving birth to the twin streams of gold,
Making its own sunset.
For miles it traced that gold
Dropping down from the west,
Its captive horde
Folding away their books,
Dousing their cigarettes,
Strapping their apprehensive diaphragms.
Slowly it lost the sun.
The gold became grey.
And as it turned for Speke
The grey became the black smoke of everyday,
The gold became pollution,
The Argonauts became the taxi queue.

MAURICE CALLANAN

Morning, Liverpool 8

In Blackburne Place and Canning Street
the terraces half-wake,
stretch their balconies;
cast-iron railings, Ionic columns
blink into daylight from
a nightmare of bulldozers,
dripping water, charred beams,
distant dreams of hopscotch,
hoofbeats on cobblestones. The mirror tells
of a bright new face, does not reflect
the past neglect. Hope Place
and Huskisson tell of the nightmare
almost gone.

ADRIAN HENRI

'What is a laugh?'

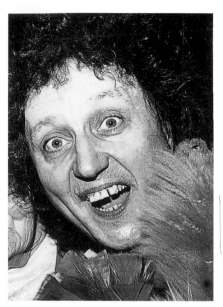

Ken Dodd (Catholic Pictorial)

I've always been obsessed by the idea of "What is a laugh?" As a child I used to haunt libraries, reading everything I could on the nature of comedy. How did it work? What made one man funnier than another? And after all these years I've come to the conclusion that somewhere there exists a little comic spirit, a muse if you like—something that is quite apart from personality and technique.

I first sensed this when I was 16 and I went to see Frank Randle play Wishee-Washee in *Aladdin* at the Liverpool Theatre of Varieties. Aristotle said that the essence of comedy is a buckled millwheel, meaning that it is everyday life out of true, and Randle had this; he was a genius. He was also a grotesque. He had a face like a medieval gargoyle. When he came onstage for the first time he simply stood and gaped at the audience with this terrible leer. And the audience shrieked with laughter for fully five minutes. Randle didn't say a word. He just stood and stared at them. It was quite incredible.

Because he looked the way he did, Randle used to collect strange people. If he saw someone with a misshaped nose or ear then he'd sign them up and take them away with him. He supported this whole entourage of grotesques. Eventually he had so many that he had to find something for them to do, so he grouped them together and called them the Mandalay Singers. The first-act finale of this production of *Aladdin* consisted of the Mandalay Singers standing in the middle of the stage. Behind them was this backcloth of a street in old Peking, while Randle, dressed as Wishee-Washee in his little smock, thrashed about wildly in the orchestra pit conducting them in the *Hallelujah Chorus.* Fabulous stuff, absolutely inspired.

Comedy is like a symphony concert in your head. When you're in full flow standing on the Palladium stage in front of 2,500 people and the belly laughs are coming thick and fast, you have this wonderful feeling of elation. You find yourself saying things and doing things that you've never thought of before. The comic muse has taken over. It's over 50 years since I first saw this happen to Frank Randle but I've never forgotten it. Watching him that night was what really made me decide to be a comedian.

KEN DODD
Sunday Telegraph (December, 1990)

Mersey Plumage

There's a stretch of mud and redrock
over the railings down a ten-foot drop
the river gradually lays bare
when the sea breathes back its waters.
Between the worn down mounds of rock
the bricks and bottles and bladderwrack,
the stranded pools and puddles wear a skin
of marbled vivid oil. It's the water's
coat-of-Joseph and its Nessus-shirt
only the hardy survive: odd pink bivalves
mottled-crabs, incorrigible lugworms.
Each winter I come back, hear underfoot
the crackle of glass and shell, the clutched
slurp of mud and the seaweed's wheezing vesicles
disgorging sewage. I follow again
the familiar profile of the skyline,
its comb of coolingtowers and chimneys
bathed in their vapours, brewing up
one more prismatic sunset. Everything
is covered with a loving grey drizzle
the gull's wings cut right through
en route for the Pier Head where they assemble
skirling the ferries into harbour
from Dublin, Belfast, the Isle of Man.
The gulls are as usual here as the stones
they could have hatched from, but this year
I'm sure there are more birds than ever:
knots peeping into the air in flocks
at the first crank of a dockside crane;
mallards at anchor in the khaki tide,
even a curlew nearby, heard not seen.
It's as if the despaired-of dove returned
with a sprig of olive in her bill
or the tamed familiar Liver Birds
had shaken their sooty pinions free
of slaveships, hovels and merchant banks,
the one-way-deal of industry.
No, it's hard to imagine the Mersey clear
divested of petrochemicals at last
a home and sanctuary for all,
with the first salmon for centuries
passing the estuary, heading inland
and all that broken glass blended and rounded
making a rainbow of the riverbed.

JAMIE MCKENDRICK

Father and Son

Your latest gadget - a "monocular" ...
You showed it to me on our homeward walk

beside the Mersey, past that stuck-up sign,
This Park is Private - then used it

to spot birds ("more now the river's cleaner"):
"plovers and, look, they're dunlins by the tide."

I looked and joked - "Your fault my vision's poor" -
but swung round to the cranes at Garston Docks

as though the city would reveal itself.
"Each to his own picture." Perhaps I meant:

Don't you see what we share - your legacy -
this sense of belonging nowhere?

Engrossed by detail, lens in hand,
you unriddled the name on a ship's bow.

MICHAEL O' NEILL

The Birth of the Ark Royal, 1952 (E. Chambré Hardman)

Portrait of a Not So Candid Camera

Three years after his death, his spectacles still rest comfortably on the workbench, the ancient electric iron is in its box ready for use and the 1930s' vacuum cleaner propped against a wall.

Time has stood still inside the 18th century Liverpool terrace house in Rodney Street where the great and the famous once went for their flattering portraits ("We bring out your best points and overlook your defects", ran the advertising).

When the photographer E. Chambré Hardman died in April, 1988, he left behind not only a rambling home cluttered with a lifetime's ephemera but a glorious collection of photographic history. There were ancient cameras, studio props, printing equipment, accessories and order books. And, above all, there were the photographs, thousands of them. Hardman, with his business partner Kenneth Burrell, had over several decades created a Liverpool institution, a photographic studio known outside the city for its excellence.

Anyone who wanted to be someone had to have an E. Chambré Hardman portrait, a formal affair, brilliantly lit and with just a flash of character. There were also the superb landscapes, typically British with their looming clouds and timeless countryside, and city scenes often set in rain or snow. As he neared the end of his life, Hardman realised that his collection might well be in peril. Both his partner and wife had died and he had no immediate family.

So he was delighted when local enthusiasts suggested the setting up of a trust to preserve the work. He bequeathed his home and belongings to the trust. But when the E. Chambré Hardman Trust took possession, they were both delighted and appalled with what faced them. Hardman was a man who obviously found it difficult to throw anything away. Yellowing newspapers, old tram tickets, letters, catalogues - all had been saved in a haphazard fashion. Some rooms were virtually impassable with the junk piled up.

Viv Tyler, development director of the Trust, says it was at first a matter of attempting to put things in order and then cataloguing. Three years later, the work is still proceeding. She had met Hardman before he died and purchased some of his landscapes ("He was unable to print new ones so I made certain that there were other copies") and had noticed the state of the house. But even she was surprised by how many items he had kept. "It was like an Aladdin's cave. It wasn't just the photographic items but the ephemera he had hoarded over the years. It was a house where time had stood still."

Typically, he had saved the old love letters between himself and his wife, Margaret, who had originally joined the firm as an assistant. They had pet names for each other, he as "Gobbles" and she as "Pearly". There were crumbling copies of the *Liverpool* (as it was then) *Daily Post* containing his work, bottles, picture postcards, brushes, combs, kitchen equipment, and a lot more, much of it dating back to the 1920s and 1930s.

Irish-born, Hardman had been a keen amateur photographer when he had joined the Indian Army in 1918, seeing action on the North West Frontier and taking snaps of India which still hang in the house. More importantly, he met a fellow officer, Kenneth Burrell, who had important contacts in his home town of Liverpool. The pair decided in 1923 to set up a photographic studio in Bold Street; Burrell as the business head, Hardman as the photographer. In 1948, Hardman moved lock, stock and hoard to Rodney Street.

They charged high prices but the quality and service were excellent: the house still contains instructions to receptionists on how to answer the telephone, "When the telephone rings, reply 'Burrell and Hardman' brightly and happily (no matter how you may be feeling at the moment) ."

They quickly established themselves as the photographic studio in the city, early clients including Lord Derby and Miss Emma Holt. Visiting theatre stars also placed themselves memorably before his cameras, including Michael Redgrave, Ivor Novello and Margot Fonteyn.

No expense was spared in the studio with hundreds of toys purchased to keep the kids happy and Greek columns used to supply dignity to the most undignified of clients (one snap on display shows a small dog posed uncertainly on top of a Greek plinth). All the items are still there, some toys stuffed in drawers, others on display and the Greek columns looking incongruous in a faded bedroom.

Later in life, Hardman's reputation spread further afield, his masterpiece, The Birth of the Ark Royal (the building of the ship seen from the top of a Birkenhead hill), now accepted as one of the great British photographs and subject of the first video produced by Bradford's National Museum of Photography, Film and Television.

The cataloguing of the prints and negatives in the house is a huge task, some of it undertaken by Philip Plant: "The work really captures the social history of Liverpool and Britain.' Pete Hagerty, conservation manager of the trust and a driving force behind it, admits that Hardman may not be a major name in world terms. "But he is an important figure in British photographic history."

But what will eventually become of the house and its contents? The E. Chambré Hardman Trust want it preserved as a museum, not only for its work but its unique preservation of a provincial photographic studio. The house has a nostalgic fascination that is totally captivating. It is the early 20th Century objects on view as much as the photographic collection that appeal but the two together seem to be an unbeatable combination.

PHILIP KEY
Daily Post (11 July, 1991)

Liverpool from the Museum Steps, 1946 (E. Chambré Hardman)

Sefton Park (Keith Medley)

City Parks

Sefton, Princes, Wavertree,
Calderstones, Newsham, Stanley...

city parks
preside, entice:
landscaped lungs
purpose-built
pre-dating smokeless fuel.

Tall trees - some more ancient
than the parks - survivors
of soot-lacquered days,
bristle brightly now
in clean-air zones.

Old lads, under the boughs,
walk slowly where once
they skimmed with balls,
sailed high in prams.

Lakes, lodges, lawns
lasting through seasons
of peace and war.
Observers of generations,
the thick-ridged boles
growing through seasons
of human budding -
babies, children, lovers,
mothers, the employed,
the unemployed.

Great roots grapple
the banked earth
border old sandstone walls
reach under back-gardens
where bunting billows
on strung-out lines.

Unrehearsed, from unwritten scripts
dramas are performed each day
against the constant backcloth
of the park...
Sefton, Princes, Wavertree,
Calderstones, Newsham, Stanley.

GLADYS MARY COLES

The Blue Cornet

There was this big lad in our school once, y'know, about three years older than us. Mickey Thacker his name was, and hey, I mean *big* - he was the kind of kid who had a beer gut in the Infants, a beard in the Juniors and a face straight out of Jungle Book. You know the kind I mean, don't y' - you're there readin' y' Beano an' he's like this (TURNING THE PAPER UPSIDE DOWN) -with the Playboy. It's right, second year of the Seniors he got caught playin' Doctors and Nurses ... with the deputy headmistress.

But y'know what - he was a rat. He was. Y'd be there, eleven years old, standin' by the Lake in Newsham Park, mindin' y' own business, catchin' tiddlers with a nylon stockin' - an' lobbo - he'd be there behind y', him and his dog, grabbin' y' by the neck an' shovin' y' into the Lake in y' leaky wellies, an' then, just for laughs, he'd make y' fill y' fish can full of water an' drink it all down. *An' then*, he'd make y' thank him for a nice cup of tea, but all the time, while y' were there sayin', "Thanks Mickey, nice that ", y' knew it wasn't tea y'd drunk, it was lake water full of slime an' frog spawn, an' y'd go home cryin' an' spittin' tadpoles in y' hankie. An' there was once when I give him ten p not to touch me, an' as soon as I give it to him, he set his dog on me, bloody big snarlin' monster, I ended up hidin' in some woman's house in Elm Vale.

An' hey, listen, y' know what happened to him - he went in the Police. Yeah. Honest t' God, I saw him at the United match standin' there with a ten foot alsatian an' a mad smile on his face, prayin' someone'd get brave.

Course, that's the reason for some of them, isn't it - y' Mickey Thackers of this world - they like the feel of the uniform, the blue cornet an' the big boots, an' suddenly they're men; an' then they've got a bit of power, haven't they? An' that kind like a bit of power, they like t' move y' on, prod y' in the back, give y' a little push, grab y' by the scruff of the neck, let y' know they're about - like a school bully roamin' the streets.

Like Isiah, the bobby on the beat on our estate. Phew - he cares alright. He's dedicated - yeah - dedicated t' tryin' t' find a reason t' put us away. Borstal trainin' f' droppin' litter, that's his plan of campaign.

Knows me well, Isiah does. First time I ever got caught was by him. Robbin' crab apples, six years old, obviously headin' for a life of crime - the bastard made us sit there an' eat them all, every single one - an' we'd robbed thousands. All we needed t' make a feast of it was a can of lake water - but even so I was crappin' little green ollies f' about a fortnight after.

But y' know the biggest problem with the Law - no offence meant like - but they're thick. (No, really, they are.) Now I don't care if they've got University degrees, or they've been t' College an' passed exams, an' out of uniform they might be a bundle of fun, bright an' witty an' nice t' know, but once the straps under their chin, their brains go out of the window.

An' if y' don't believe me - one example - right - look at the big signs they have all over their cars - see what's written on them? "POLICE". Now I ask y', isn't that a dead giveaway - I mean, y' don't see robbers goin' around with a big notice on the top of their cars sayin' "THIEF" do y'? Huh, soft isn't in it.

ALAN BLEASDALE

The Surrealism Display, 28th May 1988 - March 1989, the Tate Gallery Liverpool.

The Tate Gallery and its Liverpool University link

The opening displays and exhibitions at Tate Gallery Liverpool in May 1988 included the very successful *Surrealism* display which showed ethnographic objects as well as Surrealist Art. Since then there has been a varied selection of exhibitions, part of a coherent policy. *Degas: Images of Women,* was one of the most popular, emphasising the use of the figure in art. Following on from *Degas* were the *W. S. Sickert* display, *Francis Bacon* and the work of *Lucian Freud.* At present there is a display of paintings by *Stanley Spencer,* which again emphasises the figure in art. To complement the display of German Expressionist Art an exhibition of German Expressionist woodblock prints was mounted and the public were given the opportunity to try the technique for themselves. Tate Gallery Liverpool presents a coherent thematic display and exhibition programme of the best of modern art from the National Collection. The Gallery aims to make the work accessible to all sections of the community by offering a wide range of education provision.

As lecturer in Art and Art History at Liverpool University's Centre for Continuing Education, I am also part of the Tate Gallery Education Team, organising and teaching collaborative courses at the Gallery for the general public. The range of work has been extended to include major art history conferences, artists fora, critical studies courses for students in further and higher education, and gallery seminars for undergraduates studying art history. Ongoing are the events for the general public related to current displays from the National Collection of Modern Art at Tate Gallery Liverpool. The Gallery and the University of Liverpool have recently pledged even closer collaboration with new initiatives planned in their continuing commitment to the community.

ANNE MACPHEE

Laughing all the way to the Tate

I know something of how to deal with art.
I know just what I like and how to treat
the rest. These sculptors are a breed apart.

So when the Tate moved north, I thought it smart
to go there for a laugh, show the effete
I know something of how to deal with art.

I'd strike a scornful attitude, impart
my gems of acid to amuse the elite.
(The rest, these sculptors, are a breed apart.)

Standing among the shapes, I feel the start
of understanding. Minimal defeat
I know; something of how to deal with art.

The bricks and lights and mirrors make my heart
throb stronger, sing new rhythms to each beat,
then rest. These sculptors are a breed apart.

Their skills invade me, fill my every part.
New comprehension makes me feel complete.
I know something of how to deal with art;
the rest? - these sculptors are a breed apart.

ALISON CHISHOLM

Toxteth where I reside (Dub poem)

Come with me yes I'll be your guide
to the city where I reside
let's take a walk
so we can talk
about Liverpool on Merseyside

In the sixties Liverpool
made its name
It went international
well crucial
admired at home and abroad
everybody wanted to speak scouse
Liverpool you're hard

But dread times came
and you lost your fame
pressure hit Liverpool

Now check out Toxteth my dwelling place
can you believe your eyes
there are beautiful houses on elegant streets
I bet you are surprised
because the media painted a picture
of us in a negative light
they magnify the rundown places
and ignore the ones which are out of sight

So forget the ghetto mentality
because we are not ghettoites
we are a talented people
with a lot to give
the oldest Black community in Europe
and we're positive

Now I admit in Toxteth
that things they can get rough
but if you lived down here you would understand
we just don't get enough
so we need a chance the opportunity
to make a positive contribution
so we can feel good in this neighbourhood
and improve our situation.

LEVI TAFARI

284

Clay Pipes by the Mersey

The small boys playing
discovered treasure-trove of broken
white clay pipes - uncovered by the tide?

They were playing on the river-side
down by the jutting rocks which form
Job's Ferry, once private landing-place

at Eastham for big Carlett house.
Highly excited, the boys mud-scrabbled
hoping for pipes which they could bubble-blow,

but, although bowls were whole,
all stems were shattered. We were hard put
to explain the hoard. Old sailors, true,

used to puff pipes like these, yet who
would dump a life-time's smoke here
at high-tide-line? Did they hope mud

would suck them under, hide
the evidence of such depravity?
Or was it vengeance by some wrathful wife?

Or, in departing life,
had some old seaman asked for burial
of all his pipes in waters he had loved

and lived beside, had roved
since boyhood? The receding Mersey lapped
but did not say, gave no direction

for disposal of this odd collection.
The boys therefore, already muddy,
covered them reverently
and left them for the final Resurrection.

MARY HODGSON

The Albert Dock, 1992 - poems by two writers from abroad

From Inside Albert Dock

The dead speak out from inside Albert Dock
'Stop taking us for granted
We are a part of you -
In endless lines we suffered,
Sam, Nell and baby Tom,
Endured again across the sea
Fenced off at Ellis Island.'

Time's passageway bled long
Before another Thomas asked about his ancestors.
He hadn't cared - had thought America
Was all there was.
His emptiness untied the bonds
Built up by pride's indifference.
At last he came to find his roots
Still anchored here in Liverpool.

BARBARA CURRY
(Kansas City, U.S.A.)

Albert Dock

As the curtain rises on another misty dawn,
The water gently lapping at the Weather Map,
The gulls scratch noisily in search of food.
Two boats lie side by side, a silent sentry to the dock.

Then, there were myriads, all clamouring to be served.
A bustling, shouting crowd of burly fishermen,
Rolling barrels filled with sorted, salted fish;
meanwhile, their piercing eyes in search of wife or family.

Now, they come in gushing waves of young and old,
Spilling from their cars to invade enticing shops,
Strolling easily in tune to Beatle songs of days gone by,
Looking for fulfilment of their slow and endless time.

And when the dusk creeps on and gulls will claim their rights,
No lively step resounds on luxury boat or creaking board.
Only sad ghosts of ages past still silently will tread;
The stoney faces of the Liver Birds stand guard over the docks.

HELEN W. HOOGENDYK
(The Hague, Netherlands)

Container Ships

Mixed cargo carried in 'break bulk' form is almost a thing of the past because all valuable cargo is containerized except where port facilities do not exist to handle the containers. Instead of carefully storing a mixed bag of goods in open holds, the specialized container ship has a grid of slots in which standard size steel boxes can be fitted. Once the hatches are closed another two or three tiers can be added on deck. The container can travel in the ship and also on a lorry trailer or railway wagon. It can be unloaded by a special container crane and thus the whole process of loading and unloading can be speeded up. A container ship may spend no more than twelve hours in Royal Seaforth Dock. The containers are taken away to be unpacked (or packed) at inland destinations....The container users of Royal Seaforth Dock make a distinctive contribution to the landscape of the port.

MICHAEL STAMMERS
Liverpool: the Port and its Ships (1991)

A port within a port: Royal Seaforth Dock. The grain terminal can hold about 100,000 tons.
(Mersey Docks & Harbour Board)
Royal Seaforth Dock (officially opened by HRH Princess Anne, July 1973), covers 500 acres,
and handles 25 million tons of cargo a year (as much as the Port did in the 1950s and 1960s).

287

Bridgebuilding

At the first crossing point
of the River Mersey, Warrington
is waiting on an old stone bridge
with a piece of wire as a rod
trying to catch its first live fish
in the industrial flotsam.

At Junction 7
on the M62, Warrington
is waiting with divided loyalties
like a newspaper salesman,
Manchester Evening News in one hand
Liverpool Echo in the other.

On a roundabout
at the end of a boulevard
of adolescent trees, Warrington
is waiting like the stump
of a new exit road on the edge
of a field earmarked for development.

At a flashing red light
by the Ship Canal, Warrington
is waiting to fall like a swing bridge
uniting Greenall's brewery and
Grappenall's church, Lancashire
and Cheshire, north and south .

Outside "Mr. Smith's", Warrington
is waiting on a wire fence
in tracksuit and reeboks
for the queue to die down
and the bouncers' permission
to enter the talent competition.

On the stone bridge
over St.Helen's Canal, Warrington
is waiting like rival gangs
warring over words like private
and rented, money and pride, east
and west, borough and new town .

On the bowling green
by the "King and Queen", Warrington
is waiting to strike it lucky
before the incentive funding
runs out with the third strike
and the tournament ends.

Under graffiti
warning "Unite - don't pay", Warrington
is waiting to bolt together
past and present like a brand new
steel bridge across a river winding
its inevitable way to the sea.

KEVIN FEGAN

Where the Mersey ends

Irk, Irwell, Medlock and Tame
When they do meet with Mersey
Do lose their name.

OLD RHYME

...the Mersey officially ends, swallowed by the sea, at Liverpool Bar, thirteen miles from St George's landing stage at Pier Head. This channel is marked by buoys, but great care is needed since the sands are notoriously mobile. For many years huge blocks of stone were dropped into trenches to build underwater retaining walls in an effort to prevent yet further disasters on a coast already littered with wrecks.

Before joining the sea, however, the Mersey has one more tributary to swallow, the small but interesting River Alt. The Alt has two main sources, one in Croxteth, the other in Knowsley Park. Both these stately homes are now major tourist attractions...with Knowsley Safari Park bringing the roar of the African jungle to mingle with the song of an English blackbird. A far cry indeed from the traditional meander of the Alt, easing itself gently through fertile fields and watermeadows around Sefton...

The Alt reaches the Mersey at a point equidistant between Crosby and Formby. Crosby was originally a tiny village, now appropriately called Little Crosby and remaining aloof from development. The name derives from the Norse "the place of crosses", and one of these crosses still remains. ...

I chose to write the last lines of (my) book heading out from Crosby. There behind a ridge of flower-rich dunes lies Formby, and close to the Alt estuary is Hightown, its surrounding dunes used occasionally as a firing range. A look back at Liverpool is essential, for the city and its river are forever linked....

RON FREETHY
The River Mersey (1985)

Guardians of the Dawn:
the Liverpool Pilots

Centuries long,
The river has flowed
Through an hour glass,
Carrying in suspension
The sands of time.

Tides have turned,
Carrying our changes of fortune,
All our histories.
Gull-shades of our ancestors
Swoop on dark estuarine waves.

We men of the dawn
Came from seawards.
Learning the river's ways,
We mastered
Our business in her waters.

From the bridge,
We have seen
Calm seas, prosperous voyages,
Tempests, and have heard
Bell-buoys tolling in the storm-torn night.

Now, on the eve,
On the flood of another tide,
How fares the wind for Liverpool?
We must set yet another course,
There's a new dawn breaking.

JOHN CURRY

from On Oxton's Hill

Winter is black twigs and a giant moon
Riding the windy battlements and towers
Of gothic mansions built in carriage days
By bold philanthropists. Now boys in anoraks
Race round on Chopper bikes, delivering *Echos*
And the *Wirral Globe,* then home for tea.
The streets fall silent; lighted fir trees shine
From Roslin, Talbot House and Holly Lodge
And foxes stir in frozen shrubbery.
Then, suddenly, St. Saviour's bells ring out, ships hoot
And rockets shoot across the sky to sounds
Of cheering from the river. And, in a corner
Somewhere, high on Oxton's hill, a bud bursts
And another year begins...

HEATHER WILSON

The Return of the Tall Ships, August 1992; Grand Regatta Columbus

The Tall Ships in the Mersey (Liverpool Echo).

Columbus' voyage marked one of the great turning points of history and it is fitting five hundred years later that this anniversary is to be celebrated by this magnificent gathering of Tall Ships. I am pleased that the final destination for this Grand Regatta is the Port of Liverpool where all those who have taken part can be assured of the warmest of welcomes. ELIZABETH R.

The Spanish Royal Navy Training Ship, Juan Sebastian de Elcano, leading the Grand Parade up the Mersey Channel, with water-cannon salute. (Lloyd Wright)

Grand Regatta Columbus 1992

The eyes of the world fastened on the Mersey's famous waters as a dazzling flotilla of ships earned a parting salute like none other. Nearly one-and-a-half million people swamped the river's banks to salute the largest parade of sail since the Battle of Trafalgar in 1805. The flotilla of mighty Tall Ships glittered in the afternoon sunshine as they nosed gracefully out of Liverpool, bringing the Grand Regatta Columbus to a spectacular conclusion.

The crowds packed both banks of the Mersey from early morning to see the huge sail-past which was preceded by an air display of vintage American warplanes. The massive armada was then led along the Mersey by the graceful Spanish schooner *Juan Sebastian de Elcano*, resplendent under full sail beneath blue skies. The ships pushed towards the mouth of the estuary at New Brighton, where a mass of sight-seers had gathered for a Leaving of Liverpool beyond compare.

Crews on many of the towering vessels hung precariously from masts and rigging to acknowledge Merseyside's emotional salute. Cannon on Fort Perch Rock and the training ship *Sir Francis Drake* fired again and again in the traditional goodbye....As the first of the ships made for the open sea, Mike Roberts, officer of the watch at Crosby Coastguard Station fired a final salute of two flares.

GRAEME WILSON
Daily Post, 17 August, 1992

New Brighton: Crowds watching the departure of the Tall Ships (Liverpool Echo)

LIST OF ILLUSTRATIONS, WITH ACKNOWLEDGEMENTS

Colour Plates

Acknowledgements to the Board of Trustees of the National Museums and Galleries on Merseyside (NMGM) for kind permission to reproduce paintings in the collections of the Merseyside Maritime Museum (MMM) and the Walker Art Gallery (WAG), as detailed below; and to the photographers who have kindly given permission for their work to be reproduced.

1. Liverpool in 1682, unsigned; courtesy of MMM.
2. Liverpool from the Bowling Green, c.1768, Michael Angelo Rooker; courtesy of WAG.
3. View of Liverpool, c.1811, Henry Freeman James; courtesy of MMM.
4. Liverpool from Seacombe, c.1815, John Jenkinson; courtesy of MMM.
5. Bidston Old Lighthouse and Flagpoles, 1825, Robert Salmon; courtesy of MMM.
6. Sir John Moore, c.1834, Samuel Walters attributed; courtesy of MMM.
7. American Ships in the Mersey, off Liverpool, c.1840, Robert Salmon; courtesy of WAG.
8. Sweethearts and Wives, 1860, John J. Lee; courtesy of WAG.
9. Liverpool from Tranmere, 1863, William Collingwood; courtesy of WAG.
10. St. George's Hall, 1854, J. Penn, Lithograph Raphael Isaacs; courtesy of Lyver and Boydell Gallery.
11. The Port of Liverpool, c.1873, Samuel Walters; courtesy of WAG.
12. Liverpool Overhead Railway, from the original poster; courtesy of NMGM.
13. The Enemy Raid, May 3rd 1941, George Grainger Smith; courtesy of WAG.
14. The Soviet Training Ship "Kruzenshtern" in the Mersey, Tall Ships, August 1984; photograph by John Calderbank.
15. The Two Cathedrals; photograph by John Calderbank.
16. The Anchor of HMS *Conway*; photograph by Gladys Mary Coles.
17. Canning Dock with the Pier Head buildings, 1992; photograph by Gladys Mary Coles.
18. Floodlit Splendour of the Tall Ships in Vittoria Dock, Birkenhead, Grand Regatta Columbus, August 1992; photograph by Stephen Shakeshaft, courtesy of the *Daily Post*.

Black and White Illustrations

Grateful acknowledgement is made for permission to reproduce illustrations in this book, as detailed below:

Trustees of the National Museums and Galleries on Merseyside: Merseyside Maritime Museum: pages 34, 35, 56 (bottom), 71, 79, 91, 98, 113, 121, 125, 129, 154, 162, 175

The Walker Art Gallery: 38, 39, 49, 53, 56 (top), 61, 83, 86 (top), 133

Merseyside Museum of Labour History: 131, 135 (top), 136, 139, 140, 197

Tate Gallery Liverpool: 282

Liverpool City Council, Libraries and Arts; Record Office and Local History Library: 6, 7, 11, 13, 24, 27, 41, 86 (bottom), 110, 181

Metropolitan Borough of Wirral Council, Leisure Services: Williamson Art Gallery and Museum: 8; Libraries: 150

Living Memories Ltd: 122 (bottom), 158, 159

Liverpool Daily Post and Echo Ltd: 188, 192, 196, 244, 246, 291, 292, 293

Catholic Pictorial: 274

Mersey Docks and Harbour Board: 287.

Illustrated London News Library: 73, 96, 99

E. Chambré Hardman Trust: 173, 190, 259, 276, 279

Keith G. Medley: 187, 195, 198, 204, 208 (bottom), 212, 222, 235, 270, 280

Lloyd Wright: 292

H. L. Major: 122 (top)

Peter Kennerley and the Dean and Chapter, Anglican Cathedral, 251

Richard Lloyd-Jones, 201, 225, 247

Lever Bros. Ltd., 115

Bill Tidy: 223, 224

Lindsay Coles: 207, 242

D.J. Kewley, 171; G.S. Cooper: 178

Margaret Roberts of Peter Kaye Photography: The Beatles, 208

Palace Pictures & Film Four International, Frank Clarke & Chris Bernard: *Letter to Brezhnev*, 240

Jane Whitton: Sir Adrian Boult, 141

Graham Maddocks: 145, 146

Liverpool Scottish Regiment: portrait of Capt. Noel Chavasse by P.J. Connelly, 149

Honora Collins: 157

Scouse Press: 104, 188

Metropolitan Cathedral of Christ the King: 215, 216

Myson Combustion Products Ltd for C.E. Turner's "The Britannia on her maiden voyage", 66

Paramount Pictures: Pauline Collins, 249

Kenneth Burnley, *The Wirral Journal*: 44, 77

Sam J. M. Browne: cover, courtesy of Maritime Prints, and 120

Gladys Mary Coles: 117 (grand-parents John and Elizabeth Manlond, great-grandfather Johan Mannelund); 135 (bottom), 232, 236, 245, 262, 263; line drawings, 2, 3, 9, 218, 241

ACKNOWLEDGEMENTS

Thanks to the following authors, owners of copyright, publishers and executors for kind permission to reprint the poems, passages of prose and extracts from scripts included in this anthology.

John Addy and Routledge (Publishers) for the extract from *Sin and Society in the Seventeenth Century* (1989).

Pat Anderson for the extract from *Janet and John*.

The Estate of Thomas Armstrong, and William Collins & Son Ltd for the extract from *King Cotton* (1962).

The Estate of Arthur Askey, and The Woburn Press for the extract from *Before Your Very Eyes: An Autobiography* (1975).

Beryl Bainbridge and Duckworth & Co. Ltd for extracts from *Young Adolf* (1978) and *The Dressmaker* (1973).

Julia Baird and Geoffrey Guiliano, and Grafton Books (Collins) for the extract from *John Lennon, My Brother* (1988).

Elizabeth Bartlett and Headland Publications for "Irish Hair" from *Instead of a Mass* (1991).

The Estate of Sir John Betjeman, and John Murray Publishers for "The Manor House, Hale" from *Collected Poems* (1958).

Paul Booth for his translation of a Medieval Ghost Story.

Keith Birch for the Final Episode of his local radio "soap opera" *The Merseysiders* (1988-90).

Alan Bleasdale for his monologue "The Blue Cornet".

Alan Brack for the extracts from *Liverpool: The Official Book* (1978) and "A Street named Hope" in *Liverpool '67*; and Phillimore & Co. Ltd. for the extract from *The Wirral* (1988).

The Estate of John Brophy and William Collins & Son Ltd for the extract from *The City of Departures* (1946).

D. Brown & Sons for the extract from Julius Rodenberg's *An Autumn in Wales*, trans. William Linnard (1985).

Margaret Browne for "A Liverpool Morning."

Harold Brough and the *Daily Post* for the extract from "In the Underground Citadel" in *Darkest Hour* (February 1991).

Kenneth Burnley and Robert Hale Ltd for the poem by Frank Jocelyn Priest in The *Illustrated Portrait of Wirral* (1987).

Ramsey Campbell and Tom Doherty Associates (USA) for his story "Calling Card" from *Dark Companions* (1982).

Gladys Mary Coles and Duckworth & Co Ltd for "The Coming in of Ancestors", "Old Man", "Liverpool Dock: 1982", "Albert Dock: Regeneration, 1984 ", "The International Garden Festival, 1984" and "City Parks" from *Liverpool Folio* (1984).

The Estate of George Chandler, and B. T. Batsford Ltd. for the extract from *William Roscoe of Liverpool* (1953).

John Chapman (and Carla Lane), and the English Theatre Guild for the extract from the play *The Liver Birds* (1975).

David Charters and Merseyside County Council for the extract from *Ferries Forever: A Closer Look at the Mersey Ferries of Past and Present* (1984).

Alison Chisholm and Stride for "Laughing all the way to the Tate" from *Paper Birds* (1990).

Honora Collins for the extract from "Shining Morning"; and for "The Argonauts" by Maurice Callanan.

Paul Cosgrove for "Iron".

Ceri Courtenay for "High Rise Visit".

Michael Cunningham for "Birkenhead Tunnel".

Barbara Curry for "Inside Albert Dock".

John Curry for "Guardians of the Dawn: the Liverpool Pilots".

Ken Dodd and the *Sunday Telegraph* for "What is a Laugh?"

The Estate of John Drinkwater for his "Ode for the Liverpool Repertory Theatre on the Coming of Age, 1932".

Gordon and Harry Dison and Robbins Music Corporation Ltd for the extract from "Back Buchanan Street".

Alice Thomas Ellis for "Alice Thomas Ellis's Liverpool".

The Estate of Norman Ellison, and Robert Hale Ltd for the extract from *The Wirral Peninsula* (1955).

David Evans and Windows for the version of "The middle-aged couple at the back of the bus" from *Convictions* (1983).

Kevin Fegan and Cheshire Libraries Arts and Archives for "Bridgebuilding" from *on legs made for flying* (1991).

Helen Forrester and The Bodley Head Ltd for extracts from *Lime Street at Two* (1985).

Ron Freethy and Terence Dalton Ltd for the extract from *The River Mersey* (1985).

Gallery Press for the extract from Frank Shaw's *My Liverpool* (1971); and extracts from the 1968 reprint of *Her Benny* (1879).

Nicholas Garrick for "Patronise the Punch, Mister?"

The Estate of Winifred Gérin, and The Clarendon Press, Oxford for the extract from *Emily Brontë* (1971).

John Gloag and Cassell & Co Ltd for the extract from *The Eagles Depart* (1973).

Reg Green and Hodder & Stoughton Ltd for the extract from *A Race Apart: The History of the Grand National* (1988).

The Estate of Graham Greene and Heinemann Ltd for the extract from *Journey Without Maps* (1936).

Allen Ginsberg for the quotation of his comment on Liverpool.

Gwasg Gomer for the extract from Augusta Pearson's 1853 Journal, *A Spinster's Tour Through North Wales* (1988).

Henry Graham and *Ambit* for "The Last Resort".

Richard Hamer and Faber and Faber Ltd for lines from "The Battle of Brunanburh" from *A Choice of Anglo Saxon Verse* (1970).

Eric Hardy for his early essay "Monsters of the Mersey" (1934).

Harvard University Press, Belknap imprint, for the extract from *Letters of Thomas Carlyle to His Brother Alexander,* edited by Edwin W. Marrs Jnr (1968).

Adrian Henri and Penguin Books Ltd for "Mrs Albion you've got a lovely daughter" from *The Mersey Sound*, Penguin Modern Poets 10 (1967); and Allison & Busby Ltd. for "Adrian Henri's Talking Toxteth Blues" from *Collected Poems* (1986); and Jonathan Cape Ltd. for "Morning, Liverpool 8" from *Wish You Were Here* (1991).

Richard Hill for "City Tram".

Jim Hitchmough for "The Merseyside Nomad"; and Bantam/Transworld Publishers Ltd for the extract from his novel *Watching* (1990).

Mary Hodgson for "Clay Pipes by the Mersey".

Geoffrey Holloway for "New Brighton Ferry" and "Cunarders".

Helen Hoogendyk for "Albert Dock".

Maurice Hope and G.W. & A. Hesketh

Publishers for the extract from *Castles in the Sand* (1982).

Michael Jackson and Northern Songs for the extract from Lennon and McCartney's "In My Life".

The Estate of Augustus John and Jonathan Cape Ltd for the extract from *Chiaroscuro* (1952).

R. Merfyn Jones and D. Ben Rees for the extract from *Liverpool Welsh and Their Religion* (1984).

Ron Jones for the extract from *The American Connection - Liverpool's links with America from Columbus to the Beatles.* (Ron Jones, 1986).

The Estate of Carl G. Jung and William Collins & Son Ltd for the extract from *Memories, Dreams, Reflections,* trans Richard and Clara Winston (1963).

Rachel Kempson and Duckworth & Co. Ltd for the extract from *A Family and its Fortunes* (1986).

Dora Kennedy for "Dove Point, Meols", "1207 and So On"; and the National Poetry Foundation for "The Conway Bell" from *The Sheltering Coast* (1993).

Philip Key and the *Daily Post* for his feature "Portrait of a Not So Candid Camera".

Carla Lane and the English Theatre Guild for the extract from the play *The Liver Birds* (1975).

The Estate of Roger Lancelyn Green for the extract from *Poulton Lancelyn* (1948).

Eugene Lange (Muhammed Khalil) for "The Real Liverpool".

William Leece and the *Daily Post* for "Star Performance at the Everyman".

The Estate of Malcolm Lowry and Jonathan Cape Ltd for extracts from *Ultramarine* (1933) and *Under the Volcano* (1947).

The Estate of Edward Lucie-Smith and Rapp & Whiting/André Deutsch for the extract from *The Liverpool Scene* (1971; D.Carroll, 1967).

Moy McCrory and Sheba Feminist Publications for the extract from "Prize Giving" in *The Water's Edge and other stories* (1985).

Roger McGough for "Liverpool" and "Limestreetscene '64" from *The Liverpool Scene* (1967); and Jonathan Cape Ltd for "Poem for the Opening of Christ the King Cathedral, Liverpool" from *You at the Back: Selected Poems 1967-87* (1991).

Jimmy McGovern and the BBC for the extract from his radio play *Felix Randal* (broadcast 1985).

Peter McGovern and Spin Publications for the extract from "In My Liverpool Home".

Jamie McKendrick and Oxford University Press for "Mersey Plumage" from *The Sirocco Room* (1991).

Anne MacPhee for "Tate Gallery Liverpool and its University Link".

Graham Maddocks, and Leo Cooper imprint (Pen and Sword Books Ltd) for the extract from *Liverpool Pals* (1991).

Jim Mangnall and Windows for the extract from *Meridians* (1985).

Cheryl Martin for "Blacks Like Me".

The Estate of John Masefield for "Liverpool, 1890", his two poems "For the Liverpool Repertory Theatre"; and Heinemann Ltd for the extract from *The Conway* (1933).

Diane Massey and the *Daily Post* for her feature "That Long Ago Army".

George Melly and Weidenfeld & Nicolson Ltd for the extract from *Scouse Mouse* (1984).

Frank Milner and the Trustees of the National Museums and Galleries on Merseyside for the extracts from *The Pre-Raphaelites* (1988) and *Turner: Paintings in Merseyside Collections* (1990); and from the WAG guide to the 18th Century Room.

The Estate of Nicholas Monsarrat, and Cassell & Co. Ltd for the extract from *The Cruel Sea* (1951).

Christopher Morris and The Cresset Press Ltd for the extract from *The Journeys of Celia Fiennes* (1947).

Ian Nairn and BBC Publications for the extract from *Britain's Changing Towns* (1967).

Mr and Mrs Nokes and Tim Reeves of Microbiz for the poem by Celia Nokes, "Don't have to be there tonight" from *Celia's Poems* (1991).

Fred Nolan and *The Bookseller* for his article "Shaggy Sailor's Story".

Michael O'Neill and Harper Collins Ltd for "Father and Son" from *The Stripped Bed* (1990).

The Estate of George Orwell, and Secker & Warburg Ltd for the extract from "The Road to Wigan Pier Diary" from *Collected Essays, Journalism and Letters of George Orwell, Vol I, 1920-40*, ed Sonia Orwell and Ian Angus (1968).

The Estate of Harold Owen, and Oxford University Press for extracts from *Collected Letters of Wilfred Owen*, ed Harold Owen & John Bell (1967).

Oxford University Press (The Clarendon Press) for the extract from *Letters of Charles Dickens* 6 vols, ed. House, Storey and Tillotson (1974).

The Estate of William T. Palmer, and Robert Hale Ltd for the extract from *The River Mersey* (1944).

Edith Pargeter and the *Daily Post* for the quotations from her interview with Harold Brough in "In the Underground Citadel" from *Darkest Hour* (February 1991).

Gwyn Parry and Poetry Wales Press for the extract from "Liverpool, St David's Day, 1882" from *Hurricane* (1987).

Brian Patten and Penguin Books Ltd for "Seascape" from *The Mersey Sound*, Penguin Modern Poets 10 (1967).

Penguin Books Ltd for extracts from *Kilvert's Diary* ed. and sel. William Plomer (1977).

Susan Place and *Cheshire Life* for "Mersey Heritage at Stanley Dock" from "Time to Turn the Tide".

Richard Poole and Poetry Wales Press for "Two Little Girls and Matthew Arnold".

Peggy Poole and Headland Publications for "The Estuary" from *Cherry Stones* (1983).

The Estate of J.B.Priestley, and Heinemann Ltd for the extracts from *English Journey* (1934) and *The Good Companions* (1929).

Simon Rae, *The Guardian* and Bloodaxe Books Ltd for "The Ballad of Hillsborough" from *Soft Targets* (1991).

The Estate of Michael Redgrave, and Weidenfeld & Nicolson Ltd for the extract from *In My Mind's Eye; An Autobiography* (1983).

D. Ben Rees (and R. Merfyn Jones) for the extract from *Liverpool Welsh and Their Religion* (1984).

Christopher Reid and Faber and Faber Ltd for "Maritime Liverpool" from *Arcadia* (1979).

John P. Reid for "The Landing Stage".

John Reynolds for "Leaving" and "After the Baths".

Joe Riley and the *Liverpool Echo* for the extract from "The Battle of Derby House" from *Front Line: When Merseyside Went to War* (1979); and SPCK for the extract from *Today's Cathedral* (1978).

Jenny Roche for "Netherley, 1985".

Willy Russell and Methuen Drama for the extract from *Shirley Valentine* (1988).

The Estate of Siegfried Sassoon, and Faber & Faber Ltd for extracts from *Memoirs of an Infantry Officer* (1930).

Scouse Press and Fritz Spiegl for extracts from *Liverpool and Slavery* by a Genuine Dicky Sam (reprint 1984), and *Lern Yerself Scouse, Vols One and Two* (1990 reprints).

The Estate of George Bernard Shaw, and Constable & Co. Ltd for the extract from *Sixteen Self-Sketches* (1949).

Bishop David Sheppard (and Archbishop Derek Worlock) and Hodder & Stoughton Ltd for the extract from *Better Together* (1988).

Nigel Simeone and Simon Mundy, and Midas Books for extracts from recollections by Lawrence Tanner and Jerrold Northrop Moore from *Sir Adrian Boult, Companion of Honour - A Tribute* (1980).

Susan Skinner for "Closed Factory: Kirkby Industrial Estate".

Matt Simpson and Bloodaxe Books for "John Middleton, Childe of Hale", "Homecoming" and "Seaforth Shore Revisited" from *An Elegy for the Galosherman* (1991); and Headland Publications for "A Scouser's Birthday Card " from *The Pigs' Thermal Underwear* (1993).

Michael Stammers and Alan Sutton Publishing Ltd for the extract from *Liverpool: The Port and Its Ships* (1991).

Copland Smith for "Liverpool Cathedral, 1987".

John Stapledon and Mary Shenai, and the University Press of New England for extracts from *The Love Letters of Olaf Stapledon and Agnes Miller, Talking Across the World* 1913-19, ed Robert Crossley (1987).

Levi Tafari for the extract from "Nuh Blame Rasta"; and Headland Publications for "Toxteth Where I Reside" from *Rhyme Don't Pay* (1993).

Stainton de B. Taylor for extracts from *Two Centuries of Music in Liverpool* (1976).

The Estate of A.S.J. Tessimond, and Penguin Books Ltd for the extract from "Earthfast".

The Estate of J.R. Tolkien, and Allen & Unwin Ltd for the extract from his translation of *Sir Gawain and the Green Knight* (1975).

John Toshack and Duckworth & Co Ltd for "A Goalden Night" from *Gosh it's Tosh* (1976).

Geoffrey Tresise and the Trustees of the National Museums and Galleries on Merseyside for the extract from *The Invisible Dinosaur* (1990).

Marij Van Helmond and the Trustees of the National Museums and Galleries on Merseyside for the extract from *Votes For Women: The Events on Merseyside 1870-1928* (1992).

Van den Bergh Diary transcription: Trustees of the National Museums and Galleries on Merseyside; Merseyside Maritime Museum.

The Estate of F.T.Wainwright and Phillimore & Co Ltd for the extract from Annals of Ireland from *Scandinavian England* (1975).

Brian Wake and Headland Publications for "High Windows" from *Into Hiding* (1993).

Brenda Walker for "Barricade the Stars" and "This Game of War".

T.J.Walsh for Alec S. Paton's essay "Wilfred Owen - His Childhood in Birkenhead" in *A Tribute to Wilfred Owen* (1964).

Dave Ward and Windows for "Jambo".

John Ward and Littlewood Arc for "Proving Catherine's Age" and "Liverpool Overhead Railway in the Thirties" from *Grandfather Best and the Protestant Work Ethic* (1991).

Derek Whale and the *Liverpool Echo* for the extract from his article on Matthew Arnold.

Richard Whittington-Egan and Gallery Press for the extract from *Liverpool, This is My City* (1972).

The Estate of Emlyn Williams, and Hamish Hamilton Ltd for the extract from *George* (1961).

Graeme Wilson and the *Daily Post* for "The Return of the Tall Ships: Grand Regatta Columbus " (August 1992).

Heather Wilson and the Metropolitan Borough of Wirral Council, Dept. of Leisure Services for "Morpeth Dock" and the extract from "On Oxton's Hill" from *Wirral Visions* (1982).

Maria Lin Wong and Liver Press for extracts from *Chinese Liverpudlians: A History of the Chinese Community in Liverpool* (1989).

The Estate of Virginia Woolf, and the Hogarth Press for the extract from *A Passionate Apprentice: The Early Journals of Virginia Woolf,* ed Mitchell A. Leaska (1990).

Archbishop Derek Worlock (and Bishop David Sheppard) and Hodder & Stoughton Ltd for the extract from *Better Together* (1988).

Kit Wright and Hutchinson & Co. Ltd. for "The Mole of Edge Hill" from "The Losing of Liverpool" from *Bump-starting the Hearse* (1983).

FULL LIST OF CONTENTS

302

Part Four

THE EDITOR

Gladys Mary Coles was born in Liverpool, spending her childhood there and in North Wales - contrasting environments which were deeply formative, and to both of which she is passionately attached. She was educated at Liverpool University (in preference to Oxford), where she read History and English. There, too, she won the Felicia Hemans Prize for Poetry, edited *Sphinx,* and was awarded a Postgraduate Studentship.

After her postgraduate degree, Gladys Mary Coles held a research post at London University and wrote biographies of Elizabethan M.P.s (published in *The House of Commons, 1558-1603* HMSO, 1981), following which she became a full-time writer and freelance lecturer.

Of Gladys Mary Coles' eight collections of poetry, the most recent are *Liverpool Folio* (1984), *Leafburners: New and Selected Poems* (1986) and *The Glass Island* (1992), all published by Duckworth & Co. Ltd (London). Her poems are anthologised in *The Faber Book of English History in Verse* (1988), *The Virago Book of Wicked Verse* (1992), *The Forward Book of Poetry: Best Poems of 1992* (1992), and in various other volumes.

She has won a number of national poetry competitions, including recently the 1991 Aberystwyth (University of Wales) Open and the 1992 Outposts Competition, and major prizes in the National Poetry Competition (Poetry Society), the Cardiff International, the Scottish International, and others; and has received a Welsh Arts Council Writer's Award. In 1992, she was selected to represent British Poetry in the Euro-Literature Project. Her work was silk-screen printed for an exhibition, 'European Lyrics'.

Gladys Mary Coles' poetry has been broadcast on BBC TV and BBC Radio 4, selected for 'Poetry Please', and featured on BBC Radio Network North-West, BBC Radio Wales and BBC Radio Merseyside. She has given readings of her poetry across Britain and in Literature Festivals such as Cheltenham, Chester and Cardiff.

Also a critic and literary reviewer, she has written two biographies of the Shropshire author, Mary Webb - the first, an acclaimed pioneering study *The Flower of Light* (Duckworth, 1978); the second, a new biography, *Mary Webb,* in the Seren Books Borderlines Series (1990). Her other publications include two editions of Mary Webb's poetry. Gladys Mary Coles is President of the Mary Webb Society, and lectures extensively; her broadcasts include a BBC Radio 4 'Kaleidoscope' half-hour feature.

Gladys Mary Coles won the Award for Literature in the regional Arts Awards of the *Daily Post and Liverpool Echo,* 1992. She is a tutor in Imaginative Writing at both Liverpool University and Liverpool John Moores University, and for the Taliesin Trust.